CAMBRIDGE TE
HISTORY OF POLIT.

CW00969000

———

RICHARD PRICE
Political Writings

CAMBRIDGE TEXTS IN THE
HISTORY OF POLITICAL THOUGHT

Series Editors:

RAYMOND GEUSS *Columbia University*
QUENTIN SKINNER *Christ's College, Cambridge*

The series is intended to make available to students the most important texts required for an understanding of the history of political thought. The scholarship of the present generation has greatly expanded our sense of the range of authors indispensable for such an understanding, and the series will reflect those developments. It will also include a number of less well-known works, in particular those needed to establish the intellectual contexts that in turn help to make sense of the major texts. The principal aim, however, will be to produce new versions of the major texts themselves, based on the most up-to-date scholarship. The preference will always be for complete texts, and a special feature of the series will be to complement individual texts, within the compass of a single volume, with subsidiary contextual material. Each volume will contain an introduction on the historical identity and contemporary significance of the work or works concerned, as well as a chronology, notes on further reading and (where appropriate) brief biographical sketches of significant individuals mentioned in each text.

For a list of titles published in the series, please see end of book

RICHARD PRICE

Political Writings

EDITED BY

D. O. THOMAS

(Formerly Reader in Philosophy
The University College of Wales, Aberystwyth)

The right of the
University of Cambridge
to print and sell
all manner of books
was granted by
Henry VIII in 1534
The University has printed
and published continuously
since 1584

CAMBRIDGE UNIVERSITY PRESS
Cambridge   New York   Port Chester
Melbourne   Sydney

CAMBRIDGE UNIVERSITY PRESS
Cambridge, New York, Melbourne, Madrid, Cape Town, Singapore, São Paulo, Delhi

Cambridge University Press
The Edinburgh Building, Cambridge CB2 8RU, UK

Published in the United States of America by Cambridge University Press, New York

www.cambridge.org
Information on this title: www.cambridge.org/9780521409698

First published 1991

A catalogue record for this publication is available from the British Library

Library of Congress Cataloguing in Publication data
Price, Richard, 1723–1791.
[Selections. 1992]
Political writings / Richard Price: edited by D. O. Thomas.
p.   cm. – (Cambridge texts in the history of political
thought)
Includes bibliographical references and index.
ISBN 0 521 40162 3. – ISBN 0 521 40969 1 (paper)
1. Political science.   2. Civil rights.   I. Thomas, David Oswald.
II. Title.   III. Series
JC176.P726   1992
323'.092 – dc20   91–12548   CIP

ISBN 978-0-521-40162-3 hardback
ISBN 978-0-521-40969-8 paperback

Transferred to digital printing 2009

Contents

Contents

Introduction

Richard Price was born at Tyn-ton in the parish of Llangeinor near Bridgend in the county of Glamorgan on 23 February 1723. His father, Rice Price, was a Dissenting minister who had been an assistant to Samuel Jones, founder of the Academy at Brynllywarch. By all the accounts that have survived, Rice Price was a strict Calvinist who maintained an austere discipline in the home. Richard, however, rebelled against his father's theology at an early age, and though he upheld the puritan values inculcated by his parents, his religious beliefs became much more liberal and much more rationalist.

Price's father died on 28 June 1739 and his mother, Catherine, scarcely a year later. Richard then went up to London, where his uncle, Samuel Price, was an assistant minister to the famous hymn-writer Isaac Watts, at St Mary Axe in Bury Street. Once established in London, Price was entered at Coward's Academy in Tenter Alley, Moorfields, where he came under the instruction and the influence of John Eames, who had been a friend and a disciple of Isaac Newton. It was at this Academy that he was prepared for the ministry, which was to remain his vocation and his first concern throughout an extremely active career. It was at this Academy too that he received the training in mathematics that enabled him to make important contributions to the theory of probability, to actuarial science and to the growth and development of insurance. When he left the Academy (probably in 1744), he became a family chaplain to George Streatfield, a wealthy businessman living in Stoke Newington. Very little is known about his life during these years, except that for a period he was an assistant to Samuel Chandler at the Meeting Place at Old Jewry, but it would seem that he had ample leisure to devote himself to intellectual pursuits. Those bore fruit in 1758 in the form of a work now regarded as a classic of eighteenth-century moral philosophy, *A Review of the Principal Questions and Difficulties in Morals*. The main aim of this work was to defend the objectivity of moral judgement against the kinds of subjectivism and voluntarism that were fashionable in his day. Price believed that he could demonstrate this by showing that moral judgement is an exercise of reason. If moral judgement is rational, its objectivity is secured, for reason apprehends necessary truths. It is on these grounds that Price is classified as a rationalist among moral philosophers.

It is, however, important to bear in mind that there is another element in Price's account of moral judgement that cannot be easily reconciled with the view that moral principles are instances of necessary truth. On the latter view we should expect to find that Price held that moral principles are indefeasible: necessary truths do not admit of exceptions. But when Price dealt with the problems occasioned by the conflict of duties, he conceded that an obligation to perform an action indicated by a moral principle may be overridden or outweighed by an obligation indicated by a principle of greater weight. On this latter view at least some moral principles are defeasible. One very important implication of the latter view which has important consequences for Price's political philosophy is that his moral philosophy was not so completely dominated by abstract principles as it has often been supposed to be. His teaching as to how conflicts of duty are to be resolved implies that we cannot determine what action we ought to take in any situation in an 'a priori' way: we have to examine the context in which action is to be taken to ensure that we do justice to all the obligations that may be said to arise in it, and only when we have done so can we determine what we ought to do. For this reason Price's moral philosophy is much more pragmatic and much more heavily influenced by empirical considerations than it has often been thought to be.

In the *Review* Price also attacked utilitarianism in the name of an intuitionist account of moral principles, and he defended a libertarian account of free-will. The relevance of this work to his political philosophy must engage our attention later on; what I first wish to emphasize is the relevance of Price's vocation as a minister of the Gospel to an understanding of his thought. It is not just that Price held that his duties as a minister had the first call upon his time and energy, but also that the world in which he lived was orientated towards and dominated by the worship and service of God. When towards the end of his life he expressed in his shorthand journal the hope that his life had been useful, he was revealing an abiding fear that he had failed to discharge the duties he owed to God. In one who accomplished so much the remark is a striking testimony to his humility of mind.

Throughout his career Richard Price's thought on moral and political matters was heavily influenced by the problems faced by the Dissenters in the eighteenth century. As is well known, at that time in England and Wales the Dissenters were struggling to obtain fuller legal recognition of the right to worship God in the way they thought fit. They strove to remove the legal disabilities from which they suffered. Those who rejected orthodox Trinitarianism did not fall within the protection of the Toleration Act of 1689, and, as the law then stood, they were liable to suffer severe penalties. Those who did not take the sacrament according to the rites of the Anglican Church were debarred from holding office under the Crown or under municipal corporations. They suffered other severe disabilities: they could not, for example, matriculate at Oxford, and though they could study at Cambridge, they could not take a degree there.

The leaders of the Dissenters were anxious to remove these disabilities. They sought to establish that everyone has a right not to toleration – for that would imply a condescension in those in authority – but to worship God according to the dictates of conscience. They wanted to establish not simply that everyone should not be hindered in worshipping according to conscience, but also that no one should suffer handicaps or disabilities in doing so. To establish this position the Dissenters were anxious to deny that the State has any responsibility for man's spiritual welfare; the only responsibility the magistrate has in religious matters is to guarantee to each individual the enjoyment of freedom of worship by inhibiting those who would attempt to invade it and by removing privileges or special protection to any particular sect or denomination. The defence of religious liberty dominated Price's thinking from the first of his pamphlets, *Britain's Happiness* (1759), to the last, the celebrated *A Discourse on the Love of our Country* (1789).

In addition to defending the right to freedom of worship, Price also emphasized the importance of establishing and safeguarding the right of inquiry. Although the fundamentals of the faith are accessible to all persons of sound understanding, there is much in the field of religion that is obscure. In addition to emphasizing the duty and the right to act in accordance with conscience, he also stressed the duty to inform conscience. Although we are blameless if we do what we sincerely believe to be our duty, that consolation is only available if we have made every effort to find out what our duties really are. We have obligations of candour in both the speculative and the practical realms. We have a duty to seek the truth and a duty to act upon what we find. Price believed that the pursuit of knowledge would eventually lead us to realise in our lives and in our institutions the truths of the Gospels. The practical implications of this belief can be seen in his discussion of the role of education. Students should not be told what to believe, but rather how to discover the truth for themselves. His optimism was such that he believed passionately that opening society to rational inquiry would inevitably lead to the establishment of a purified form of the Christian religion, to economic progress, and to social harmony. The role of the State in promoting progress is, however, strictly limited. The experience of the Dissenters had led them to mistrust State intervention, especially in religious matters. But minimizing the role of government was not based solely on the fear that power would be abused: it was also based on the conviction that there are many things that are better done if done by the individual or if done by people acting together in small associations. Price believed very firmly in the virtues of self-dependence.

The basic principles of Price's theological position can be stated quite simply: that there is an omnipotent, omniscient and benevolent God, that there is a Providence that adjusts the course of events to secure the realization of His ultimate purpose, that this life is a period of probation after which the virtuous will receive the reward of eternal life and the vicious will be annihilated (although there is some evidence that in his later years he was beginning to incline to the view that ultimately all men will be restored to communion with God). Our overriding interest is to secure eternal life, the pearl for which all else must be sacrificed, and to this end what is essential is that we seek to do our duty. What is crucially important morally and politically, therefore, is that everyone is, as far as is possible, guaranteed the freedom to act conscientiously. Since, however, we are all fallible and weak creatures, no one's virtue of itself will merit the reward of eternal life. At this point Price stressed the indispensability of Christ's saving Grace. He was thus an Arian, holding what may be termed a midway position between the Calvinist view that redemption is secured wholly and entirely by Divine Grace and the Socinian view that Christ's redeeming role is confined to His teaching and His example.

The tendency towards the secularization of politics in Price's thought, which I shall discuss below, should not blind us to the fact that political activity is placed by Price within a context in which God is relied upon to redress the apparent injustices of life on earth. It needs to be recognized, however, that Price allotted two contrasting roles to Providence, both of which play a part in his thinking throughout his career, but each receiving greater emphasis at some times than at others. In periods of depression and gloom when all his projects seem to be frustrated, as in 1781, when there seemed to be no prospect of a favourable end to the War of American Independence, Price stressed the part played by God's Providence in securing justice for the virtuous in another life; it was in this mood that he composed his *Fast Sermon* of 1781. In more hopeful times, for example, after the Americans had won their independence, Price saw the hand of Providence working in human history. The success of the Americans and the prospect of reform at home revived millennial expectations: these are clearly in evidence in *Observations on the Importance of the American Revolution* (1784), and in *The Evidence for a Future Period of Improvement in the State of Mankind* (1787). They are also manifest in *A Discourse on the Love of our Country* (1789), particularly in the way in which he welcomed the opening events of the French Revolution and the prospect of harmony between England and France.

Scholars of the millennium distinguish millenarian views from millennialist ones; the former find in the Book of Revelation the prophecy that Christ will come again to inaugurate a period in which He and His saints will rule for a thousand years before the Day of Judgement, when all men will each receive their just deserts; the millennialists hold that the millennium will precede Christ's coming, and will, if it has not indeed already begun, be a time when the condition of man on earth will improve gradually so as to be fit for the rule of Christ and His saints. Price belonged to the latter group, and in his mind the millennialist doctrine meshed in with the more secular doctrine of progress held by thinkers such as Turgot and Condorcet. Particular emphasis was placed on the contribution to enlightenment and progress made possible by religious freedom and the freedom of inquiry. It is in the light of these expectations that we must understand the enthusiasm of his reflections on the achievements of the American Revolution and the ardour with which he greeted the French Revolution.

Against this background it may seem strange to argue that there are marked tendencies in his thought towards the secularization of politics, so the claim needs careful explanation. Following in a tradition which owed much to John Locke, Price believed in the separation of the spiritual from the secular, and in confining government as far as possible to the defence of life, liberty and property. The State has no responsibility for man's spiritual welfare, except, as I noted earlier, for its duty to guarantee to every one the enjoyment of the right to religious liberty. The great achievement of this tradition, which Price played an important part in developing, was to establish the separation of the secular from the spiritual so strongly in conceptual terms that the separation seemed to many to be the keystone in the arch of liberal ideology.

Price's patron, George Streatfield, died in 1757, and in the following year Price became minister to the Presbyterian chapel at Newington Green where he remained until 1783. It was at this chapel on 29 November 1759 – a day appointed for a General Thanksgiving – that he preached the sermon later published under the title *Britain's Happiness, and the Proper Improvement of it*. In it Price expressed many of the beliefs that dominated his thinking on religious and political topics throughout his career: the conviction that there is an omnipotent and benevolent God, that there is a Providence that adjusts the course of events so as to secure the ultimate realization of the Divine purpose, that there is general amendment in human affairs which justifies millennial expectations; that men have a duty to worship God, and to cultivate the virtues, that everyone has a right to worship God in the way he thinks most fitting, and to act in accordance with his conscience, that the people of Britain are especially fortunate in enjoying a large measure of religious liberty, and that the Glorious Revolution had established a form of constitutional government that, although imperfect, was able to secure the protection of everyone's life, liberty and property.

To those more familiar with Price's writings during the War of American Independence and at the outbreak of the French Revolution, it may come as a surprise to find him exulting in the nation's prowess in arms and talking of the good fortune that the British enjoyed under George II with an almost undiluted praise. It is equally surprising to find one who attacked imperialism and the 'spirit of domination' with such passion claiming that the extension of military and commercial power was a sign of Providence's intention to use the British people as an instrument in the amelioration of the state of mankind. But Price was not completely uncritical: he did not altogether disguise his belief that much remained to be done to make Britain the seat of liberty that he wished it to become, pre-eminently by extending the benefits of freedom of worship to all sects and by reclaiming those who had fallen from Grace to the paths of virtue.

The defects were, however, only lightly sketched in, and it is not until his later pamphlets that we find the sweeping denunciations of the administration of the day. In 1759, even if he had wanted to indulge in heavier criticism of British institutions, he might have felt that it would not have been appropriate in a thanksgiving sermon, and especially not in a year when the French had been so decisively defeated by Wolfe at Quebec and by Hawke at Quiberon Bay.

In addition to his duties as a minister Price had many intellectual pursuits – he edited an essay by Thomas Bayes on the theory of probability, in recognition of which he became a Fellow of the Royal Society in 1765; and in the mid sixties he was invited to advise the newly founded Society for Equitable Assurances on demographic and actuarial problems and entered upon a period of intense study which culminated in the publication of his *Observations on Reversionary Payments* in 1771. During this period his interest in the problems of government finance was awakened, and he devoted a chapter in the first edition of *Observations on Reversionary Payments* to a discussion of the problem of the National Debt. This essay he extended to a pamphlet that was published separately in 1772 under the title *An Appeal to the Public on the Subject of the National Debt*. After the Glorious Revolution and the introduction into this country of what Disraeli was later to term 'Dutch finances' the Government fell into the habit of financing much of its activity by borrowing and funding debt. The interest required to service the debt became an annual charge on the nation's revenue. As the debt grew, and it grew rapidly in wartime, the burden of the annual charge upon the nation's income became proportionately heavier. Price was alarmed that it might grow to such an extent that it would threaten national bankruptcy. Earlier in the century a sinking fund had been established with the ultimate aim of wiping it out. The scheme was a simple one. By taxation the government was to create a surplus of income over current expenditure and place it in a fund that would be used to buy back debt. Instead of cancelling the debt as it was bought up, interest should be paid on it and used to buy up further debt. The fund would then grow at compound interest until a sum large enough to liquidate the whole debt would be created. Price was scandalized by the failure of successive ministries to maintain this scheme. Ministers had found it difficult to impose the level of taxation necessary to supply it, and in times of financial stringency, so far from supplying the fund, they had found it all too tempting to raid it.

There were further reasons for reforming government finance. The fears of early redemption of stocks had led the market to prefer to take up stocks bearing low rates of interest at a high discount rather than high interest stocks at par: for example, a nominal £100 stock bearing 3 per cent interest issued at £60 was more attractive than a £100 stock bearing 5 per cent issued at par. The rate of return was the same on both issues, but the stock issued at a discount was more attractive because if the government wanted to redeem the stock it would have to pay £100 for every £60 it had received. Price complained that the government was irresponsibly extravagant in creating a large capital debt in return for much smaller sums raised.

Lord North's defence of this policy rested on the assumption that the burden to the nation's resources lay only in the annual charge that the debt created, and that since this was so, the government should always accept the lowest rates of borrowing it could find. This was tantamount to declaring that the National Debt was a permanent charge upon the nation since there was no intention that the debt should ever be repaid. This contention proved completely unacceptable to Price: he retained the notion many still retain today that a debt, whether public or private, is something that ought to be repaid. His abhorrence of the thought that the government should ease its own burden by creating a permanent charge on the nation's income was reinforced by his extreme distaste for contracting debt. Morality required that one should repay one's debts; prudence required that one should, wherever possible, avoid contracting them. The need to redeem debt became almost an obsession with Price: he spent a great deal of time and energy inveighing against the ways in which the Government raised money and in advocating the re-establishment of sinking fund procedures for redeeming debt. When he came to advise the Americans on the construction of a new State in *Observations on the Importance of the American Revolution*, Price was particularly concerned to warn them of the evils of public indebtedness. There were other reasons for reducing debt: the existence of the debt itself led to the maintenance of a class that lived off the funds, it led to the unwholesome stockjobbing practices of the Alley, and since a large portion of the fund was held by Dutch financial houses, it led to an annual export of specie that the nation could ill afford.

There were further reasons for reforming the ways in which the government raised money. There are many affinities between Price's political thought and what Hans Baron has identified as the tradition of 'civic humanism': among them the fear that power may be used corruptly and the consequent need to prevent the accumulation of power beyond what is strictly necessary to discharge the duties of government. Price suspected that the ways in which government loans were raised – by private allocations on very favourable terms – opened the way to corruption: it was only too easy for those in government to gain support for their policies in Parliament by allowing loans to be taken up at rates substantially below their market value. Subscribers could then make a quick profit by selling stock shortly after they received it. Price's allegations were difficult to prove because there were ways in which unsavoury operations could be concealed, but there were good reasons to suspect that his charges were well founded in the fact that the prices of stocks rose substantially after they were issued, thus presenting an easy profit to those who had been allowed to subscribe.

Up to the outbreak of the War of American Independence Price was known primarily to the relatively small circle of those who read his writings on moral philosophy, theology, probability theory, assurance and the nation's finances. It was his defence of the American rebels that brought him to the attention of a much wider public. In February 1776 he published his *Observations on the Nature of Civil Liberty*, of which, according to his nephew, William Morgan, 60,000 copies were sold. It was followed a year later by *Additional Observa-*

tions, in which he clarified some of the positions he had adopted in the earlier pamphlet and published more accurate accounts of the nation's finances. According to Horace Walpole, one of the reasons why the first pamphlet had caused such a stir was that it laid bare the financial ruin threatened by the prosecution of the war. In 1778 the two pamphlets were republished in one volume under the title *Two Tracts*.

In these political pamphlets Price's main aim was to establish that in their quarrel with the British administration right was on the side of the American rebels. He used several different kinds of argument to establish this. The British administration were in the wrong in seeking to impose their will on the colonies and doubly wrong in seeking to do so by military force. In opening hostilities the British government were entering upon a war they could not win; they were embarking on a course that would be heavily expensive in men and resources, one so expensive that it carried with it the threat of national bankruptcy and ruin. The main argument, however, was that the British administration were in the wrong because they had violated a basic principle. Political authority, Price argued, originates with the people: the forms of government are just the ways in which they choose to govern themselves. Following Locke and Hoadly he repudiated the theory of Divine Right, claiming instead that the authority of the ruler derives from the social compact whereby the people agree among themselves to accept the constraints of law and choose the forms under which they will be governed. If authority derives from the people, it follows, Price claimed, that every community has a right to govern itself.

No community can have a right to make other communities subject to it. There are no grounds for justifying imperialism, conquest or dominion. Applying this principle to the claims of the colonists, Price held that if they so chose, the Americans had the right to rid themselves of rule from London and become independent. He did not want to see the break-up of the British Empire; he would rather have seen it become a confederation of political societies, each participating on an equal basis and submitting to a Federal authority for the regulation of those matters that were of common concern. This was the ideal, but if the Americans did not wish to participate in this way, they should be left free to go their own way.

Price showed considerable polemical skill in identifying what he wanted to justify, namely national self-government, with what is universally conceived to be a high value, namely liberty or freedom, and by stressing the analogies between national autonomy and other forms of self-government that are highly prized. The aim was to persuade the reader to attach to his political goal – autonomy for the American colonies – the values associated with other forms of liberty. This procedure produced a bewilderingly complex treatment of liberty, and whatever the gains polemically – and they were considerable – they were bought at a heavy cost in conceptual confusion and lack of clarity. In classifying the differing kinds of liberty Price distinguished physical, moral, religious and civil liberty. Physical liberty he characterized as the capacity of the agent to make decisions without being subject to external determining forces: I enjoy physical liberty if and only if I can truly be said to be the author of my actions. Moral liberty Price characterized as the capacity to follow one's own conscience and not be prevented from doing so by the passions. It is important to note that Price holds that every individual *really* wants to act conscientiously. It is this assumption that enables him to say that when I do what I believe to be my duty I am governing myself, and that when I follow my desires against the call of duty, I have fallen a slave to the passions. This conflation of two different notions – that I am free when I do what I want to do and that I am free when I do what I believe to be my duty – has, I believe, unfortunate consequences. It leads Price to imply that I am only morally free when I act in accordance with conscience or in doing God's will; it also leads him to imply that when I follow my desires against the call of duty, I have been overpowered by desire.

Religious liberty is another form of self-government. I enjoy it when I am free to worship God according to my own conception of what God requires of me. Here again Price conflates two different notions that are better kept apart: the idea that I am free only when I am under the direction of my own will and the idea that I am free only when I do what I think God requires of me.

Civil liberty, conceived as a form of self-government, applies both to individuals and to communities. A community is free when it governs itself, and is not subject to the alien will of another community. An individual enjoys civil liberty (a) when he is a member of a community that governs itself, and (b) when he participates in some form in the government of his own society. In the course of publishing his pamphlets on the American problem Price changed his definition of civil liberty to accommodate the latter point. In the early editions of *Observations on the Nature of Civil Liberty* he defined civil liberty as 'the power of a Civil Society or State to govern itself by its own discretion; or by laws of its own choosing, without being subject to any foreign discretion, or to the impositions of any extraneous will or power'. In the seventh edition, for the phrase 'any extraneous will or power' he substituted the following: 'any power, in appointing and directing which the collective body of the people have no concern, and over which they have no controul'. In *Additional Observations* Price expanded this definition. He distinguished the liberty of the citizen, the liberty of the government, and the liberty of the community. 'A citizen is free when the power of commanding his own conduct and the quiet possession of his life, person, property and good name are *secured* to him by being his own legislator . . . a *government* is free when constituted in such a manner as to give this *security*. And the freedom of a community, or nation is the same among nations, that the freedom of a citizen is among his fellow citizens.'

It is instructive to compare Price's treatment of civil and political liberty with that given by Joseph Priestley, his friend and fellow Dissenter. In *An Essay on the First Principles of Government*, the first edition of which appeared in 1768, Priestley made a clear distinction between civil liberty and political liberty: the former he defined as 'that power over their own actions, which the members of the state reserve to themselves, and which their officers must not infringe', and the latter he defined as 'the power, which the members of the state reserve to themselves, of arriving at the public offices, or, at least, of having votes in the nomination of those who fill them'. Although he believed that the possession of political liberty is needed to secure civil liberties, Priestley preferred for reasons of clarity to make a firm distinction between them. Price, on the other hand, thought the possession of political liberty so essential to the security of civil liberty that he chose to make it part of the definition of civil liberty.

Ideally, following Rousseau, Price believed that civil liberty required that all members of the community should participate in the legislative process; but he realized that this would be impracticable in large communities, so he, unlike Rousseau, was prepared to sanction representation. In his practical recommendations Price was not prepared to advocate universal suffrage. From his definitions of freedom (and slavery) one would expect him to give unqualified support to the implementation of democratic institutions, but this is not what we find. In discussing his moral philosophy I pointed out how he conceded that where there are conflicts of principle a principle of lesser weight could be outweighed by one of greater weight. Similar considerations apply to his treatment of political principles. There is need to balance the claims of liberty with those of prudence. Price thought that it would not be safe to entrust the vote to those who were likely to sell it: consequently he would restrict the franchise to those capable of independent judgement. This qualification indicates that Price's main aim in securing parliamentary reform was in line with the Real Whig tradition, namely that of preventing the abuse of power. Those reforms should be introduced which would make the Commons less subservient to the Executive and more responsive to the weight of public opinion: it was for these reasons that Price gave priority to producing 'a fair and equal representation', the abolition of rotten boroughs, the enfranchisement of new towns, the removal of places and pensions and the introduction of annual Parliaments. These elements in Price's political philosophy need to be borne in mind when estimating the validity of Edmund Burke's criticism of him as one who dealt entirely in abstract speculations, and inalienable natural rights to the disregard of the claims of prudence.

In the preface to the fifth edition of *Observations on the Nature of Civil Liberty*, which he wrote in defence of the American rebels in their contest with the British administration, Price claimed that he followed in the footsteps of his mentor John Locke. Undoubtedly he owed a great deal to him. He accepted his rebuttal of the doctrine of the Divine Right of Kings. He follows him in maintaining that political authority is a creation of the people, that the forms of government are ways in which they choose to order their affairs, that civil society is instituted by the people coming together and agreeing among themselves to be bound by rules, and that government is a trust vested in those who have authority by the people. Price followed Locke too in holding that that political authority is limited, that its limits are determined by natural rights and by consideration of the common good, that political power should not be concentrated in one pair of hands but distributed over different estates, and that the functions of 'powers' of government should be distributed to different agencies of the State. Furthermore, Price followed Locke in holding that as far as

possible the State should be restricted to dealing with civil interests –
the maintenance of law and order, the defence of natural rights and
the protection of property – and that it should not concern itself with
spiritual matters other than preserving religious liberty by inhibiting
infringements of it.

But whether he was aware of it or not, Price's thought on political
matters can be seen to involve a more radical interpretation of the
doctrine of the social contract than Locke would have canvassed.
Locke supposed that when the people come together to form a political society, they agree among themselves to entrust the responsibili-
ties and the powers of government to those whom they choose to
govern them, undertaking to obey their rulers as long as their rulers
rule in accordance with the articles of the trust by which their authority was created. For as long as their rulers honour the trust placed in
them, the powers they have delegated to them are not revocable.
Although Price uses the concept of a trust of government, he intro-
duces a new idea: government is conceived to be an agency for executing the will of the people. The forms of government are just the ways
in which the people choose to regulate their affairs. Governors in all
they do are the servants of the people. Whereas Locke had held that
the right in the people to dismiss the government only arose when the
government had betrayed its trust, Price held that the people had the
right to change when they saw fit, and that, if it was their pleasure,
they had the right to reconstitute the forms of government. There is
therefore a tension in Price's thought between the notion that the
people have a right to resist government when power is abused and a
more radical thesis that the people have a right to refashion government as they please. There is also a tension between the view that
government is an instrument in the hands of the people, who are
sovereign, and the defence of the balanced constitution. It is difficult
to see how the notion that omnipotence lies with the people or their
chosen representatives can be reconciled with the view that the
exercise of power should be dispersed, except on the supposition that
the people will always be sufficiently wise to demand that there always
are constitutional checks to the exercise of power.

Observations on the Importance of the American Revolution is in part an
essay in congratulation, in part a tendering of advice. Price was
unbounded in his enthusiasm for the creation of a new kind of society
in America: a society without kings, without nobles, without bishops;

a society which dispensed with the need for a religious establishment; a society which secured religious liberty equally to all sects and denominations. Price thought that after the foundation of Christianity the American Revolution was the most important event in the history of mankind. The advice he gave to the new society illustrates his ideals, and evinces a strong strain of pragmatism in his thinking. The new society should defend religious liberty and the freedom of inquiry. It should not be tempted to pursue material wealth at all costs: it should remain sensitive to the dangers inherent in an extensive foreign trade, in the pursuit of luxury, in the growth of public indebtedness, in standing armies and in the emergence of inequalities. It should not deny freedom to the Negro. Price saw the dangers of an exaggerated emphasis on the autonomy of the various states that comprised the Union and counselled that the Federal Government should be given adequate powers to maintain law and order and to conduct the kind of foreign policy that would make the united states (notice how Price uses the lower case in this instance) respected in the world.

In *A Discourse on the Love of our Country*, although in a brief compass, Price eloquently expressed the ideals that had inspired him throughout a long career. He hoped that the spirit of reform kindled in America and productive of significant changes in France would inspire radicals at home. He defended the notion of natural, inalienable rights, the right to religious liberty, the right of inquiry, the right to participate in the process of government: he believed that reform to secure the universal enjoyment of these rights would lead to the betterment of the human condition and provide a basis for creating peace and harmony between nations. He saw in these reforms the workings of a Providence that was bringing about new and better forms of society. Above all, the *Discourse* was a celebration of a patriotism that is consistent with the Christian ethic of universal benevolence. Gone is the belief that we can glory in the spirit of conquest and domination: to be acceptable our love of our own must not infringe the equal rights of others and must be consistent with the prosperity of all. The unqualified optimism of the *Discourse* made Price an easy target for the denunciation of Edmund Burke, but it should be noted that his sermon did not do justice to Price's thought in its most mature form. In a sermon there was not enough time to make all the qualifications and all the reservations that the larger scope of a book or an extended pamphlet would have allowed. There was not enough space for Price to express the caution that he had shown in earlier pamphlets when discussing the dangers and the difficulties of putting 'a priori' principles into practice. The pragmatic element, the need to consider circumstance which Edmund Burke was to elaborate at great length in *Reflections on the Revolution in France*, and which had characterized Price's earlier work, was missing. Because of Burke's attack some commentators have fallen into the habit of referring to Price as 'the unfortunate Dr Price'. It may well be asked whether that epithet is deserved; his defence of religious liberty, of the freedom of inquiry, of the right to participate in the process of government, of national autonomy, of the equal partnership of different communities in one federation, above all, his concept of patriotism, deserve to be celebrated as an enduring contribution to the thought that has shaped our political traditions.

Chronology

1777 *Additional Observations.*
1778 *Two Tracts.*
      October: Invited by American Congress to become a citizen
      of the United States.
1781 *A Fast Sermon.*
1781 24 April: LL.D. at Yale.
1782 30 January: Elected to a Fellowship of the American
      Academy of Arts and Sciences at Boston.
1782 July: Shelburne becomes First Lord of the Treasury and
      William Pitt becomes Chancellor of the Exchequer.
1783 Relinquishes afternoon service at Newington Green.
      20 January: Preliminary Articles of Peace signed at
      Versailles.
      February: Shelburne resigns.
      December: William Pitt becomes First Lord of the
      Treasury and Chancellor of the Exchequer.
1784 *Observations on the Importance of the American Revolution.*
1785 Elected a member of the American Philosophical Society at
      Philadelphia.
1786 27 September: Sarah Price dies.
      29 March: Pitt's Sinking Fund Bill introduced in the
      House of Commons.
      Foundation of New College, Hackney.
1787 Price moves to St Thomas's Square, Hackney.
      *The Evidence for a Future Period of Improvement in the State of
      Mankind.*
1789 14 July: Fall of the Bastille.
      4 November: Meeting of the Revolution Society at the Old
      Jewry.
      A Discourse on the Love of our Country.
1791 Retires from his ministry at Gravel Pit, Hackney.
      19 April: dies.

Bibliographical note

Biography

Price's first biographer was his nephew, William Morgan, who published *Memoirs of the Life of The Rev. Richard Price, D.D.F.R.S.* in London in 1815. This is still an important, if occasionally unreliable, source. Additional material is to be found in Caroline Williams, *A Welsh Family*, 2nd edn (London, 1893). The first modern biography, a pioneering achievement, was Roland Thomas, *Richard Price: Philosopher and Apostle of Liberty* (Oxford, 1924), followed by Carl B. Cone, *Torchbearer of Freedom: the Influence of Richard Price on Eighteenth Century Thought* (Lexington, 1952): an impressive work, drawing on American sources not available to Roland Thomas.

Price's works

There is no collected edition of Price's works, although the British Library has a bound collection of various editions of his publications. A facsimile reprint of *Two Tracts* was published in New York in 1972. A scholarly edition with extensive annotation of *Two Tracts*, the 1779 *Fast Sermon* and *Observations on the Importance of the American Revolution*, together with extracts from contemporary criticism of Price, extracts from his correspondence and a critical introduction was published by Bernard Peach under the title *Richard Price and the Ethical Foundations of the American Revolution* at Durham, N.C., in 1979. A bilingual (in English and Welsh) version of *A Discourse on the Love of our Country*, edited and translated by P. A. L. Jones, was published under the title *Cariad at ein gwlad* at Aberystwyth in 1989. Price's main contribution to philosophy, indispensable for an understanding of his political philosophy, *A review of the Principal Questions and Difficulties in Morals*, was published in 1758: it was republished with a critical introduction by D. D. Raphael at Oxford in 1948 (revised impression, 1974). A facsimile edition of *Four Dissertations*, first published in 1767, with an introduction by John Stephens, appeared in Bristol in 1990. Price's correspondence is in the process of being published; the first volume, *The Correspondence of Richard Price*, edited by D. O. Thomas and Bernard Peach, was published at Durham, N.C., and Cardiff in 1983. Price's shorthand journal, deciphered by Beryl Thomas and edited by D. O. Thomas, was published in *The National Library of Wales Journal*, vol. 21, no. 4 (1980). A comprehensive bibliography of Price's works edited by D. O. Thomas, John Stephens and P. A. L. Jones is shortly to appear in the St Paul's bibliographies.

Price's thought

In 1970 Henri Laboucheix published *Richard Price: théoricien de la Revolution Américaine, le philosophe et le sociologue, le pamphlétaire et l'orateur*, a comprehensive study of the origins of Price's thought. An English translation of this work by Sylvia and David Raphael was published under the title *Richard Price as Moral Philosopher and Political Theorist* at Oxford in 1982. *The Honest Mind: the Thought and Work of Richard Price* by D. O. Thomas was published at Oxford in 1977. Other relevant works by the same author are *Richard Price and America* (Aberystwyth, 1975), *Richard Price* (Cardiff, 1976), and *Ymateb i chwyldro: Response to Revolution* (Cardiff, 1989). Important contributions to the study of Price's moral philosophy are to be found in W. D. Hudson, *Reason and Right* (London, 1970) and D. D. Raphael, *The Moral Sense* (Oxford, 1947). The millennialist elements in Price's thought are fully investigated in Jack Fruchtman, Jr, 'The Apocalyptic Politics of Richard Price and Joseph Priestley', *Transactions of the American Philosophical Society*, vol. 73, part 4 (1983).

Articles devoted to Price's wide-ranging intellectual concerns are to be found in *The Price–Priestley Newsletter* (1977–80) and its successor, *Enlightenment and Dissent* (1982–), edited by Martin Fitzpatrick and D. O. Thomas.

Criticism and background

Valuable criticisms of Price's thought and/or expositions of the cultural and political background are to be found in: Max Beloff (ed.), *The Debate on the American Revolution, 1761–1783* (2nd edn, London, 1960); Colin Bonwick, *English Radicals and the American Revolution* (Chapel Hill, N.C., 1979); Peter Brown, *The Chathamites* (London, 1967); Alfred Cobban (ed.), *The Debate on the French Revolution, 1789–1800* (London, 1950); Albert Goodwin, *The Friends of Liberty: the English Democratic Movement in the age of the French Revolution* (London, 1979); J. A. W. Gunn, *Beyond Liberty and Property* (Kingston and Montreal, 1983); Ursula Henriques, *Religious Toleration in England, 1787–1833*; Robert Hole, *Pulpits, Politics, and Public Order in England, 1760–1832* (Cambridge, 1989); Anthony Lincoln, *Some Political and Social Ideas of English Dissent, 1763–1800* (Cambridge, 1938; reprinted New York, 1971); Caroline Robbins, *The Eighteenth-Century Commonwealthman* (Cambridge, Mass., 1959); Thomas Schlereth, *The Cosmopolitan Ideal in Enlightenment Thought* (Notre Dame and London, 1977); Leslie Stephen, *History of English Thought in the Eighteenth Century*, 3rd edn (2 vols., London, 1902); M. R. Watts, *The Dissenters: from the Reformation to the French Revolution* (Oxford, 1978).

Biographical notes

ADAMS, John (1735–1826), President of the United States of America (1796–1801). Author of *A Defence of the Constitutions of Government of the United States of America, against the Attack of M. Turgot in his Letter to Doctor Price dated the twenty second of March 1778* (3 vols., London, 1787–8). During his stay in London as Minister Plenipotentiary to the Court of St James, Adams and his wife Abigail were frequent attenders at Gravel Pit Meeting Place, Hackney, where Price was a minister.

BURGH, James (1714–75), schoolmaster and author. In 1747 he opened a school in Stoke Newington and later became a close friend of Price; he and his pupils attended Price's Meeting House at Newington Green. He wrote several influential works, among them *Political Disquisitions* (3 vols., London, 1774–5), which proved to be a mine of information heavily exploited by writers sympathetic to radical causes. He defended the American rebels and was a strong advocate of parliamentary reform.

BURKE, Edmund (1729–97), one of the most influential of all British Conservative political thinkers. He enters the biography of Price as a critic of what he conceived to be Price's abstract speculations, in *A letter to the Sheriffs of Bristol* (1777), but his best-known denunciation of Price's natural rights philosophy occurs in *Reflections on the Revolution in France* (1790), a critique provoked by *A Discourse on the Love of our Country*. Burke's animosity towards Price was heightened by his hatred of Price's patron, the Earl of Shelburne.

Biographical notes

BUTLER, Joseph (1692–1752), Bishop of Bristol (1738–50), Bishop of Durham (1750–2). Author of *The Analogy of Religion, Natural and Revealed, to the Constitution and Course of Nature* (London, 1736).

CARTWRIGHT, Major John (1740–1824), entered the navy at the age of eighteen and saw active service under Lord Howe. In 1770 medical problems forced him to return home. In 1775 he became a major in the Nottinghamshire militia, but his military career was cut short by his refusal, on account of his sympathies with the American rebels, to join Lord Howe's command. His career as a political reformer began in 1775, and in 1776 he published *Take your Choice*, in which he advocated annual Parliaments, universal suffrage and a secret ballot. He deserves wider recognition than he has received for the part he played in promoting radicalism and democratic politics.

CHATHAM, William Pitt the Elder, first Earl of (1708–78), statesman and orator. He was much revered by Price, partly because with Shelburne he headed the political groups whose aims Price accepted, and partly because of the support he gave to the Dissenters in their struggle to be relieved of subscription to the Thirty-nine Articles.

CLARKE, Samuel (1675–1729), Rector of St James's, Piccadilly. Author of *A Discourse concerning the Being and Attributes of God, the Obligations of Natural Religion, and the Truth and Certainty of the Christian Revelation* (London, 1705–6). In *A Review of the Principal Questions in Morals* Price refers to Clarke (along with Newton and Butler) as one of the three greatest names the world has ever known (ed. Raphael, p. 291).

FERGUSON, Adam (1723–1816), became Professor of Natural Philosophy at Edinburgh in 1759 and Professor of Moral Philosophy, also at Edinburgh, in 1764. Author of *An Essay on the History of Civil Society* (Edinburgh, 1767). In 1778 he was appointed secretary to the Carlisle Commission sent to America to negotiate a settlement.

FILMER, Sir Robert (*c.* 1588–1653), author of *Patriarcha, or the Natural Power of Kings* (London, 1680), which was published posthumously in an attempt to bolster the authority of the Stuarts. It embodied the theory of the Divine Right of Kings, a theory which was comprehensively attacked by John Locke in his *First Treatise on Civil Government* (London, 1690).

FRANKLIN, Benjamin (1706–90), first met Price during his visit to England in the period July 1757 to August 1762, and they remained firm friends and frequent correspondents until Franklin's death in 1790. They were both Fellows of the Royal Society and members of the Club of Honest Whigs, a group that had considerable influence on the development of the political thought of those groups hostile to the policy of the administration, and, under Franklin's guidance, in support of the American colonists.

HOADLY, Benjamin (1676–1761), successively Bishop of Bangor, Hereford, Salisbury and Winchester. One of Price's heroes. Price particularly admired his attack on the theory of Divine Right set out in *The Measures of Submission to the Civil Magistrate, Consider'd* (London, 1706), and his support of the Dissenters in their struggle to secure the repeal of the Test and Corporation Acts.

HUME, David (1711–76), philosopher and historian. Although Price was vehemently opposed to Hume's scepticism and to his subjectivism in ethics, their personal relationships seem to have been very amicable and they were both in agreement on many political issues, as, for example, the dangers of ever-increasing public indebtedness.

KIPPIS, Andrew (1725–95), DD, FRS, a leading Dissenting minister. From June 1753 until 1786 pastor of Princes Street Chapel, Westminster. Became tutor in classics and philology at Hoxton Academy in 1763 and Professor of Belles-Lettres at New College, Hackney in 1786. Edited *Biographia Britannica*. He delivered the address celebrating the foundation of New College, Hackney in 1786, and on 4 November 1788 addressed the Revolution Society, a year before Price delivered to them his *Discourse on the Love of our Country*.

LOCKE, John (1632–1704), the philosopher whose work in a wide range of subjects was for long considered to be, not without reason, the most formative influence on the development of eighteenth-century thought in Britain. Author of *Two Treatises on Government* (1689/90) and *An Essay concerning Human Understanding* (1690). In the preface to the fifth edition of *Observations on the Nature of Civil Liberty* Price claimed that his principles on political matters 'are the same as those taught by Mr. Locke'.

MARKHAM, William (1719–1807), Bishop of Chester (1771–6), Archbishop of York (1776–1807). He was highly critical of Price's defence of the American colonists, and appeared to threaten the Dissenters with penal sanctions.

MIRABEAU, Comte Honoré Riquetti de (1749–91), politician, orator. He translated, or arranged for the translation, into French of Price's *Observations on the Importance of the American Revolution*. He also included an abstract of Price's pamphlet in his own publication, *Considérations sur l'ordre de Cincinnatus* (1785).

MONTESQUIEU, Charles Louis de Secondat, Baron de La Brède et (1689–1755), author of *De l'esprit des lois*, a highly influential work in the development of political thought in the eighteenth century, especially in defence of the theory of the balanced constitution.

NECKER, Jacques (1732–1804), held the post of Director-General of Finance in France from 1777 to 1781, and from 1788 to December 1790, except for a brief period in 1789. Author of *Traité de l'administration des finances de France* (1784).

PRIESTLEY, Joseph (1733–1804), DD, FRS, Dissenting minister, celebrated chemist and polymath. He first met Price in January 1766 when he was on a visit to London from Warrington, where he was a tutor at the Academy, and was taken by Price as a guest to a meeting of the Royal Society. Thereafter they remained firm friends even though they disagreed on many theological and philosophical topics. Whereas Price was an Arian, Priestley became a Socinian; whereas Price was an intuitionist, Priestley was a utilitarian; whereas Price was a dualist and a libertarian, Priestley was a determinist and a materialist. In 1778 they together published *A Free Discussion of the Doctrines of Materialism and Philosophical Necessity*, in which they debated their disagreements vigorously but amicably. Priestley was Shelburne's librarian from 1774 to 1780, when he moved to Birmingham to become minister at the New Meeting House. His home, library and laboratory were destroyed in the riots of 1791, after which he moved to London to become a minister at Gravel Pit Meeting Place at Hackney. In 1794 he emigrated to America and did not return to this country.

SHELBURNE, Sir William Petty (1737–1805), second Earl of, became First Lord of Trade in Grenville's administration in 1763 and from 1766 to 1768 was Secretary of State for the Southern Department. Thereafter he remained in Opposition to the government until in 1782 he became Home Secretary in Rockingham's administration. He was Prime Minister from July 1782 until February 1783. Created Marquis of Lansdowne in 1784. Price first met Shelburne in 1771 and thereafter became a frequent visitor at Bowood and at Shelburne House, advising Shelburne on matters of government finance. Price dedicated the third edition of *Observations on Reversionary Payments* to him.

TUCKER, Josiah (1712–99), Dean of Gloucester. Prominent as an advocate of the view that the colonies were more of a burden than a benefit to Britain.

TURGOT, Anne Robert Jacques (1727–81), economist, Minister of Finance in France (1774–6). It was Turgot's celebrated letter to Price of 22 March 1778, published in Price's *Observations on the Importance of the American Revolution*, that provoked John Adams to write his three-volume *A Defence of the Constitutions of Government of the United States of America*. Like Price and Priestley, celebrated by Condorcet as a defender of the notion of the 'infinite perfectibility of man'.

WILKES, John (1727–97), politician, Lord Mayor of London, exile and MP. He was at the centre of the controversies regarding the publication of an obscene libel, the issue of general warrants, and the Middlesex election. In the House of Commons on 10 December 1777, Wilkes moved the repeal of the Declaratory Act. Although Price was scandalized by his private life, he supported Wilkes's various stands on constitutional issues. For his part Wilkes had a warm regard for Price's advocacy of parliamentary reform and defence of the colonists.

A note on the texts

Britain's Happiness, and the Proper Improvement of it

This sermon is reproduced from the pamphlet published in 1759 by A. Millar and R. Griffiths in the Strand.

Two Tracts on Civil Liberty, the War with America, and the Debts and Finances of the Kingdom

The first tract, *Observations on the Nature of Civil Liberty, the Principles of Government, and the Justice and Policy of the War with America*, was published in February 1776; the second tract, *Additional Observations on the Nature and Value of Civil Liberty, and the War with America*, appeared a year later. In 1778 Price decided to republish both with a new 'General Introduction'. Because of his habit of adding supplements and appendices (some of which were also published separately) and because these different elements or combinations of them were bound up in different ways, this is one of the most bibliographically complex productions of the eighteenth century. The text of the selections printed here is based on the first edition, published by Thomas Cadell in 1778 and reprinted in the Da Capo Press Reprint Series in New York in 1972, except for the passages from the 'General Introduction' which are taken from the version in Bernard Peach, *Richard Price and the Ethical Foundations of the American Revolution* (Durham, N.C., 1979). The selection includes passages from the 'General Introduction', the whole of *Observations on the Nature of Civil*

Liberty as it appeared in *Two Tracts* (that is, excluding the section on the nation's finances that had appeared in the 1776 editions), and the first section of *Additional Observations*.

A Fast Sermon (1781)

This sermon is reproduced from the pamphlet published by Thomas Cadell in that year, omitting Price's postscript and advertisement.

Observations on the Importance of the American Revolution and the means of making it a Benefit to the World

This pamphlet is reproduced from the 1785 edition published by Thomas Cadell, omitting Turgot's letter to Price dated 22 March 1778, and the appendix.

The Evidence for a Future Period of Improvement in the State of Mankind

This address is reproduced from the pamphlet published by Thomas Cadell and J. Johnson in 1787.

A Discourse on the Love of our Country

The text of this address is taken from the sixth edition (1790) published by Thomas Cadell, omitting Price's appendices.

Price added many notes to his texts before publication and in successive editions. These have been scaled down. He composed in a way that as a preacher he would have found convenient, with a liberal use of capitals, with a lavish use of underlining and dashes and with heavy punctuation. In these respects his text has been modernized, although his spelling remains virtually unchanged. The notes preceded by a number are Price's; those preceded by a letter of the alphabet are mine. I wish to thank Mr P. A. L. Jones, my wife Beryl and my daughter Janet for their kindness in helping me to prepare the text. I also wish to thank Ms Pauline Marsh and Ms Jayne Matthews for the skill they have shown and the great care they have taken in preparing the text for publication and supervising the production process.

Britain's Happiness, and the Proper Improvement of it
(1759)

Britain's Happiness,
and
the proper improvement of it,
represented in a
sermon,
preach'd
at Newington-Green, Middlesex,
on Nov. 29. 1759.
Being the Day appointed for a
General Thanksgiving.
(1759)

Psal. cxlvii. 20.
He hath not dealt so with any nation: And as for his judgments,
they have not known them. Praise ye the Lord.

This psalm contains a warm exhortation, addressed to the Jewish
people, to praise God for the blessings and benefits which he had
conferred upon them.

Praise the Lord, for it is good to sing praises unto our God, and praise is
comely.

Praise the Lord, O Jerusalem. Praise thy God, O Zion. For he hath
strengthened the bars of thy gates.

He hath blessed thy children within thee. He maketh peace in thy borders
and filleth thee with the finest of the wheat. He sheweth his word unto Jacob,

his statutes and his judgments unto Israel. He hath not dealt so with any nation: and as for his judgments, they have not known them. Praise ye the Lord. The whole of this passage is applicable, with great propriety, to this Kingdom on the present occasion. We have like reasons for joy and thanksgiving, and may now take up these words and say: *Praise thy God, Oh Britain! For he hath strengthened the bars of thy gates. He hath blessed thy children within thee. He maketh peace in thy borders and filleth thee with the finest of the wheat. He hath shewed his word unto thee, his statutes and his judgments. He hath not dealt so with any nation, and as for his judgments they have not known them. Praise ye the Lord.*

My present design is (I) to shew you how happily we are distinguished as a nation, and (II) what effects the consideration of our peculiar happiness ought to have upon us.

In speaking on the former of these heads, the circumstance I shall first mention is our situation as an island, by which our internal peace and tranquillity are secured.

Nothing can be more affecting than to think of the dismal state of many of the countries about us, where the noise and tumults of war fill every ear, where powerful armies march in dreadful pomp spreading devastation around them, and numberless innocent persons are driven from their houses and families and all that is dear to them. In those countries garments are continually rolled in blood, and none can enjoy any thing in comfort or security. They live in perpetual terror. *They plant vineyards without knowing who shall eat the fruit thereof. They carry seed into the field, without knowing who shall gather in the harvest,* and their wives and their children and themselves often fall a prey to relentless insult and cruelty.

But we are exempted from all these miseries. *We can sit every man under his own vine and under his fig-tree, and no one maketh us afraid.* As long as we agree among ourselves, it is scarcely possible that we should become the seat of war. The ocean is our wall of defense, which guards us on all sides, and cuts off our communication with the neighbouring nations, so that no hostile feet or destroying armies can easily alarm our borders. We live in the quiet and full possession of all our properties and blessings, without being in any danger from the inroads of enemies or the depredations of lawless savages. We *hear* indeed of the dreadful calamities and desolations of war, but we only *hear* of them. We neither *feel* nor *see* them. And so little is the difference between the state of most of us now, and what it was before the commencement of war, that, was it not for the accounts we read and the reports conveyed to us, we should scarcely know that we are engaged in war.

How great a privilege is this? How distinguishingly happy are we to possess thus, among contending nations and in the midst of desolation and bloodshed, tranquillity and security and almost all the enjoyments and sweets of peace?

Secondly. Another part of our peculiar happiness, as a nation, is the plenty and opulence we enjoy. God has given us the appointed weeks of harvest. He has satisfied our poor with bread, and crowned our seasons with his goodness. We want nothing that can contribute to make us easy and happy. All the conveniences and even the elegancies of life are poured upon us in the greatest profusion. Such plenty have we, that we help to feed and cloath other nations. Such is our opulence, that there is not a kingdom upon earth which can in this respect be compared with us. Notwithstanding all the drains of war, we feel no very sensible scarcity of any kind. Our wealth increases continually; and it may be questioned whether any nation ever raised, with so much ease, such large expences as have been laid out by this nation in the present war. Our commerce is extended from one end of the earth to the other. Our naval force is unrivaled. Our enemies dare not shew themselves before our fleets; and we are acknowledged by all the world as the sovereigns of the sea.

But there is a still higher instance of our distinguished happiness to be mentioned; I mean the LIBERTY we are blessed with. There is no country where this is enjoyed in such extent and perfection. The greatest part of the rest of mankind are *slaves*. They are subject to arbitrary and insolent masters, who say to them bow down before us that we may go over you, and who have their properties and lives entirely at their mercy. How melancholy a situation must this be; and how disgraceful to human nature is it, that men should be capable of enduring such encroachments on their natural rights; or that, in so many countries, such slavish forms of government should take place, human beings descend, by hereditary right, like beasts, from one tyrant to another, and the will of, perhaps, the most silly and contemptible creature in a nation, be established as its supreme guide and law?

But our case is totally different. While other nations groan under

3

slavery, we rejoice in the possession of liberty and independency. Our rights and properties are, in general, secured to us beyond the possibility of violation. Every man among us can enjoy the fruits of his industry without restraint or disturbance. We can have no burdens laid upon us without our own consent, and the laws by which we are governed are not such as a senseless tyrant may please to appoint, but such as we ourselves by our representatives concur in making. The meanest of our fellow-subjects cannot have the least injury done him without being able to find redress. No life can be taken away, or any punishment inflicted on any one, without a fair and equitable trial. The King himself has not power to touch the person, to seize any part of the property, or to make the smallest infringement on the liberty, of any one man in his dominions.

But our religious liberty is the crown of all our national advantages. There are other nations who enjoy civil liberty as well as we, tho' perhaps not so completely. But with respect to religious liberty we are almost singular and unparalleled.

In other countries not only the lives and fortune, but the souls and consciences of men are subject to the absolute will of their governors. In those countries a person dare not speak his mind about religious matters, or avow any opinions different from those commonly received, without exposing himself to the greatest dangers. Nothing, surely, can be more dismal than for men to have their minds thus shackled, to be obliged to receive without examination the decisions of ignorant pretenders to spiritual authority, or to be deprived of a liberty which is the very last thing a wise man would consent to part with, I mean, that of worshiping God according to his conscience, and of professing those principles of religion, which he thinks, come nearest to the simplicity of the Gospel.

If it is a disgrace to human nature, as I have observed before, that men should be capable of enduring civil slavery, how much more ignominious and dastardly is it to suffer themselves to be inslaved in religious matters, or to follow blindly the direction of earthly masters in things that concern their everlasting salvation?

But we, Brethren, are unspeakably happier. We see the shameful folly of this. The principles of liberty have been thoroughly explained and are now generally understood and embraced among us. We well know that Christ is the only law-giver of Christians, that there can be no such thing as human authority in religious matters, and that the office of the magistrate is not to interpose in any religious differences, but to keep the peace, to secure the civil rights of men, and to protect and encourage all good subjects of all sects and persuasions. In this nation every one may judge for himself, and act agreeably to his judgment, without molestation or fear. A free and publick discussion is allowed of all points, even such as in other nations it would be imprisonment or death to discover any doubts about. All sects enjoy the benefit of toleration, and may worship God in whatever way they think most acceptable to him; and nothing exposes any person to civil penalties or censures, but overt acts inconsistent with the peace and security of society. The researches of learned men among us have been pushed farther than ever they were in any nation. An absolute and unbounded scope is given to enquiries of all kinds; and the consequence of this has been, that the greatest improvements have been made in all the sciences, and that we are now become the Fountain-head of knowledge, and the Instructors of the world.

Religious knowledge, I think, in particular owes more to us that [than?] to all the world besides. It would be wonderful indeed if it did not, considering our distinctions in other respects. Christianity has been cleared among us of a great deal of that shocking rubbish, which has been thrown upon it by Popery. And, perhaps, there never was a time, since that of the Apostles, in which the nature and design of the Gospel were so well understood, and its evidences and excellency so well explained, as in the present age and kingdom.

Blessed are our eyes, for they see, while those of others are shut. Blessed are our minds, for they are free, while those of others are fettered and enslaved. Here light and knowledge prevail, and from hence the arts and sciences diffuse their influence, and are propagated to the nations around us. In this Island peace and liberty have fixed their abode, and from hence superstition, persecution, and slavery are fled, while in other nations they still remain to confound and terrify and oppress the souls of men.

How is it possible to reflect on these things without joy and exultation? How happy is it for us that our lot has been cast in such a land? A land favoured with so many invaluable privileges and advantages. A land where, peace, plenty, knowledge and liberty abound and flourish. A land which has the best constitution of government, the best laws, the best king and the best religion in the world.

To this account of our happiness I shall add once more, that we have among us many persons of characters eminent for virtue and piety founded upon rational principles. I wish however I had more to say on this head. It must be acknowledged that our improvements in goodness have by no means been proportionable to those which we have made in other respects. But tho' this is true; yet, without doubt, there are in this kingdom many truly worthy and good men; and were they to be collected together from the different persuasions of Christians among us, they would, whatever they might be in comparison with the rest of the nation, appear, I imagine, a great multitude. These are, indeed, the flowers of the nation. They are the cause of all its happiness and its chief glory. Were these taken away, its whole beauty would be destroyed, its prosperity would be blasted, and immediate ruin would overtake it. That we have then any considerable number of these in the nation must be matter of great consolation to us, and it ought to be our whole study and business to add to this number by at least adding ourselves to it.

To say no more here. One branch of virtue at least there is which shines with peculiar lustre among us. Our charities exceed all that ever was known in any kingdom. And tho' there is among us a prodigious rabble of loose and irreligious persons, yet I cannot but hope and presume, that there is not a spot on earth of equal size which has an equal number of good persons in it, or where there are so many who understand so well what true religion is, and who so uniformly and steddily practise it.

What I have hitherto said, contains chiefly an account of such particulars of our happiness as constitute what seems to be our permanent and settled state as a nation, and what has been its state for a course of many years.

But there are some particulars to be added which relate peculiarly to the present time, and which, on this occasion, it would be inexcusable not to remember. During the course of this year, this happy and memorable year, you all know what occasions of joy we have met with, and what additions have been made to our glory.

The tumults of party seem to be laid asleep among us; and God grant they may never wake more. Scarcely one murmur is there to be heard any where. Our counsels have been wise, our measures vigorous and our enterprizes successful. Our Navy and our Army have gained the highest honour by their unanimity and bravery. Our enemies have been taught to fear and to feel our superiority. They have fled before us every where. They have been conquered by sea and by land, and in all the quarters of the world. Their towns, their ships and their fortresses have been delivered up into our hands; and we now appear among the nations great, rich, prosperous and form-idable, whilst they appear mean and wretched, and are impoverished, distracted and confounded. With the utmost propriety, therefore, may we on this joyful day adopt the words of my text, and say: *Surely God hath not dealt so with any nation.*

One circumstance, indeed, there is, relating to our late successes and victories, which cannot but deeply affect our minds. They have cost us some of the best blood that was ever shed. When we think of those brave men who have sacrificed their lives in our defence, all the springs of grateful anguish must be opened within us, and it becomes almost impossible to avoid mingling tears with the joy of this day. But, my Brethren and Countrymen, amidst the concern we must feel on this account, let us remember how gloriously they have fallen, and that they are more the objects of envy than lamentation. Their exam-ple, we may expect, will kindle courage in others, and their spirit be transfused into thousands who will emulate their virtues and aspire to their glory. There ought not indeed to be one person in this nation, whose heart does not glow with this emulation, and who does not earnestly wish, that he could die the same death, and that his latter end might be like theirs. How much better is it to expire thus in a blaze of glory earned by virtue, and to go down to the grave followed by the acclamations and the tears of a nation, than to drag a worthless life beneath universal contempt and infamy?

Having now represented to you our happiness as a nation, it is proper that I should next endeavour to shew you what improvement we ought to make of it, or what effects the consideration of it should have upon us.

In the first place, it must be very obvious that we ought to be thankful for our happiness. We ought to have a deep sense of it upon our hearts, and to praise God for assigning us our passage thro' life in such a country, and blessing it with so many mercies and advantages.

'Tis to God we owe all that makes us happy. 'Tis he that bringeth down one nation, and that exalteth another. 'Tis from him that all the distinctions among the communities, as well as the individuals of mankind, are derived. All events are subject to his superintendency, *and he doeth whatsoever he pleaseth in the armies of heaven and among the*

7

inhabitants of the earth. We ought therefore, in all circumstances, to acknowledge and adore his hand. We ought to ascribe all our successes to his goodness, and, with grateful hearts, to direct our regards to his providence, and to fix our dependence upon his favour, as the original sources of all prosperity and bliss. So distinguishing and invaluable are our national privileges, that it is not possible for us to be thankful enough for them; and miserably base and disingenuous would it be in us to discover in such happy circumstances no thankful emotions, or, amidst such a profusion of blessings, to forget and neglect the supreme Author of all blessings. There are, I believe, many among us who are capable of this detestable impiety and profaneness; and it cannot but give every good man great pain to think of their characters; or to observe that inattention to providence, and that readiness to ascribe all our advantages to our own merit, without any thought of the Deity, which prevail among us. It is with the greatest pleasure that I can observe to you here, that we have had a better example set us from the throne, which has been since followed in both houses of Parliament. May the influence of so noble an example extend itself every where, and be communicated to every heart in the nation. There are indeed, in the successes we have lately met with, so many appearances of a providential disposal of things in our favour, as one would think sufficient to kindle devotion in the coldest breast, and to extort acknowledgement and praise from the most blind and atheistical. In all events we ought to look higher than second causes, but in cases, where the fate of nations is concerned, to ascribe events (of so striking a kind especially as those we this day celebrate) to human agency merely, would show an insensibility and ignorance of the most shocking nature. Let us study carefully to avoid such guilt; and, while we honour and admire the instruments of our happiness, let us remember that they are no more than the instruments of it, and that our thoughts ought always to be directed primarily and chiefly to that Almighty Being who is the cause of all causes, the ruler of all events, and the *giver of every good and perfect gift.*

The antient heathens thought they did the greatest honour to their Heroes and Warriors, when they represented them as favoured of heaven, and indebted to superior power for their successes.

The Psalmist, after mentioning in my text the peculiar happiness of the Jewish nation, adds immediately, *Praise ye the Lord.* No exhortation could be more properly added. We have as much reason to praise the Lord as the Jews had. We seem to be, as they were, his peculiar and favourite people; and nothing can be more fit than that, with joy and triumph, we should *magnify his holy name.*

Secondly, the peculiar happiness we enjoy ought to lead us to the general practise of virtue and religion. This, above all things, ought to be the effect of God's goodness to us. The unspeakable riches of his forbearance and love should engage us to amend our evil ways, and to fear and obey him. We shall shew the most shameful perverseness, if we convert the benefits he heaps upon us into instruments of rebellion against him, or make the plenty and the liberty with which he distinguishes us, the occasions of luxury and licentiousness.

We are now, God be praised, a great, a free and powerful people. As far as we have among us any principles of true ingenuity, the consideration of this will make us ambitious to shew ourselves worthy of our advantages by our integrity, humanity, and piety. The continuance of our happiness depends entirely on the practise of righteousness among us. It is this alone that exalteth a nation, and that can maintain its dignity and superiority. If our remarkable successes produce no other effect than to increase irreligion among us, or to make us more proud and wanton, and mad after pleasure; then may we well fear, that our glory will be soon laid in the dust, and our enemies, now under our feet, raised up to humble and chastise us. Let then every one of us labour to the greatest extent of his power to practise virtue himself, and to promote it in others. Thus shall we be the means of strengthening in the best manner the foundations of our public happiness, and do the greatest service to our country. Nothing need give us the least pain about this kingdom, except the vice and irreligion which prevail in it. Every vicious man is a canker at the root of our happiness, and a curse to his country. Sin, without doubt, is the worst enemy a nation can have; and our sins are peculiarly aggravated by being committed in a land blest with such light as ours enjoys. But, yet, we find that heaven smiles upon us, and that we are happy beyond example. What then should we be, and how should we be favoured, did publick virtue prevail among us in proportion to our successes and advantages?

Thirdly, a sense of our peculiar happiness ought to engage us to endeavour to establish and improve it. After advancing so far, it will be inexcusable to stop short, or to neglect doing our utmost to push things to that point of perfection which we have brought so nearly within our reach. Our glory is great. How ambitious should we be to place it above all danger, and to wipe off from it every stain? Is it not too sadly notorious, and has it not been often lamented by the wisest and best men amongst us, that, in our constitution, both civil and ecclesiastical, there are many particulars, which greatly want amendment, and some of which are inconsistent with that liberty, which is the chief subject of our boast and triumph, and really a scandal to a great and wise people?

It would be very easy to give a particular recital of these, and to mention many alterations and amendments, which would make us greater and happier. What an addition, for instance, to our strength and riches would be produced by encouraging foreign Protestants to settle among us? What a dreadful load of prevarication and perjury, which overwhelms the integrity, and destroys the souls of multitudes about us, might be taken off by abolishing all useless tests and lessening the number of oaths? At the time that our present religious establishment was made, the nation was but just emerging from Popery. Is it possible then, that it should be entirely agreeable to the purity of the Christian doctrine and worship, or that it should want no review in order to secure its safety, and adapt it to a more improved and enlightened age?

But I will not enlarge here, lest I should offend any worthy men, and deviate into what would be inconsistent with the design of this day.

Were those alterations and amendments made effectually but willingly, which almost every body now sees to be necessary, and which, as generous sentiments spread, are daily growing more and more necessary; and were we likewise heartily to love one another amidst our religious differences, and to study above all things to imbibe the spirit and to obey the precepts of our holy religion, nothing would be wanting to raise us to the highest pitch of grandeur and prosperity, and to make us the pride and wonder of the earth.

In the mean time, however, it is, I think, our duty, as private men, to do what we can towards removing those offences which dishonour our country, by declaring our sentiments about them, on all proper occasions, with modesty and humility; by never complying in any instance contrary to our sentiments; and giving as far as possible, a publick testimony in favour of universal liberty and the simplicity of the Gospel. As long as wise men will not do this, or indulge timidity and indolence, it is certain, that corruptions must continue, and that no alterations or improvements can ever be expected. Had the primitive Christians, or the first reformers, acted thus, neither Christianity nor the reformation would ever have taken in the world.

Fourthly, the consideration of our unparalleled happiness should engage us to do every thing in our power, to preserve and defend it against all dangerous attacks. Who would not exert himself to the utmost in such a cause? Who would not sooner sacrifice every thing in the world than part with so much bliss? What shame ought to confound that man who, in such a country, can entertain one factious thought, or discover the least reluctance in contributing his part towards its support?

How do I wish that, on this occasion, I had a voice which could reach and penetrate the hearts of all my countrymen, that I might make them more deeply sensible of their unspeakable happiness, and convince them effectually that there never was a people, who had so much reason to shew themselves valiant; that I might inspire them with the most ardent gratitude to the Author of all good for their blessings, and engage them to pray continually for the peace of our Jerusalem, to forget private interest and party prejudices in zeal for virtue and their country, and to concur, as one man, in striving to exalt this nation to the highest, and to make it an example of all that is great and excellent!

We are engaged in a most important and decisive war. Upon the issue of it depends, in a great measure, all that is valuable to us, and the state of Europe, perhaps, for many ages to come. Let us, joyfully, give every aid possible towards making it successful, and towards humbling that cruel and faithless nation, which has so long been the plague of Europe, and in whose weakness our only security lies: Remembring that we have *every thing* to fight for, they *nothing* except their breaden God and their chains; and that the consequence of our being conquered by them would be our sinking into the lowest infamy, our becoming, what they are, ignoble and miserable slaves, and the prevalency once more among us of that religion which would crush all our liberties and privileges, which would teach us to cut one another's throats in order to do God service, and which is the shame and the scourge of mankind. Oh! frightful prospect! Can any *British* heart bear to view it with patience?

But, thanks be to God, there seems at present no danger of any such event. We are the bulwark of the Protestant interest in the world, and this is an interest which, we may hope, God will not forsake. We have been hitherto wonderfully prospered; and we have shewn our enemies what they may expect, if they go on to contend with us. This year will always shine among the brightest in our Annals. Never, never was *Britain* so glorious.

But, let us not be too much elated. The struggle is not yet over, and the issues of war are still uncertain. 'Tis *possible* that we may lose the advantages we have gained, and our joy and triumph be suddenly changed to misery and despair. Let us then rejoyce with trembling, and suppress carefully in ourselves all vain confidence, placing our chief trust in God, and discovering, in all events, that regard to the common welfare of mankind and those equitable, reasonable, and pious dispositions, which are the best proofs of true magnanimity, and the best means of securing the continuance of the divine protection.

Lastly, the account, which has been given of the happy state of this nation, may lead our thoughts to that time when the whole world shall enjoy the like happiness. The scriptures, I think, give us abundant reason to expect such a time; a time when Popish darkness and oppression shall be exceeded by universal peace and liberty, *and nation no more lift up a sword against nation*; when the everlasting Gospel in its native purity shall prevail thro' the whole earth, and the *kingdoms of this world become the kingdoms of the Lord and of his Christ.*

The invention of printing followed by the reformation and the revival of Literature; the free communication which has been opened between the different parts of the world, and the late amazing improvements in knowledge of every kind, have remarkably prepared the way for this joyful period. The world is now advanced far beyond its infancy. There are many indications of an approaching general amendment in human affairs. The season fixed by prophecy for the destruction of the *man of sin* cannot be far distant, and the glorious light of *the latter days* seems to be now dawning upon mankind from this happy Island.

Nothing can be more pleasing than to indulge such views and hopes; and it should be a great encouragement to those who have espoused the principles of liberty, and who stand up against anti-christian usurpations and corruptions, to consider, that it is by such principles this period is likely to be introduced, and that, in the end, they must prevail over all opposition. This should engage them to adhere steddily to them under all difficulties, and to strive, by all the methods consistent with true wisdom and benevolence, to diffuse and propagate them, thro' the world. There have been many in this nation who have nobly distinguished themselves in this work, and may their names be had in everlasting remembrance and honour.

Two Tracts
(1778)

Two Tracts
on
Civil Liberty,
the
War with America,
and
The Debts and Finances of
the Kingdom:
with
A General Introduction and
Supplement.
(1778)

General Introduction

The first of the following tracts was published in the beginning of the
year 1776 and the second in the beginning of last year.

The principal design of the first part of the second tract was . . . to
remove the misapprehensions of my sentiments on civil liberty and
government into which some had fallen. It gives me concern to find
that it has not answered that end in the degree I wished. I am still
charged with maintaining opinions which tend to subvert all civil
authority. I paid little regard to this charge while it was confined to the
advocates for the principles which have produced the present war; but

as it seems lately to have been given the public from the authority of a writer of the first character, it is impossible I should not be impressed by it; and I find myself under a necessity of taking farther notice of it.

There are two accounts, directly opposite to one another, which have been given of the origin of civil government. One of them is that 'civil government is an expedient contrived by human prudence for gaining security against oppression, and that, consequently, the power of civil governors is a delegation or trust from the people for accomplishing this end'.

The other account is that 'civil government is an ordinance of the Deity, by which the body of mankind are given up to the will of a few, and, consequently, that it is a trust from the Deity, in the exercise of which civil governors are accountable only to him'.

The question 'which of these accounts we ought to receive' is important in the highest degree. There is no question which more deeply affects the happiness and dignity of man as a citizen of this world. If the former account is right, the people (that is, the body of independent agents in every community) are their own legislators. All civil authority is properly their authority. Civil governors are only public servants, and their power, being delegated, is by its nature limited. On the contrary, if the latter account is right the people have nothing to do with their own government. They are placed by their Maker in the situation of cattle on an estate, which the owner may dispose of as he pleases. Civil governors are a body of masters, constituted such by inherent rights, and their power is a commission from Heaven, unbounded in its extent and never to be resisted.

I have espoused, with some zeal, the first of these accounts; and in the following tracts endeavoured to explain and defend it. And this is all I have done to give countenance to the charge I have mentioned. Even the masterly writer who, after a croud of writers infinitely his inferiors, seems to have taken up this accusation against me, often expresses himself as if he had adopted the same idea of government. Such indeed is my opinion of his good sense, and such has been the zeal which he has discovered for the rights of mankind, that I think it scarcely possible his ideas and mine on this subject should be very different. His language, however, sometimes puzzles me, and particularly when he intimates that government is an institution of divine authority; when he scouts all discussions of the nature of civil liberty, the foundation of civil rights, and the principles of a free government;

and when he asserts the competence of our legislature to revive the High-Commission Court and Star-Chamber, and its boundless authority not only over the people of Britain, but over distant communities who have no voice in it.

But whatever may be Mr. Burke's sentiments on this subject, he cannot possibly think of the former account of government that 'it is a speculation which destroys all authority'. Both accounts establish an authority. The difference is that one derives it from the people and makes it a limited authority; and the other derives it from heaven and makes it unlimited. I have repeatedly declared my admiration of such a constitution of government as our own would be, were the House of Commons a fair representation of the kingdom and under no undue influence. The sum of all I have meant to maintain is, 'that legitimate government as opposed to oppression and tyranny, consists in the dominion of equal laws made with common concent or of men over themselves and not in the dominion of communities over communities, or of any men over other men'. How then can it be pretended, that I have aimed at destroying all authority? Does our own constitution destroy all authority? Is the authority of equal laws made with common consent no authority? Must there be no government in a state that governs itself? Or, must an institution, contrived by the united counsels of the members of a community for restraining licentiousness and gaining security against injury and violence, encourage licentiousness and give to every one a power to commit what outrages he pleases?

The Archbishop of York [William Markham] (in a sermon preached before the Society for Propagating the Gospel in Foreign Parts, 21 Feb. 1777) has taken notice of some loose opinions, as he calls them, which have been lately current on civil liberty; some who mean delinquency having given accounts of it 'by which every man's humour is made to be the rule of his obedience, all the bad passions are let loose, and those dear interests abandoned to outrage for the protection of which we trust in law'. It is not difficult to guess at one of the delinquents intended in these words. In opposition to the horrid sentiments of liberty which they describe, but which in reality no man in his senses ever entertained, the Archbishop defines it to be simply the supremacy of law, or government by law, without adding to 'law' as I had done, the words 'equal and made with common consent'; and without opposing a government by law to a government by men, as others had done. According to him, therefore, the supremacy of law must be liberty, whatever the law is, or whoever makes it. In despotic countries government by law is the same with government by the will of one man, which Hooker has called 'the misery of all men'; but, according to this definition, it is liberty. In England formerly the law consigned to the flames all who denied certain established points of faith. Even now, it subjects to fines, imprisonment and banishment all teachers of religion who have not subscribed the doctrinal articles of the church of England; and the good Archbishop, not thinking the law in this case sufficiently rigorous, has proposed putting Protestant Dissenters under the same restraints with the Papists. And should this be done, if done by law, it will be the establishment of liberty.

The truth is that a government by law, is or is not liberty, just as the laws are just or unjust; and as the body of the people do or do not participate in the power of making them. The learned prelate seems to have thought otherwise, and therefore has given a definition of liberty which might as well have been given of slavery.

At the conclusion of his sermon, the Archbishop adds words which he calls comfortable, addressed to those who had been 'patient in tribulation', and intimating that they might 'rejoice in hope', 'a ray of brightness then appearing after a prospect which had been long dark'. And in an account which follows the sermon, from one of the missionaries in the province of New-York, it is said that, 'the rebellion would undoubtedly be crushed, and that then will be the time for taking steps for the increase of the church in America, by granting it an episcopate'. In conformity to the sentiments of this missionary the Archbishop also expresses his hope, that the opportunity which such an event will give for establishing episcopacy among the colonists, will not be lost; and advises that measures should be thought of for that purpose, and for thereby rescuing the church from the persecution it has long suffered in America.

This is a subject so important, and it has been so much misrepresented, that I cannot help going out of my way to give a brief account of it.

It does not appear that the lay members themselves of the church in America have ever wished for bishops. On the contrary, the assembly of Virginia (the first episcopal colony) some years ago returned thanks to two clergymen in that colony who had protested against a resolution of the other clergy to petition for bishops. The church here cannot have a right to impose bishops on the church in another country; and, therefore, while churchmen in America are averse to bishops, it must be persecution to send bishops among them. The Presbyterians and other religious sects there are willing, from a sense of the reasonableness of toleration, to admit bishops whenever the body of episcopalian laity shall desire them, provided security is given that they shall be officers merely spiritual, possessed of no other power, than those which are necessary to the full exercise of that mode of religious worship. It is not bishops, as spiritual officers, they have opposed; but bishops on a state-establishment; bishops with civil powers; bishops at the head of ecclesiastical courts, maintained by taxing other sects, and possessed of a pre-eminence which would be incompatible with the equality which has long subsisted among all religious sects in America. In this last respect, the colonies have hitherto enjoyed a happiness which is unparalleled, but which the introduction of such bishops as would be sent from hence would destroy. In Pensilvania (one of the happiest countries under heaven before we carried into it desolation and carnage) all sects of christians have been always perfectly on a level, the legislature taking no part with any one sect against others, but protecting all equally as far as they are peaceable. The state of the colonies north of Pensilvania is much the same; and, in the province of Massachusett's Bay in particular, civil authority interposes no farther in religion than by imposing a tax for supporting public worship, leaving to all the power of applying the tax to the support of that mode of public worship which they like best. This tax the episcopalians were, at one time, obliged to pay in common with others; but so far did the province carry its indulgence to them, that an act was passed on purpose to excuse them. With this let the state of Protestant Dissenters in this country be compared. Not only are they obliged to pay tithes for the support of the established church, but their worship is not even tolerated unless their ministers will subscribe the articles of the church. In consequence of having long scrupled this subscription, they have lost all legal right to protection, and are exposed to the cruellest penalties. Uneasy in such a situation, they not long ago applied twice to Parliament for the repeal of the penal laws against them. Bills for that purpose were brought into the House of Commons, and passed that House. But, in the House of Lords, they were rejected in conse-

quence of the opposition of the Bishops.*a* There are few I reverence
so much as some on the sacred bench, but such conduct (and may I
not add the alacrity with which most of them support the present
measures?) must leave an indelible stain upon them, and will probably
exclude them for ever from America.

On this occasion, I cannot help thinking with concern of the
learned prelate's feelings. After a prospect long dark, he had discovered a ray of brightness shewing him America reduced, and the
church triumphant. But lately, that ray of brightness has vanished,
and defeat has taken place of victory and conquest. And what do we
now see? What a different prospect, mortifying to the learned prelate,
presents itself? A great people likely to be formed in spite of all our
efforts into free communities under governments which have no religious tests and establishments?[1] A new aera in future annals, and a
new opening in human affairs beginning, among the descendants of
Englishmen, in a new world; A rising empire, extended over an
immense continent, without bishops, without nobles, and without
kings.

O the depth of the riches of the wisdom of God! How unsearchable
are his judgments!

---

a The Bill for the Relief of the Protestant Dissenters was presented to Parliament on 3
April 1772. The measure was given a second reading by the House of Commons on 14
April but was defeated in the Lords on 19 May, largely due to the intervention of the
bishops. In the following year another attempt was made to relieve the Dissenters, but
this too failed in the House of Lords.

[1] I am sorry to mention one exception to the fact here intimated. The new constitution for
Pennsylvania (in other respects wise and liberal) is dishonoured by a religious test. It
requires an acknowledgement of the divine inspiration of the Old and the New Testament, as a condition of being admitted to a seat in the House of Representatives;
directing however, at the same time, that no other religious test shall *for ever* hereafter be
required of any civil officer. This has been, probably, an accommodation to the prejudices of some of the narrower sects in the province, to which the more liberal part have for
the present thought fit to yield; and, therefore, it may be expected that it will not be of
long continuance.

Religious tests and subscriptions in general, and all establishments of particular
systems of faith, with civil emoluments annexed, do inconceivable mischief, by turning
religion into a trade, by engendering strife and persecution, by forming hypocrites, by
obstructing the progress of truth, and fettering and perverting the human mind; nor will
the world ever grow much wiser, or better, or happier, till, by the abolition of them, truth
can gain fair play, and reason free scope for exertion.

Observations on the Nature of Civil Liberty (1776)

Observations
on the Nature of
Civil Liberty, the Principles of Government,
and the Justice and Policy
of the War with America.
(1776)

Preface to the Fifth Edition

The favourable reception which the following Tract has met with makes me abundant amends for the abuse it has brought upon me. I should be ill employed were I to take much notice of this abuse: but there is one circumstance attending it which I cannot help just mentioning. The principles on which I have argued form the foundation of every state as far as it is free, and are the same with those taught by Mr. Locke and all the writers on civil liberty who have been hitherto most admired in this country. But I find with concern that our governors chuse to decline trying by them their present measures. For, in a pamphlet[b] which has been circulated by government with great industry, these principles are pronounced to be 'unnatural and wild, incompatible with practice, and the offspring of the distempered imagination of a man who is biassed by party, and who writes to deceive'. I must take this opportunity to add that I love quiet too well to think of entering into a controversy with any writers, particularly nameless ones. Conscious of good intentions and unconnected with any party, I have endeavoured to plead the cause of general liberty and justice. And happy in knowing this, I shall, in silence, commit myself to that candour of the public of which I have had so much experience.

March 12th. 1776.

---

[b] [James Macpherson], *The Rights of Great Britain asserted against the Claims of America: being an Answer to the Declaration of the General Congress* (London, 1776).

Our colonies in North America appear to be now determined to risk and suffer every thing under the persuasion that Great Britain is attempting to rob them of that liberty to which every member of society, and all civil communities, have a natural and unalienable title. The question, therefore, whether this is a right persuasion, is highly interesting and deserves the careful attention of every Englishman who values liberty and wishes to avoid staining himself with the guilt of invading it. But it is impossible to judge properly of this question without just ideas of liberty in general, and of the nature, limits, and principles of civil liberty in particular. The following observations on this subject appear to me of some importance, and I cannot make myself easy without offering them to the public at the present period, big with events of the last consequence to this kingdom. I do this with reluctance and pain urged by strong feelings, but at the same time checked by the consciousness that I am likely to deliver sentiments not favourable to the present measures of that government under which I live and to which I am a constant and zealous well-wisher. Such, however, are my present sentiments and views, that this is a consideration of inferior moment with me, and, as I hope never to go beyond the bounds of decent discussion and expostulation, I flatter myself, that I shall be able to avoid giving any person reason for offence.

The observations with which I shall begin are of a more general and abstract nature; but being necessary to introduce what I have principally in view, I hope they will be patiently read and considered.

Sect. I
Of the Nature of Liberty in General

In order to obtain a more distinct view of the nature of liberty as such it will be useful to consider it under the four following general divisions.

First, physical liberty; secondly, moral liberty; thirdly, religious liberty; and fourthly, civil liberty. These heads comprehend under them all the different kinds of liberty. And I have placed civil liberty last because I mean to apply to it all I shall say of the other kinds of liberty.

By physical liberty I mean that principle of spontaneity, or self-determination, which constitutes us agents, or which gives us a command over our actions, rendering them properly ours, and not effects of the operation of any foreign cause. Moral liberty is the power of following, in all circumstances, our sense of right and wrong, or of acting in conformity to our reflecting and moral principles, without being controuled by any contrary principles. Religious liberty signifies the power of exercising, without molestation, that mode of religion which we think best, or of making the decisions of our own consciences respecting religious truth, the rule of our conduct, and not any of the decisions of our fellow-men. In like manner civil liberty is the power of a civil society or state to govern itself by its own discretion or by laws of its own making, without being subject to the impositions of any power in appointing and directing which the collective body of the people have no concern and over which they have no controul.

It should be observed that, according to these definitions of the different kinds of liberty, there is one general idea that runs through them all; I mean the idea of self-direction, or self-government. Did our volitions originate not with ourselves, but with some cause over which we have no power; or were we under a necessity of always following some will different from our own, we should want physical liberty.

In like manner, he whose perceptions of moral obligation are controuled by his passions has lost his moral liberty, and the most common language applied to him is that he wants self-government.

He likewise who, in religion, cannot govern himself by his convictions of religious duty, but is obliged to receive formularies of faith, and to practise modes of worship imposed upon him by others, wants religious liberty. And the community also that is governed, not by itself, but by some will independent of it, wants civil liberty.

In all these cases there is a force which stands opposed to the agent's own will, and which, as far as it operates, produces servitude. In the first case, this force is incompatible with the very idea of voluntary motion; and the subject of it is a mere passive instrument which never acts, but is always acted upon. In the second case, this force is the influence of passion getting the better of reason, or the brute overpowering and conquering the will of the man. In the third case, it is human authority in religion requiring conformity to particular modes of faith and worship, and superseding private judgment.

And in the last case, it is any will distinct from that of the majority of a community which claims a power in making laws for it and disposing of its property.

This it is, I think, that marks the limit between liberty and slavery. As far as, in any instance, the operation of any cause comes in to restrain the power of self-government, so far slavery is introduced. Nor do I think that a preciser idea than this of liberty and slavery can be formed.

I cannot help wishing I could here fix my reader's attention, and engage him to consider carefully the dignity of that blessing to which we give the name of liberty, according to the representation now made of it. There is not a word in the whole compass of language which expresses so much of what is important and excellent. It is, in every view of it, a blessing truly sacred and invaluable. Without physical liberty, man would be a machine acted upon by mechanical springs, having no principle of motion in himself, or command over events; and, therefore, incapable of all merit and demerit. Without moral liberty, he is a wicked and detestable being, subject to the tyranny of base lusts, and the sport of every vile appetite. And without religious and civil liberty, he is a poor and abject animal, without rights, without property, and without a conscience, bending his neck to the yoke, and crouching to the will of every silly creature who has the insolence to pretend to authority over him. Nothing, therefore, can be of much consequence to us as liberty. It is the foundation of all honour, and the chief privilege and glory of our natures.

In fixing our idea on the subject of liberty, it is of particular use to take such an enlarged view of it as I have now given. But the immediate object of the present enquiry being civil liberty, I will confine to it all the subsequent observations.

Sect. II
Of Civil liberty and the Principles of Government

From what has been said it is obvious that all civil government, as far as it can be denominated free, is the creature of the people. It originates with them. It is conducted under their direction, and has in view nothing but their happiness. All its different forms are no more than so many different modes in which they chuse to direct their affairs, and to secure the quiet enjoyment of their rights. In every free state every man is his own Legislator. All taxes are free-gifts for public services. All laws are particular provisions or regulations established by common consent for gaining protection and safety. And all magistrates are trustees or deputies for carrying these regulations into execution.

Liberty, therefore, is too imperfectly defined when it is said to be 'a government by laws, and not by men'. If the laws are made by one man, or a junto of men in a state, and not by common consent, a government by them does not differ from slavery. In this case it would be a contradiction in terms to say that the state governs itself.

From hence it is obvious that civil liberty, in its most perfect degree, can be enjoyed only in small states where every independent agent is capable of giving his suffrage in person, and of being chosen into public offices. When a state becomes so numerous, or when the different parts of it are removed to such distances from one another as to render this impracticable, a diminution of liberty necessarily arises. There are, however, in these circumstances, methods by which such near approaches may be made to perfect liberty as shall answer all the purposes of government, and at the same time secure every right of human nature.

Tho' all the members of a state should not be capable of giving their suffrages on public measures, individually and personally, they may do this by the appointment of substitutes or representatives. They may entrust the powers of legislation, subject to such restrictions as they shall think necessary, with any number of delegates; and whatever can be done by such delegates within the limits of their trust, may be considered as done by the united voice and counsel of the community. In this method a free government may be established in the largest state, and it is conceivable that by regulations of this kind any number of states might be subjected to a scheme of government that would exclude the desolations of war, and produce universal peace and order.

Let us think here of what may be practicable in this way with respect to Europe in particular. While it continues divided, as it is at present, into a great number of independent kingdoms whose interests are continually clashing, it is impossible but that disputes will often arise which must end in war and carnage. It would be no remedy to this evil to make one of these states supreme over the rest, and to give it an absolute plenitude of power to superintend and controul them. This would be to subject all the states to the arbitrary discretion of one, and to establish an ignominious slavery not possible to be long endured. It would, therefore, be a remedy worse than the disease; nor is it possible it should be approved by any mind that has not lost every idea of civil liberty. On the contrary, let every state, with respect to all its internal concerns, be continued independent of all the rest, and let a general confederacy be formed by the appointment of a senate consisting of representatives from all the different states. Let this senate possess the power of managing all the common concerns of the united states, and of judging and deciding between them, as a common arbiter or umpire, in all disputes; having, at the same time, under its direction the common force of the states to support its decisions. In these circumstances, each separate state would be secure against the interference of sovereign power in its private concerns, and, therefore, would possess liberty, and at the same time it would be secure against all oppression and insult from every neighbouring state. Thus might the scattered force and abilities of a whole continent be gathered into one point, all litigations settled as they rose, universal peace preserved, and nation prevented *from any more lifting up a sword against nation.*

I have observed that tho' in a great state all the individuals that compose it cannot be admitted to an immediate participation in the powers of legislation and government, yet they may participate in these powers by a delegation of them to a body of representatives. In this case it is evident that the state will be still free or self-governed, and that it will be more or less so in proportion as it is more or less fairly and adequately represented. If the persons to whom the trust of government is committed hold their places for short terms, if they are chosen by the unbiassed voices of a majority of the state, and subject to their instructions, liberty will be enjoyed in its highest degree. But if they are chosen for long terms by a part only of the state, and if during that term they are subject to no controul from their constituents, the very idea of liberty will be lost and the power of chusing representatives becomes nothing but a power, lodged in a few, to chuse at certain periods a body of masters for themselves and for the rest of the community. And if a state is so sunk that the majority of its representatives are elected by a handful of the meanest[2] persons in it,

---

[2] In Great Britain, consisting of near six millions of inhabitants, 5,723 persons, most of them the lowest of the people, elect one half of the House of Commons, and 364 chuse a

whose votes are always paid for, and if also there is a higher will on which even these mock representatives themselves depend, and that directs their voices: in these circumstances, it will be an abuse of language to say that the state possesses liberty. Private men, indeed, might be allowed the exercise of liberty, as they might also under the most despotic government; but it would be an indulgence or connivance derived from the spirit of the times, or from an accidental mildness in the administration. And, rather than be governed in such a manner, it would perhaps be better to be governed by the will of one man without any representation, for a representation so degenerated could answer no other end than to mislead and deceive, by disguising slavery, and keeping up a form of liberty when the reality was lost.

Within the limits now mentioned, liberty may be enjoyed in every possible degree, from that which is complete and perfect, to that which is merely nominal; according as the people have more or less of a share in government, and of a controuling power over the persons by whom it is administered.

In general, to be free is to be guided by one's own will; and to be guided by the will of another is the characteristic of servitude. This is particularly applicable to political liberty. That state, I have observed, is free which is guided by its own will, or (which comes to the same) by the will of an assembly of representatives appointed by itself and accountable to itself. And every state that is not so governed, or in which a body of men representing the people make not an essential part of the legislature, is in slavery. In order to form the most perfect constitution of government, there may be the best reasons for joining to such a body of representatives an hereditary council, consisting of

ninth part. This may be seen distinctly made out in [James Burgh], *Political Disquisitions*, [3 vols., London, 1774–5] vol. 1, Bk. 2, ch. 4, [pp. 39–54] a work of important and useful instruction. [Burgh's claim, repeated by Price, that 254 members were chosen by 5,723 votes, was misleading. What Burgh did was to compute for each constituency a bare majority of those entitled to vote. Then he added these numbers for 254 constituencies to give, not the number of those who had actually voted for sitting members at any one election, but the lowest number that *could* conceivably have secured their election. Price's use of these figures is misleading in another respect. What Burgh's computation established was not that half the members of the House of Commons, but half the greatest number known to have been present at a debate at any one time, *could* have been elected by 5,723 votes. At this time there were 558 members of the Commons; the greatest number known to have been present at any one time at a debate was 502, and that in 1741. Price's assertion that a ninth part of the members for Great Britain were chosen by 364 votes is also inaccurate. What Burgh claimed was that a ninth part of the members for *England* were chosen by 364 votes.]

men of the first rank in the state, with a supreme executive magistrate as the head of all. This will form useful checks in a legislature, and contribute to give it vigour, union, and dispatch, without infringing liberty; for, as long as that part of a government which represents the people is a fair representation, and also has a negative on all public measures, together with the sole power of imposing taxes and originating supplies, the essentials of liberty will be preserved. We make it our boast in this country that this is our own constitution. I will not say with how much reason.

Of such liberty as I have now described, it is impossible there should be an excess. Government is an institution for the benefit of the people governed, which they have the power to model as they please; and to say that they can have too much of this power, is to say that there ought to be a power in the state superior to that which gives it being, and from which all jurisdiction in it is derived. Licentiousness, which has been commonly mentioned, as an extreme of liberty, is indeed its opposite. It is government by the will of rapacious individuals in opposition to the will of the community made known and declared in the laws. A free state, at the same time that it is free itself, makes all its members free by excluding licentiousness, and guarding their persons and property and good name against insult. It is the end of all just government, at the same time that it secures the liberty of the public against foreign injury, to secure the liberty of the individual against private injury. I do not, therefore, think it strictly just to say that it belongs to the nature of government to entrench on private liberty. It ought never to do this, except as far as the exercise of private liberty encroaches on the liberties of others. That is, it is licentiousness it restrains and liberty itself only when used to destroy liberty.

It appears from hence that licentiousness and despotism are more nearly allied than is commonly imagined. They are both alike inconsistent with liberty and the true end of government; nor is there any other difference between them than that the one is the licentiousness of great men, and the other the licentiousness of little men; or that, by the one, the persons and property of a people are subject to outrage and invasion from a king or a lawless body of grandees; and that, by the other, they are subject to the like outrage from a lawless mob. In avoiding one of these evils, mankind have often run into the other. But all well constituted governments guard equally against both.

Indeed of the two, the last is, on several accounts, the least to be dreaded and has done the least mischief. It may be truly said that if licentiousness has destroyed its thousands, despotism has destroyed its millions. The former, having little power and no system to support it, necessarily finds its own remedy; and a people soon get out of the tumult and anarchy attending it. But a despotism, wearing the form of government and being armed with its force, is an evil not to be conquered without dreadful struggles. It goes on from age to age, debasing the human faculties, levelling all distinctions, and preying on the rights and blessings of society. It deserves to be added that in a state disturbed by licentiousness, there is an animation which is favourable to the human mind and which puts it upon exerting its powers; but in a state habituated to a despotism, all is still and torpid. A dark and savage tyranny stifles every effort of genius, and the mind loses all its spirit and dignity.

Before I proceed to what I have farther in view, I will observe that the account now given of the principles of public liberty and the nature of an equal and free government shews what judgment we should form of that omnipotence, which, it has been said, must belong to every government as such. Great stress has been laid on this, but most unreasonably. Government, as has been before observed, is, in the very nature of it, a trust, and all its powers a delegation for gaining particular ends. This trust may be misapplied and abused. It may be employed to defeat the very ends for which it was instituted, and to subvert the very rights which it ought to protect. A parliament, for instance, consisting of a body of representatives, chosen for a limited period to make laws and to grant money for public services, would forfeit its authority by making itself perpetual, or even prolonging its own duration; by nominating its own members; by accepting bribes; or subjecting itself to any kind of foreign influence. This would convert a parliament into a conclave or junto of self-created tools; and a state that has lost its regard to its own rights, so far as to submit to such a breach of trust in its rulers, is enslaved. Nothing, therefore, can be more absurd than the doctrine which some have taught with respect to the omnipotence of parliaments. They possess no power beyond the limits of the trust for the execution of which they were formed. If they contradict this trust, they betray their constituents and dissolve themselves. All delegated power must be subordinate and limited. If omnipotence can, with any sense, be ascribed to a legislature, it must be lodged where all legislative authority originates; that is, in the people. For their sakes government is instituted, and theirs is the only real omnipotence.

I am sensible that all I have been saying would be very absurd, were the opinions just which some have maintained concerning the origin of government. According to these opinions, government is not the creature of the people, or the result of a convention between them and their rulers; but there are certain men who possess in themselves, independently of the will of the people, a right of governing them, which they derive from the Deity. This doctrine has been abundantly refuted by many excellent writers. It is a doctrine which avowedly subverts civil liberty and which represents mankind as a body of vassals, formed to descend like cattle from one set of owners to another, who have an absolute dominion over them. It is a wonder that those who view their species in a light so humiliating should ever be able to think of themselves without regret and shame. The intention of these observations is not to oppose such sentiments, but, taking for granted the reasonableness of civil liberty, to shew wherein it consists, and what distinguishes it from its contrary. And, in considering this subject, as it has been now treated, it is unavoidable to reflect on the excellency of a free government and its tendency to exalt the nature of man. Every member of a free state, having his property secure and knowing himself his own governor, possesses a consciousness of dignity in himself and feels incitements to emulation and improvement to which the miserable slaves of arbitrary power must be utter strangers. In such a state all the springs of action have room to operate and the mind is stimulated to the noblest exertions. But to be obliged from our birth to look up to a creature no better than ourselves as the master of our fortunes, and to receive his will as our law – what can be more humiliating? What elevated ideas can enter a mind in such a situation? Agreeably to this remark, the subjects of free states have, in all ages, been most distinguished for genius and knowledge. Liberty is the soil where the arts and sciences have flourished and the more free a state has been, the more have the powers of the human mind been drawn forth into action, and the greater number of brave men has it produced. With what lustre do the antient free states of Greece shine in the annals of the world? How different is that country now, under the great Turk? The difference between a country inhabited by men and by brutes, is not greater.

These are reflexions which should be constantly present to every mind in this country. As moral liberty is the prime blessing of man in his private capacity, so is civil liberty in his public capacity. There is nothing that requires more to be watched than power. There is nothing that ought to be opposed with a more determined resolution than its encroachments. Sleep in a state, as Montesquieu says, is always followed by slavery.

The people of this kingdom were once warmed by such sentiments as these. Many a sycophant of power have they sacrificed. Often have they fought and bled in the cause of liberty. But that time seems to be going. The fair inheritance of liberty left us by our ancestors, many of us are willing to resign. An abandoned venality, the inseparable companion of dissipation and extravagance, has poisoned the springs of public virtue among us; and should any events ever arise that should render the same opposition necessary that took place in the times of King Charles the First and James the Second, I am afraid all that is valuable to us would be lost. The terror of the standing army, the danger of the public funds, and the all-corrupting influence of the treasury, would deaden all zeal and produce general acquiescence and servility.

Sect. III
Of the Authority of One Country over Another

From the nature and principles of civil liberty, as they have been now explained, it is an immediate and necessary inference that no one community can have any power over the property or legislation of another community which is not incorporated with it by a just and adequate representation. Then only, it has been shewn, is a state free when it is governed by its own will. But a country that is subject to the legislature of another country in which it has no voice, and over which it has no controul, cannot be said to be governed by its own will. Such a country, therefore, is in a state of slavery. And it deserves to be particularly considered that such a slavery is worse, on several accounts, than any slavery of private men to one another, or of kingdoms to despots within themselves. Between one state and another there is none of that fellow-feeling that takes place between persons in private life. Being detached bodies that never see one another, and residing perhaps in different quarters of the globe, the state that governs cannot be a witness to the sufferings occasioned by its oppressions; or a competent judge of the circumstances and abilities of the people who are governed. They must also have in a great degree separate interests; and the more the one is loaded the more the other may be eased. The infamy likewise of oppression, being in such circumstances shared among a multitude, is not likely to be much felt or regarded. On all these accounts there is, in the case of one country subjugated to another, little or nothing to check rapacity; and the most flagrant injustice and cruelty may be practised without remorse or pity. I will add that it is particularly difficult to shake off a tyranny of this kind. A single despot, if a people are unanimous and resolute, may be soon subdued. But a despotic state is not easily subdued, and a people subject to it cannot emancipate themselves without entering into a dreadful and, perhaps, very unequal contest.

I cannot help observing farther, that the slavery of a people to internal despots may be qualified and limited; but I don't see what can limit the authority of one state over another. The exercise of power in this case can have no other measure than discretion, and, therefore, must be indefinite and absolute.

Once more, it should be considered that the government of one country by another can only be opposed by a military force, and, without such a support must be destitute of all weight and efficiency.

This will be best explained by putting the following case. There is, let us suppose, in a province subject to the sovereignty of a distant state, a subordinate legislature consisting of an assembly chosen by the people; a council chosen by that assembly; and a governor appointed by the sovereign state, and paid by the province. There are, likewise, judges and other officers, appointed and paid in the same manner, for administering justice agreeably to the laws by the verdicts of juries fairly chosen.

This forms a constitution seemingly free, by giving the people a share in their own government and some check on their rulers. But, while there is a higher legislative power to the controul of which such a constitution is subject, it does not itself possess liberty, and therefore cannot be of any use as a security to liberty; nor is it possible that it should be of long duration. Laws offensive to the province will be enacted by the sovereign state. The legislature of the province will remonstrate against them. The magistrates will not execute them. Juries will not convict upon them, and, consequently, like the Pope's bulls which once governed Europe, they will become nothing but forms and empty sounds to which no regard will be shewn. In order to remedy this evil and to give efficiency to its government, the supreme state will naturally be led to withdraw the governor, the council, and the judges from the controul of the province by making them entirely dependent on itself for their pay and continuance in office, as well as for their appointment. It will also alter the mode of chusing juries on purpose to bring them more under its influence. And in some cases, under the pretence of the impossibility of gaining an impartial trial where government is resisted, it will perhaps ordain that offenders shall be removed from the province to be tried within its own territories. And it may even go so far in this kind of policy as to endeavour to prevent the effects of discontents by forbidding all meetings and associations of the people except at such times, and for such particular purposes, as shall be permitted them.

Thus will such a province be exactly in the same state that Britain would be in were our first executive magistrate, our House of Lords, and our judges, nothing but the instruments of a sovereign democratical power; were our juries nominated by that power; or were we liable to be transported to a distant country to be tried for offences committed here; and restrained from calling any meetings, consulting about any grievances, or associating for any purposes, except when leave should be given us by a Lord Lieutenant or Viceroy.

It is certain that this is a state of oppression which no country could endure, and to which it would be vain to expect, that any people should submit an hour without an armed force to compel them.

The late transactions in Massachusett's Bay are a perfect exemplification of what I have now said. The government of Great Britain in that province has gone on exactly in the train I have described; till at last it became necessary to station troops there not amenable to the civil power; and all terminated in a government by the sword. And such, if a people are not sunk below the character of men, will be the issue of all government in similar circumstances.

It may be asked, 'Are there not causes by which one state may acquire a rightful authority over another, though not consolidated by an adequate representation?' I answer that there are no such causes. All the causes to which such an effect can be ascribed are conquest, compact, or obligations conferred.

Much has been said of the right of conquest; and history contains little more than accounts of kingdoms reduced by it under the dominion of other kingdoms, and of the havock it has made among mankind. But the authority derived from hence, being founded on violence, is never rightful. The Roman Republic was nothing but a faction against the general liberties of the world; and had no more right to give law to the provinces subject to it than thieves have to the property they seize, or to the houses into which they break. Even in the case of a just war undertaken by one people to defend itself against the oppressions of another people, conquest gives only a right to an indemnification for the injury which occasioned the war and a reasonable security against future injury.

Neither can any state acquire such an authority over other states in virtue of any compacts or cessions. This is a case in which compacts are not binding. Civil liberty is, in this respect, on the same footing with religious liberty. As no people can lawfully surrender their religious liberty by giving up their right of judging for themselves in religion, or by allowing any human beings to prescribe to them what faith they shall embrace, or what mode of worship they shall practise, so neither can any civil societies lawfully surrender their civil liberty by giving up to any extraneous jurisdiction their power of legislating for themselves and disposing their property. Such a cession, being inconsistent with the unalienable rights of human nature, would either not bind at all, or bind only the individuals who made it. This is a blessing which no one generation of men can give up for another, and which, when lost, a people have always a right to resume. Had our ancestors in this country been so mad as to have subjected themselves to any foreign community, we could not have been under any obligation to continue in such a state. And all the nations now in the world who, in consequence of the tameness and folly of their predecessors, are subject to arbitrary power have a right to emancipate themselves as soon as they can.

If neither conquest nor compact can give such an authority, much less can any favours received or any services performed by one state for another. Let the favour received be what it will, liberty is too dear a price for it. A state that has been obliged is not, therefore, bound to be enslaved. It ought, if possible, to make an adequate return for the services done to it, but to suppose that it ought to give up the power of governing itself and the disposal of its property, would be to suppose, that, in order to show its gratitude, it ought to part with the power of

33

ever afterwards exercising gratitude. How much has been done by this kingdom for Hanover? But no one will say that on this account we have a right to make the laws of Hanover; or even to draw a single penny from it without its own consent.

After what has been said, it will, I am afraid, be trifling to apply the preceding arguments to the case of different communities which are considered as different parts of the same empire. But there are reasons which render it necessary for me to be explicit in making the application.

What I mean here is just to point out the difference of situation between communities forming an empire; and particular bodies or classes of men forming different parts of a kingdom. Different communities forming an empire have no connexions which produce a necessary reciprocation of interests between them. They inhabit different districts and are governed by different legislatures. On the contrary, the different classes of men within a kingdom are all placed on the same ground. Their concerns and interests are the same, and what is done to one part must affect all. These are situations totally different and a constitution of government that may be consistent with liberty in one of them may be entirely inconsistent with it in the other. It is, however, certain that, even in the last of these situations, no one part ought to govern the rest. In order to a fair and equal government, there ought to be a fair and equal representation of all that are governed; and as far as this is wanting in any government, it deviates from the principles of liberty, and becomes unjust and oppressive. But in the circumstances of different communities, all this holds with unspeakably more force. The government of a part in this case becomes complete tyranny, and subjection to it becomes complete slavery.

But ought there not, it is asked, to exist somewhere in an empire a supreme legislative authority over the whole, or a power to controul and bind all the different states of which it consists? This enquiry has been already answered. The truth is, that such a supreme controuling power ought to exist nowhere except in such a senate or body of delegates as that described in page 25; and that the authority or supremacy of even this senate ought to be limited to the common concerns of the Empire. I think I have proved that the fundamental principles of liberty necessarily require this.

In a word, an empire is a collection of states or communities united by some common bond or tye. If these states have each of them free constitutions of government, and, with respect to taxation and internal legislation, are independent of the other states, but united by compacts, or alliances, or subjection to a great council, representing the whole, or to one monarch entrusted with the supreme executive power; in these circumstances the empire will be an empire of freemen. If, on the contrary, like the different provinces subject to the Grand Seignior, none of the states possess any independent legislative authority, but are all subject to an absolute monarch whose will is their law, then is the empire an empire of slaves. If one of the states is free, but governs by its will all the other states; then is the empire, like that of the Romans in the times of the Republic, an empire consisting of one state free, and the rest in slavery. Nor does it make any more difference in this case that the governing state is itself free than it does in the case of a kingdom subject to a despot that this despot is himself free. I have before observed that this only makes the slavery worse. There is, in the one case, a chance that in the quick succession of despots a good one will sometimes arise. But bodies of men continue the same and have generally proved the most unrelenting of all tyrants.

A great writer before[3] quoted, observes of the Roman Empire, that while liberty was at the center, tyranny prevailed in the distant provinces; that such as were free under it were extremely so, while those who were slaves groaned under the extremity of slavery; and that the same events that destroyed the liberty of the former, gave liberty to the latter.

The liberty of the Romans, therefore, was only an additional calamity to the provinces governed by them; and though it might have been said of the citizens of Rome, that they were the 'freest members of any civil society in the known world', yet of the subjects of Rome, it must have been said that they were the completest slaves in the known world. How remarkable is it that this very people, once the freest of mankind, but at the same time the most proud and tyrannical, should become at last the most contemptible and abject slaves that ever existed?

[3] Montesquieu's Spirit of Laws, vol. I, bk 11, ch. xix. [The English translation of *De l'esprit des lois* by Thomas Nugent was published under the title *The Spirit of the Laws* in London in 1750].

Part II

In the foregoing disquisitions, I have, from one leading principle, deduced a number of consequences that seem to me incapable of being disputed. I have meant that they should be applied to the great question between this kingdom and the colonies which has occasioned the present war with them.

It is impossible but my readers must have been all along making this application; and if they still think that the claims of this kingdom are reconcileable to the principles of true liberty and legitimate government, I am afraid, that nothing I shall farther say will have any effect on their judgments. I wish, however, they would have the patience and candour to go with me and grant me a hearing some time longer.

Though clearly decided in my own judgment on this subject, I am inclined to make great allowances for the different judgments of others. We have been so used to speak of the colonies as *our* colonies, and to think of them as in a state of subordination to us, and as holding their existence in America only for our use, that it is no wonder the prejudices of many are alarmed when they find a different doctrine maintained. The meanest person among us is disposed to look upon himself as having a body of subjects in America, and to be offended at the denial of his right to make laws for them, though perhaps he does not know what colour they are of, or what language they talk. Such are the natural prejudices of this country. But the time is coming, I hope, when the unreasonableness of them will be seen, and more just sentiments prevail.

Before I proceed, I beg it may be attended to that I have chosen to try this question by the general principles of civil liberty; and not by the practice of former times; or by the charters granted the colonies. The arguments for them, drawn from these last topics, appear to me greatly to outweigh the arguments against them. But I wish to have this question brought to a higher test and surer issue. The question with all liberal enquirers ought to be, not what jurisdiction over them precedents, statutes and charters give, but what reason and equity, and the rights of humanity give. This is, in truth, a question which no kingdom has ever before had occasion to agitate. The case of a free country branching itself out in the manner Britain has done, and sending to a distant world colonies which have there, from small beginnings and under free legislatures of their own, increased and formed a body of powerful states, likely soon to become superior to the parent state. This is a case which is new in the history of mankind, and it is extremely improper to judge of it by the rules of any narrow and partial policy, or to consider it on any other ground than the general one of reason and justice. Those who will be candid enough to judge on this ground, and who can divest themselves of national prejudices, will not, I fancy, remain long unsatisfied. But alas! matters are gone too far. The dispute probably must be settled another way, and the sword alone, I am afraid, is now to determine what the rights of Britain and America are. Shocking situation! Detested be the measures which have brought us into it: and, if we are endeavouring to enforce injustice, cursed will be the war. A retreat, however, is not yet impracticable. The duty we owe our gracious sovereign obliges us to rely on his disposition to stay the sword, and to promote the happiness of all the different parts of the empire at the head of which he is placed. With some hopes, therefore, that it may not be too late to reason on this subject, I will, in the following sections, enquire what the war with America is in the following respects.

1. In respect of Justice.
2. The principles of the constitution.
3. In respect of policy and humanity.
4. The Honour of the Kingdom.

And, lastly, the probability of succeeding in it.

Sect. I

Of the Justice of the War with America

The enquiry, whether the war with the colonies is a just war, will be best determined by stating the power over them, which it is the end of the war to maintain: and this cannot be better done, than in the words of an act of parliament, made on purpose to define it. That act, it is well known, declares, 'That this kingdom has power, and of right ought to have power to make laws and statutes to bind the colonies, and people of America, in all cases whatever'.ᶜ Dreadful power indeed! I defy anyone to express slavery in stronger language. It is the

---

ᶜ The Declaratory Act, 6 Geo. III c. 12.

same with declaring 'that we have a right to do with them what we please'. I will not waste my time by applying to such a claim any of the preceding arguments. If my reader does not feel more in this case, than words can express, all reasoning must be vain.

But, probably, most persons will be for using milder language; and for saying no more than that the united legislatures of England and Scotland have of right power to tax the colonies, and a supremacy of legislature over America. But this comes to the same. If it means anything, it means that the property and the legislations of the colonies are subject to the absolute discretion of Great Britain, and ought of right to be so. The nature of the thing admits of no limitation. The colonies can never be admitted to be judges how far the authority over them in these cases shall extend. This would be to destroy it entirely. If any part of their property is subject to our discretion, the whole must be so. If we have a right to interfere at all in their internal legislations, we have a right to interfere as far as we think proper. It is self-evident that this leaves them nothing they can call their own. And what is it that can give to any people such a supremacy over other people? I have already examined the principal answers which have been given to this enquiry. But it will not be amiss in this place to go over some of them again.

It has been urged, that such a right must be lodged somewhere, 'in order to preserve the unity of the British Empire'.

Pleas of this sort have, in all ages, been used to justify tyranny. They have in religion given rise to numberless oppressive claims and slavish hierarchies. And in the Romish communion, particularly, it is well known that the Pope claims the title and powers of the supreme head on earth of the Christian church in order to preserve its unity. With respect to the British Empire nothing can be more preposterous than to endeavour to maintain its unity by setting up such a claim. This is a method of establishing unity which, like the similar method in religion, can produce nothing but discord and mischief. The truth is that a common relation to one supreme executive head, an exchange of kind offices, types of interest and affection, and compacts, are sufficient to give the British Empire all the unity that is necessary. But if not – if in order to preserve its unity, one half of it must be entrusted to the other half, let it, in the name of God, want unity.

Much has been said of 'the superiority of the British state'. But what gives us our superiority? Is it our wealth? This never confers real dignity. On the contrary its effect is always to debase, intoxicate, and corrupt. Is it the number of our people? The colonies will soon be equal to us in number. Is it our knowledge and virtue? They are probably equally knowing and more virtuous. There are names among them that will not stoop to any names among the philosophers and politicians of this island.

But we are the parent state. These are the magic words which have fascinated and misled us. The English came from Germany. Does that give the German states a right to tax us? Children, having no property and being incapable of guiding themselves, the author of nature has committed the care of them to their parents, and subjected them to their absolute authority. But there is a period when having acquired property and a capacity of judging for themselves, they become independent agents; and when, for this reason, the authority of their parents ceases, and becomes nothing but the respect and influence due to benefactors. Supposing, therefore, that the order of nature in establishing the relation between parents and children ought to have been the rule of our conduct to the colonies, we should have been gradually relaxing our authority as they grew up. But, like mad parents, we have done the contrary; and, at the very time when our authority should have been most relaxed, we have carried it to the greatest extent and exercised it with the greatest rigour. No wonder then that they have turned upon us, and obliged us to remember that they are not children.

'But we have', it is said, 'protected them and run deeply in debt on their account.' The full answer to this has been already given, Will any one say that all we have done for them has not been more on our own account than on theirs? But suppose the contrary. Have they done nothing for us? Have they made no compensation for the protection they have received? Have they not helped us to pay our taxes, to support our poor, and to bear the burthen of our debts, by taking from us, at our own price, all the commodities with which we can supply them? Have they not, for our advantage, submitted to many restraints in acquiring property? Must they likewise resign to us the disposal of that property? Has not their exclusive trade with us been for many years one of the chief sources of our wealth and power? In all our wars have they not fought by our side, and contributed much to our success? In the last war, particularly, it is well known that they ran themselves deeply in debt; and that the Parliament thought it necessary to grant them considerable sums annually as compensations for going beyond their abilities in assisting us. And in this course would they have continued for many future years; perhaps, for ever. In short, were an accurate account stated, it is by no means certain which side would appear to be most indebted. When asked as freemen they have hitherto seldom discovered any reluctance in giving. But, in obedience to a demand and with the bayonet at their breasts, they will give us nothing but blood.

It is farther said, 'that the land on which they settled was ours'. But how came it to be ours? If sailing along a coast can give a right to a country, then might the people of Japan become, as soon as they please, the proprietors of Britain. Nothing can be more chimerical than property founded on such a reason. If the land on which the colonies first settled had any proprietors, they were the natives. The greatest part of it they bought of the natives. They have since cleared and cultivated it; and, without any help from us, converted a wilderness into fruitful and pleasant fields. It is, therefore, now on a double account their property, and no power on earth can have any right to disturb them in the possession of it, or to take from them, without their consent, any part of its produce.

But let it be granted that the land was ours. Did they not settle upon it under the faith of charters which promised them the enjoyment of all the rights of Englishmen, and allowed them to tax themselves, and to be governed by legislatures of their own, similar to ours? These charters were given them by an authority which at the time was thought competent; and they have been rendered sacred by an acquiescence on our part for near a century. Can it then be wondered at that the colonies should revolt when they found their charters violated, and an attempt made to force innovations upon them by famine and the sword? But I lay no stress on charters. They derive their rights from a higher source. It is inconsistent with common sense to imagine that any people would ever think of settling in a distant country, on any such condition, as that the people from whom they withdrew, should for ever be masters of their property, and have power to subject them to any modes of government they pleased. And had there been express stipulations to this purpose in all the charters of the colonies, they would, in my opinion, be no more bound by them, than if it had been stipulated with them, that they should go naked, or expose themselves to the incursions of wolves and tigers.

The defective state of the representation of this kingdom has been farther pleaded to prove our right to tax America. We submit to a parliament that does not represent us, and therefore they ought. How strange an argument is this? It is saying we want liberty, and, therefore, they ought to want it. Suppose it true, that they are indeed contending for a better constitution of government, and more liberty than we enjoy: ought this to make us angry? Who is there that does not see the danger to which this country is exposed? Is it generous, because we are in a sink, to endeavour to draw them into it? Ought we not rather to wish earnestly that there may at least be one free country left upon earth to which we may fly, when venality, luxury, and vice have completed the ruin of liberty here?

It is, however, by no means true that America has no more right to be exempted from taxation by the British Parliament, than Britain itself. Here, all freeholders and burgesses in boroughs are represented. There, not one freeholder or any other person is represented. Here the aids granted by the represented part of the kingdom must be proportionably paid by themselves; and the laws they make for others, they at the same time make for themselves. There, the aids they would grant would not be paid, but received, by themselves; and the laws they made would be made for others only. In short, the relation of one country to another country, whose representatives have the power of taxing it (and of appropriating the money raised by the taxes) is much the same with the relation of a country to a single despot, or a body of despots within itself, invested with the like power. In both cases, the people taxed and those who tax have separate interests, nor can there be any thing to check oppression, besides either the abilities of the people taxed, or the humanity of the taxers. But indeed I can never hope to convince that person of any thing, who does not see an essential difference between the two cases now mentioned; or between the circumstances of individuals, and classes of men, making parts of a community imperfectly represented in the legislature that governs it; and the circumstances of a whole community, in a distant world, not at all represented.

But enough has been said by others on this point; nor is it possible for me to throw any new light upon it. To finish, therefore, what I meant to offer under this head, I must beg that the following considerations may be particularly attended to.

The question now between us and the colonies is whether in respect of taxation and internal legislation, they are bound to be subject to the jurisdiction of this kingdom: or, in other words, whether the British Parliament has or has not of right a power to dispose of their property, and to model as it pleases their governments? To this supremacy over them, we say, we are entitled; and in order to maintain it, we have begun the present war. Let me here enquire,

First, whether, if we have now this supremacy, we shall not be equally entitled to it in any future time? They are now but little short of half our number. To this number they have grown from a small body of original settlers by a very rapid increase. The probability is that they will go on to increase, and that, in 50 or 60 years, they will be double our number and form a mighty empire, consisting of a variety of states, all equal or superior to ourselves in all the arts and accomplishments which give dignity and happiness to human life. In that period, will they be still bound to acknowledge that supremacy over them which we now claim? Can there be any person who will assert this, or whose mind does not revolt at the idea of a vast continent holding all that is valuable to it at the discretion of a handful of people on the other side of the Atlantic? But if, at that period, this would be unreasonable; what makes it otherwise now? Draw the line if you can. But there is a still greater difficulty.

Britain is now, I will suppose, the seat of liberty and virtue; and its legislature consists of a body of able and independent men who govern with wisdom and justice. The time may come when all will be reversed: when its excellent constitution of government will be subverted: when, pressed by debts and taxes, it will be greedy to draw to itself an increase of revenue from every distant province, in order to ease its own burdens. When the influence of the crown, strengthened by luxury and an universal profligacy of manners, will have tainted every heart, broken down every fence of liberty, and rendered us a nation of tame and contented vassals: when a general election will be nothing but a general auction of boroughs; and when the Parliament, the Grand Council of the nation and once the faithful guardian of the state and a terror to evil ministers, will be degenerated into a body of sycophants, dependent and venal, always ready to confirm any measures, and little more than a public court for registering royal edicts. Such, it is possible, may, some time or other, be the state of Great Britain. What will, at that period, be the duty of the colonies? Will they be still bound to unconditional submission? Must they always continue an appendage to our government and follow it implicitly through every change that can happen to it? Wretched condition, indeed, of millions of freemen as good as ourselves. Will you say that we now govern equitably, and that there is no danger of any such revolution? Would to God this were true. But will you not always say the same? Who shall judge whether we govern equitably or not? Can you give the colonies any security that such a period will never come? Once more, if we have indeed that power which we claim over the legislations, and internal rights of the Colonies, may we not, whenever we please, subject them to the arbitrary power of the crown? I do not mean that this would be a disadvantageous change, for I have before observed that if a people are to be subject to an external power over which they have no command, it is better that power should be lodged in the hands of one man than of a multitude. But many persons think otherwise and such ought to consider that, if this would be a calamity, the condition of the Colonies must be deplorable. 'A government by King, Lords, and Commons, (it has been said) is the perfection of government', and so it is when the Commons are a just representation of the people and when also it is not extended to any distant people or communities not represented. But if this is the best, a government by a king only must be the worst, and every claim implying a right to establish such a government among any people must be unjust and cruel. It is self-evident that by claiming a right to alter the constitutions of the Colonies, according to our discretion, we claim this power. And it is a power that we have thought fit to exercise in one of our Colonies and that we have attempted to exercise in another. Canada, according to the late extension of its limits, is a country almost as large as half Europe, and it may possibly come in time to be filled with British subjects. The Quebec Act*d* makes the king of Great Britain a despot over all that country. In the province of Massachuset's Bay the same thing had been attempted and begun.

The act for better regulating their government,*e* passed at the same time with the Quebec Act, gives the king the right of appointing, and removing at his pleasure, the members of one part of the legislature;

---

d The Quebec Act (1775), 16 Geo. III c. 83.

e The Massachusetts Government Act (1774), 14 Geo. III c. 45.

alters the mode of chusing juries, on purpose to bring it more under the influence of the king; and takes away from the province the power of calling any meetings of the people without the king's consent. The judges, likewise, have been made dependent on the king for their nomination and pay and continuance in office. If all this is no more than we have a right to do, may we not go on to abolish the house of representatives, to destroy all trials by juries, and to give up the province absolutely and totally to the will of the king? May we not even establish Popery in the province, as has been lately done in Canada, leaving the support of Protestantism to the king's discretion? Can there be any Englishmen who, were it his own case, would not sooner lose his heart's blood than yield to claims so pregnant with evils and destructive to every thing that can distinguish a freeman from a slave?

I will take this opportunity to add that what I have now said suggests a consideration that demonstrates on how different a footing the Colonies are with respect to our government from particular bodies of men within the kingdom who happen not to be represented. Here, it is impossible that the represented part should subject the unrepresented part to arbitrary power without including themselves. But in the Colonies it is not impossible. We know that it has been done.

Sect. II
*Whether the War with America is Justified by the
Principles of the Constitution*

I have proposed, in the next place, to examine the war with the Colonies by the principles of the constitution. I know that it is common to say that we are now maintaining the constitution in America. If this means that we are endeavouring to establish our own constitution of government there, it is by no means true, nor, were it true, would it be right. They have chartered governments of their own, with which they are pleased and which, if any power on earth may change without their consent, that power may likewise, if it thinks proper, deliver them over to the Grand Seignior. Suppose the colonies of France had, by compacts, enjoyed for many years free governments open to all the world, under which they had grown and flourished; what should we think of that kingdom, were it to attempt to destroy their governments and to force upon them its own mode of government? Should we not applaud any zeal they discovered in repelling such an injury? But the truth is, in the present instance, that we are not maintaining but violating our own constitution in America. The essence of our constitution consists in its independency. There is in this case no difference between subjection and annihilation. Did, therefore, the Colonies possess governments perfectly the same with ours, the attempt to subject them to ours would be an attempt to ruin them. A free government loses its nature from the moment it becomes liable to be commanded or altered by any superior power.

But I intended here principally to make the following observation. The fundamental principle of our government is, 'the right of a people to give and grant their own money'. It is of no consequence, in this case, whether we enjoy this right in a proper manner or not. Most certainly we do not. It is, however, the principle on which our government, as a free government, is founded. The spirit of the constitution gives it us and, however imperfectly enjoyed, we glory in it as our first and greatest blessing. It was an attempt to encroach upon this right, in a trifling instance, that produced the civil war in the reign of Charles the First. Ought not our brethren in America to enjoy this right as well as ourselves? Do the principles of the constitution give it us, but deny it to them? Or can we, with any decency, pretend that when we give to the king their money, we give them our own? What difference does it make that in the time of Charles the First the attempt to take away this right was made by one man; but that, in the case of America it is made by a body of men?

In a word, this is a war undertaken not only against the principles of our own constitution, but on purpose to destroy other similar constitutions in America, and to substitute in their room a military force. It is, therefore, a gross and flagrant violation of the constitution.

Sect. III

Of the Policy of the War with America

In writing the present section, I enter upon a subject of the last importance, on which much has been said by other writers with great force, and in the ablest manner. But I am not willing to omit any topic which I think of great consequence, merely because it has already been discussed. And, with respect to this in particular, it will, I believe, be found that some of the observations on which I shall insist have not been sufficiently attended to.

The object of this war has been often enough declared to be 'maintaining the supremacy of this country over the colonies'. I have already enquired how far reason and justice, the principles of liberty, and the rights of humanity, entitle us to this supremacy. Setting aside, therefore, now all considerations of this kind, I would observe that this supremacy is to be maintained either merely for its own sake or for the sake of some public interest connected with it and dependent upon it. If for its own sake, the only object of the war is the extension of dominion, and its only motive is the lust of power. All government, even within a state, becomes tyrannical as far as it is a needless and wanton exercise of power, or is carried farther than is absolutely necessary to preserve the peace and to secure the safety of the state. This is what an excellent writer [Jonathan Shipley] calls 'governing too much'[f] and its effect must always be, weakening government by rendering it contemptible and odious. Nothing can be of more importance in governing distant provinces and adjusting the clashing interests of different societies than attention to this remark. In these circumstances it is particularly necessary to make a sparing use of power in order to preserve power. Happy would it have been for Great Britain, had this been remembered by those who have lately conducted its affairs. But our policy has been of another kind. At the period when our authority should have been most concealed, it has been brought most in view and by a progression of violent measures, every one of which has increased distress, we have given the world reason to conclude that we are acquainted with no other method of governing than by force. What a shocking mistake! If our object is power we should have known better how to use it, and our rulers should have considered that freemen will always revolt at the sight of a naked sword, and that the complicated affairs of a great kingdom, holding in subordination to it a multitude of distant communities, all jealous of their rights and warmed with spirits as high as our own, require not only the most skilful but the most cautious and tender management. The consequences of a different management we are

[f] Jonathan Shipley, *A Sermon Preached before the Incorporated Society for the Propagation of the Gospel in Foreign Parts; at their Anniversary Meeting in the Parish Church of St. Mary-le-Bow, on Friday February 19, 1773.*

now feeling. We see ourselves driven among rocks and in danger of being lost.

The following reasons make it too probable that the present contest with America is a contest for power only, abstracted from all the advantages connected with it.

First, there is a love of power inherent in human nature, and it cannot be uncharitable to suppose that the nation in general, and the cabinet in particular, are too likely to be influenced by it. What can be more flattering than to look across the Atlantic, and to see in the boundless continent of America increasing millions whom we have a right to order as we please, who hold their property at our disposal, and who have no other law than our will? With what complacency have we been used to talk of them as our subjects? Is it not the interruption they now give to this pleasure, is it not the opposition they make to our pride, and not any injury they have done us, that is the secret spring of our present animosity against them? I wish all in this kingdom would examine themselves carefully on this point. Perhaps they might find that they have not known what spirit they are of. Perhaps they would become sensible that it was a spirit of domination more than a regard to the true interest of this country that lately led so many of them, with such savage folly, to address the throne for the slaughter of their brethren in America if they will not submit to them and to make offers of their lives and fortunes for that purpose. Indeed, I am persuaded that, were pride and the lust of dominion exterminated from every heart among us and the humility of Christians infused in their room, this quarrel would be soon ended.

Secondly, another reason for believing that this is a contest for power only is that our ministers have frequently declared that their object is not to draw a revenue from America, and that many of those who are warmest for continuing it represent the American trade as of no great consequence.

But what deserves particular consideration here is that this is a contest from which no advantages can possibly be derived. Not a revenue, for the provinces of America, when desolated, will afford no revenue, or, if they should, the expence of subduing them and keeping them in subjection will much exceed that revenue. Not any of the advantages of trade, for it is a folly, next to insanity, to think trade can be promoted by impoverishing our customers and fixing in their minds an everlasting abhorrence of us. It remains, therefore, that this war can have no other object than the extension of power. Miserable reflection! To sheath our swords in the bowels of our brethren and spread misery and ruin among a happy people for no other end than to oblige them to acknowledge our supremacy. How horrid! This is the cursed ambition that led a Caesar and an Alexander, and many other mad conquerors, to attack peaceful communities and to lay waste the earth.

But a worse principle than even this influences some among us. Pride and the love of dominion are principles hateful enough, but blind resentment and the desire of revenge are infernal principles. And these, I am afraid, have no small share at present in guiding our public conduct. One cannot help indeed being astonished at the virulence with which some speak on the present occasion against the Colonies. For what have they done? Have they crossed the ocean and invaded us? Have they attempted to take from us the fruits of our labour and to overturn that form of government which we hold so sacred? This cannot be pretended. On the contrary, this is what we have done to them. We have transported ourselves to their peaceful retreats and employed our fleets and armies to stop up their ports, to destroy their commerce, to seize their effects, and to burn their towns. Would we but let them alone and suffer them to enjoy in security their property and governments, instead of disturbing us they would thank and bless us. And yet it is we who imagine ourselves ill-used. The truth is, we expected to find them a cowardly rabble who would lie quietly at our feet and they have disappointed us. They have risen in their own defence and repelled force by force. They deny the plenitude of our power over them and insist upon being treated as free communities. It is this that has provoked us and kindled our governors into rage.

I hope I shall not here be understood to intimate that all who promote this war are actuated by these principles. Some, I doubt not, are influenced by no other principle than a regard to what they think the just authority of this country over its colonies and to the unity and indivisibility of the British Empire. I wish such could be engaged to enter thoroughly into the enquiry which has been the subject of the first part of this pamphlet and to consider particularly how different a thing maintaining the authority of government within a state is from maintaining the authority of one people over another already happy in the enjoyment of a government of their own. I wish farther they would consider that the desire of maintaining authority is warrantable only as far as it is the means of promoting some end and doing some good, and that, before we resolve to spread famine and fire through a country in order to make it acknowledge our authority, we ought to be assured that great advantages will arise not only to ourselves, but to the country we wish to conquer. That from the present contest no advantage to ourselves can arise has been already shewn, and will presently be shewn more at large. That no advantage to the Colonies can arise from it need not, I hope, be shewn. It has however been asserted that even their good is intended by this war. Many of us are persuaded that they will be much happier under our government than under any government of their own, and that their liberties will be safer when held for them by us than when trusted in their own hands. How kind is it thus to take upon us the trouble of judging for them what is most for their happiness? Nothing can be kinder except the resolution we have formed to exterminate them if they will not submit to our judgment. What strange language have I sometimes heard? By an armed force we are now endeavouring to destroy the laws and governments of America, and yet I have heard it said that we are endeavouring to support law and government there. We are insisting upon our right to levy contributions upon them and to maintain this right we are bringing upon them all the miseries a people can endure, and yet it is asserted that we mean nothing but their security and happiness.

But I have wandered a little from the point I intended principally to insist upon in this section, which is, 'the folly, in respect of policy, of the measures which have brought on this contest, and its pernicious and fatal tendency'.

The following observations will, I believe, abundantly prove this.

First, there are points which are likely always to suffer by discussion. Of this kind are most points of authority and prerogative and the best policy is to avoid, as much as possible, giving any occasion for calling them in question.

The Colonies were at the beginning of this reign in the habit of acknowledging our authority and of allowing us as much power over them as our interest required and more, in some instances, than we could reasonably claim. This habit they would have retained, and had we, instead of imposing new burdens upon them and increasing their restraints, studied to promote their commerce and to grant them new indulgences, they would have been always growing more attached to us. Luxury and, together with it, their dependence upon us, and our influence in their assemblies, would have increased till in time perhaps they would have become as corrupt as ourselves; and we might have succeeded to our wishes in establishing our authority over them. But, happily for them, we have chosen a different course. By exertions of authority which have alarmed them they have been put upon examining into the grounds of all our claims and forced to give up their luxuries and to seek all their resources within themselves. And the issue is likely to prove the loss of all our authority over them and of all the advantages connected with it. So little do men in power sometimes know how to preserve power and so remarkably does the desire of extending dominion sometimes destroy it. Mankind are naturally disposed to continue in subjection to that mode of government, be it what it will, under which they have been born and educated. Nothing rouses them into resistance but gross abuse or some particular oppressions out of the road to which they have been used. And he who will examine the history of the world will find there has generally been more reason for complaining that they have been too patient than that they have been turbulent and rebellious.

Our governors, ever since I can remember, have been jealous that the Colonies, some time or other, would throw off their dependence. This jealousy was not founded on any of their acts or declarations. They have always, while at peace with us, disclaimed any such design, and they have continued to disclaim it since they have been at war with us. I have reason, indeed, to believe that independency is, even at this moment, generally dreaded among them as a calamity to which they are in danger of being driven in order to avoid a greater. The jealousy, I have mentioned, was, however, natural and betrayed a secret opinion that the subjection in which they were held was more than we could expect them always to endure. In such circumstances, all possible care should have been taken to give them no reason for discontent and to preserve them in subjection by keeping in that line of conduct to which custom had reconciled them, or, at least, never deviating from it except with great caution, and, particularly, by avoiding all direct attacks on their property and legislations. Had we done this, the different interests of so many states scattered over a vast continent, joined to our own prudence and moderation, would have enabled us to maintain them in dependence for ages to come. But instead of this, how have we acted? It is in truth too evident that our whole conduct, instead of being directed by that sound policy and foresight which in such circumstances were absolutely necessary, has been nothing (to say the best of it) but a series of the blindest rigour followed by retraction, of violence followed by concession, of mistake, weakness and inconsistency. A recital of a few facts within every body's recollection, will fully prove this.

In the 6th of George the Second, an act was passed for imposing certain duties on all foreign spirits, molasses and sugars imported into the plantations.[g] In this act the duties imposed are said to be given and granted by the Parliament to the King, and this is the first American act in which these words have been used. But notwithstanding this, as the act had the appearance of being only a regulation of trade, the Colonies submitted to it and a small direct revenue was drawn by it from them. In the 4th of the present reign, many alterations were made in this act, with the declared purpose of making provision for raising a revenue in America.[h] This alarmed the Colonies and produced discontents and remonstrances which might have convinced our rulers this was tender ground on which it became them to tread very gently. There is, however, no reason to doubt but in time they would have sunk into a quiet submission to this revenue act as being at worst only the exercise of a power which then they seem not to have thought much of contesting, I mean, the power of taxing them externally. But before they had time to cool, a worse provocation was given them and the Stamp Act[i] was passed. This being an attempt to tax them internally, and a direct attack on their property by a power which would not suffer itself to be questioned, which eased itself by loading them, and to which it was impossible to fix any bounds, they were thrown at once, from one end of the continent to the other, into resistance and rage. Government, dreading the consequences, gave way and the Parliament (upon a change of ministry) repealed the Stamp Act without requiring from them any recognition of its authority, or doing any more to preserve its dignity than asserting, by the declaratory law, that it was possessed of full power and authority to make laws to bind them in all cases whatever. Upon this, peace was restored, and, had

[g] The Molasses Act (1733), 6 Geo. II c. 13.
[h] The Sugar Act, 4 Geo. III c. 15.
[i] The Stamp Act, 5 Geo. III c. 12.

no farther attempts of the same kind been made, they would undoubtedly have suffered us (as the people of Ireland have done) to enjoy quietly our declaratory law. They would have recovered their former habits of subjection, and our connexion with them might have continued an increasing source of our wealth and glory. But the spirit of despotism and avarice, always blind and restless, soon broke forth again. The scheme for drawing a revenue from America, by parliamentary taxation, was resumed and in a little more than a year after the repeal of the Stamp Act, when all was peace, a third act was passed, imposing duties payable in America on tea, paper, glass, painters' colours, etc.[j] This, as might have been expected, revived all the former heats and the Empire was a second time threatened with the most dangerous commotions. Government receded again and the Parliament (under another change of ministry) repealed all the obnoxious duties except that upon tea. This exception was made in order to maintain a shew of dignity. But it was, in reality, sacrificing safety to pride and leaving a splinter in the wound to produce a gangrene. For some time, however, this relaxation answered its intended purposes. Our commercial intercourse with the Colonies was again recovered and they avoided nothing but that tea which we had excepted in our repeal. In this state would things have remained, and even tea would perhaps in time have been gradually admitted, had not the evil genius of Britain stepped forth once more to embroil the Empire.

The East India Company having fallen under difficulties, partly in consequence of the loss of the American market for tea, a scheme was formed for assisting them by an attempt to recover that market. With this view an act was passed to enable them to export their tea to America free of all duties here, and subject only to 3d per pound duty payable in America. It was to be offered at a low price and it was expected the consequence would prove that the Colonies would be tempted to buy it, a precedent gained for taxing them, and at the same time the company relieved. Ships were, therefore, fitted out and large cargoes sent. The snare was too gross to escape the notice of the Colonies. They saw it and spurned at it. They refused to admit the tea and at Boston some persons in disguise threw it into the sea. Had our governors in this case satisfied themselves with requiring a compensa-

---

[j] The Townshend Revenue Act, 7 Geo. III c. 46.

tion from the province for the damage done, there is no doubt but it would have been granted. Or had they proceeded no farther in the infliction of punishment than stopping up the port and destroying the trade of Boston till compensation was made, the province might possibly have submitted and a sufficient saving would have been gained for the honour of the nation. But having hitherto proceeded without wisdom they observed now no bounds in their resentment. To the Boston Port Bill*k* was added a bill*l* which destroyed the chartered government of the province, a bill*m* which withdrew from the jurisdiction of the province persons who in particular cases should commit murder, and the Quebec Bill. At the same time a strong body of troops was stationed at Boston to enforce obedience to their bills.

All who knew any thing of the temper of the Colonies saw that the effect of this sudden accumulation of vengeance would probably be not intimidating but exasperating them and driving them into a general revolt. But our ministers had different apprehensions. They believed that the malecontents in the Colony of Massachusett's were a small party, headed by a few factious men, that the majority of the people would take the side of government as soon as they saw a force among them capable of supporting them, that, at worst, the Colonies in general would never make a common cause with this province, and that the issue would prove, in a few months, order, tranquility and submission. Every one of these apprehensions was falsified by the events that followed.

When the bills I have mentioned came to be carried into execution, the whole province was thrown into confusion. Their courts of justice were shut up, and all government was dissolved. The commander in chief found it necessary to fortify himself in Boston, and the other Colonies immediately resolved to make a common cause with this Colony.

Disappointed by these consequences, our ministers took fright. Once more they made an effort to retreat, but indeed the most ungracious one that can well be imagined. A proposal was sent to the Colonies called Conciliatory, and the substance of which was, that if any of them would raise such sums as should be demanded of them by taxing themselves, the Parliament would forbear to tax them. It will

k Boston Port Act (1774), 14 Geo. III c. 19.
l The Massachusetts Government Act (1774).
m The Administration of Justice Act, 14 Geo. III c. 39.

be scarcely believed, hereafter, that such a proposal would be thought conciliatory. It was only telling them, 'If you will tax yourselves by our order, we will save ourselves the trouble of taxing you.' They received the proposal as an insult, and rejected it with disdain.

At the time this concession was transmitted to America, open hostilities were not begun. In the sword our ministers thought they had still a resource which would immediately settle all disputes. They considered the people of New-England as nothing but a mob, who would be soon routed and forced into obedience. It was even believed that a few thousands of our army might march through all America, and make all quiet wherever they went. Under this conviction our ministers did not dread urging the Province of Massachusett's Bay into rebellion, by ordering the army to seize their stores and to take up some of their leading men. The attempt was made. The people fled immediately to arms and repelled the attack. A considerable part of the flower of the British army has been destroyed. Some of our best generals and the bravest of our troops are now disgracefully and miserably imprisoned at Boston. A horrid civil war is commenced and the Empire is distracted and convulsed.

Can it be possible to think with patience of the policy that has brought us into these circumstances? Did ever Heaven punish the vices of a people more severely by darkening their counsels? How great would be our happiness could we now recall former times and return to the policy of the last reign? But those times are gone. I will, however, beg leave for a few moments to look back to them and to compare the ground we have left with that on which we find our-selves. This must be done with deep regret, but it forms a necessary part of my present design.

In those times our Colonies, foregoing every advantage which they might derive from trading with foreign nations, consented to send only to us whatever it was for our interest to receive from them and to receive only from us whatever it was for our interest to send to them. They gave up the power of making sumptuary laws and exposed themselves to all the evils of an increasing and wasteful luxury, because we were benefited by vending among them the materials of it. The iron with which providence had blessed their country, they were required by laws, in which they acquiesced, to transport hither that our people might be maintained by working it for them into nails, ploughs, axes, etc. And, in several instances, even one Colony was not allowed to supply any neighbouring Colonies with commodities which could be conveyed to them from hence. But they yielded much farther. They consented that we should have the appointment of one branch of their legislature. By recognizing as their King, a King resident among us and under our influence, they gave us a negative on all their laws. By allowing an appeal to us in their civil disputes, they gave us likewise the ultimate determination of all civil causes among them. In short, they allowed us every power we could desire, except that of taxing them, and interfering in their internal legislations. And they had admitted precedents which, even in these instances, gave us no inconsiderable authority over them. By purchasing our goods they paid our taxes, and by allowing us to regulate their trade in any manner we thought most for our advantage they enriched our merchants and helped us to bear our growing burdens. They fought our battles with us. They gloried in their relation to us. All their gains centered among us and they always spoke of this country and looked to it as their home.

Such was the state of things. What is it now?

Not contented with a degree of power sufficient to satisfy any reasonable ambition, we have attempted to extend it. Not contented with drawing from them a large revenue indirectly, we have endeavoured to procure one directly by an authoritative seizure, and in order to gain a pepper-corn in this way have chosen to hazard millions, acquired by the peaceable intercourse of trade. Vile policy! What a scourge is government so conducted? Had we never deserted our old ground, had we nourished and favoured America with a view to commerce instead of considering it as a country to be governed, had we, like a liberal and wise people, rejoiced to see a multitude of free states branched forth from ourselves, all enjoying independent legislatures similar to our own, had we aimed at binding them to us only by the tyes of affection and interest, and contented ourselves with a moderate power rendered durable by being lenient and friendly, an umpire in their differences, an aid to them in improving their own free governments, and their common bulwark against the assaults of foreign enemies, had this, I say, been our policy and temper, there is nothing so great or happy that we might not have expected. With their increase our strength would have increased. A growing surplus in the revenue might have been gained which, invariably applied to the gradual discharge of the national debt, would have delivered us from the ruin with which it threatens us. The liberty of America might have preserved our liberty, and, under the direction of a patriot king or wise minister, proved the means of restoring to us our almost lost constitution. Perhaps, in time, we might also have been brought to see the necessity of carefully watching and restricting our paper-credit. And thus we might have regained safety and, in union with our Colonies, have been more than a match for every enemy and risen to a situation of honour and dignity never before known amongst mankind. But I am forgetting myself. Our Colonies are likely to be lost for ever. Their love is turned into hatred and their respect for our government into resentment and abhorrence. We shall see more distinctly what a calamity this is, and the observations I have now made will be confirmed by attending to the following facts.

Our American Colonies, particularly the northern ones, have been for some time in the happiest state of society or in that middle state of civilization, between its first rude and its last refined and corrupt state. Old countries consist, generally, of three classes of people, a gentry; a yeomanry; and a peasantry. The Colonies consist only of a body of yeomanry[4] supported by agriculture, and all independent and nearly upon a level; in consequence of which, joined to a boundless extent of country, the means of subsistence are procured without difficulty and the temptations to wickedness are so inconsiderable that executions are seldom known among them. From hence arises an encouragement to population so great that in some of the colonies they double their own number in fifteen years, in others in eighteen years, and in all, taken one with another, in twenty-five years. Such an increase was, I believe, never before known. It demonstrates that they must live at their ease and be free from those cares, oppressions, and diseases which depopulate and ravage luxurious states.

With the population of the Colonies has increased their trade; but much faster, on account of the gradual introduction of luxury among them. In 1723 the exports to Pensylvania were £16,000. In 1742 they were £75,295. In 1757 they were increased to £268,426, and in 1773 to half a million.

---

[4] Except the negroes in the southern Colonies, who probably will now either soon become extinct, or have their condition changed into that of freemen. It is not the fault of the Colonies that they have among them so many of these unhappy people. They have made laws to prohibit the importation of them, but these laws have always had a negative put upon them here because of their tendency to hurt our Negro trade.

The exports to all the Colonies in 1744 were £640,114. In 1758 they were increased to £1,832,948 and in 1773 to three millions. And the probability is that, had it not been for the discontents among the Colonies since the year 1764, our trade with them would have been this year double to what it was in 1773, and that in a few years more, it would not have been possible for the whole kingdom, though consisting only of manufacturers, to supply the American demand.

This trade, it should be considered, was not only thus an increasing trade, but it was a trade in which we had no rivals, a trade certain, constant, and uninterrupted, and which, by the shipping employed in it, and the naval stores supplied by it, contributed greatly to the support of that navy which is our chief national strength. Viewed in these lights it was an object unspeakably important. But it will appear still more so if we view it in its connexions and dependencies. It is well known that our trade with Africa and the West-Indies cannot easily subsist without it. And, upon the whole, it is undeniable that it has been one of the main springs of our opulence and splendour and that we have, in a great measure, been indebted to it for our ability to bear a debt so much heavier than that which, fifty years ago, the wisest men thought would necessarily sink us.

This inestimable prize and all the advantages connected with America, we are now throwing away. Experience alone can shew what calamities must follow. It will indeed be astonishing if this kingdom can bear such a loss without dreadful consequences. These consequences have been amply represented by others and it is needless to enter into any account of them. At the time we shall be feeling them: the Empire dismembered, the blood of thousands shed in an unrighteous quarrel, our strength exhausted, our merchants breaking, our manufacturers starving, our debts increasing, the revenues sinking, the funds tottering, and all the miseries of a public bankruptcy impending. At such a crisis should our natural enemies, eager for our ruin, seize the opportunity. The apprehension is too distressing. Let us view this subject in another light.

On this occasion, particular attention should be given to the present singular situation of this kingdom. This is a circumstance of the utmost importance and, as I am afraid it is not much considered, I will beg leave to give a distinct account of it.

At the Revolution, the specie of the kingdom amounted, according to Davenant's account, to eighteen millions and a half. From the accession to the year 1772 there were coined at the mint near 29 millions of gold; and in ten years only of this time or from January 1759 to January 1769 there were coined eight millions and a half. But it has appeared lately that the gold specie now left in the kingdom is no more than about twelve millions and a half. Not so much as half a million of silver specie has been coined these sixty years, and it cannot be supposed that the quantity of it now in circulation exceeds two or three millions. The whole specie of the kingdom, therefore, is probably at this time about fifteen millions. Of this some millions must be hoarded at the Bank. Our circulating specie, therefore, appears to be decreased. But our wealth, or the quantity of money in the kingdom, is greatly increased. This is paper to a vast amount, issued in almost every corner of the kingdom, and, particularly, by the Bank of England. While this paper maintains its credit it answers all the purposes of specie, and is in all respects the same with money.

Specie represents some real value in goods or commodities. On the contrary, paper represents immediately nothing but specie. It is a promise or obligation which the emitter brings himself under to pay a given sum in coin, and it owes its currency to the credit of the emitter, or to an opinion that he is able to make good his engagement, and that the sum specified may be received upon being demanded. Paper, therefore, represents coin, and coin represents real value. That is, the one is a sign of wealth. The other is the sign of that sign. But farther, coin is an universal sign of wealth, and will procure it every where. It will bear any alarm, and stand any shock. On the contrary, paper, owing its currency to opinion, has only a local and imaginary value. It can stand no shock. It is destroyed by the approach of danger or even the suspicion of danger.

In short, coin is the basis of our paper credit, and were it either all destroyed, or were only the quantity of it reduced beyond a certain limit, the paper circulation of the kingdom would sink at once. But, were our paper destroyed, the coin would not only remain but rise in value in proportion to the quantity of paper destroyed.

From this account it follows that as far as, in any circumstances, specie is not to be procured in exchange for paper, it represents nothing, and is worth nothing. The specie of this kingdom is inconsiderable compared with the amount of the paper circulating in it. This is generally believed and, therefore, it is natural to enquire how its currency is supported. The answer is easy. It is supported in the same manner with all other bubbles. Were all to demand specie in exchange for their notes payment could not be made, but at the same time that this is known every one trusts that no alarm producing such a demand will happen, while he holds the paper he is possessed of, and that if it should happen, he will stand a chance for being first paid, and this makes him easy. But let any events happen which threaten danger and every one will become diffident. A run will take place and a bankruptcy follow.

This is an account of what has often happened in private credit. And it is also an account of what will (if no change of measures takes place) happen some time or other in public credit. The description I have given of our paper-circulation implies that nothing can be more delicate or hazardous. It is an immense fabrick with its head in the clouds that is continually trembling with every adverse blast and every fluctuation of trade and which, like the baseless fabrick of a vision, may in a moment vanish, and leave no wreck behind. The destruction of a few books at the Bank, an improvement in the art of forgery, the landing of a body of French troops on our coasts, insurrections threatening a revolution in government, or any events that should produce a general panic, however groundless, would at once annihilate it and leave us without any other medium of traffic than a quantity of specie not much more than the money now drawn from the public by the taxes. It would, therefore, become impossible to pay the taxes. The revenue would fail. Near a hundred and forty millions of property would be destroyed. The whole frame of government would fall to pieces, and a state of nature would take place. What a dreadful situation? It has never had a parallel among mankind, except at one time in France after the establishment of the Royal Mississippi Bank. In 1720 this bank broke and, after involving for some time the whole kingdom in a golden dream, spread through it in one day desolation and ruin. The distress attending such an event in this free country would be greater than it was in France. Happily for that kingdom they have shot this gulph. Paper-credit has never since recovered itself there and their circulating cash consists now all of solid coin amounting, according to the lowest account, to no less a sum than 1500 millions of livres, or near 67 millions of pounds sterling. This gives them unspeakable advantages and, joined to that quick reduction of their debts which is inseparable from their nature, places them on a ground of safety which we have reason to admire and envy.

These are subjects on which I should have chosen to be silent, did I not think it necessary that this country should be apprized and warned of the danger which threatens it. This danger is created chiefly by the national debt. High taxes are necessary to support a great public debt and a large supply of cash is necessary to support high taxes. This cash we owe to our paper and, in proportion to our paper, must be the productiveness of our taxes. King William's wars drained the kingdom of its specie. This sunk the revenue and distressed government. In 1694 the Bank was established and the kingdom was provided with a substitute for specie. The taxes became again productive. The revenue rose and government was relieved. Ever since that period our paper and taxes have been increasing together and supporting one another; and one reason, undoubtedly, of the late increase in the productiveness of our taxes has been the increase of our paper.

Was there no public debt, there would be no occasion for half the present taxes. Our paper circulation might be reduced. The balance of trade would turn in our favour. Specie would flow in upon us. The quantity of property destroyed by a failure of paper-credit (should it in such circumstances happen) would be 140 millions less, and, therefore, the shock attending it would be tolerable. But in the present state of things whenever any calamity or panic shall produce such a failure, the shock attending it will be intolerable. May heaven soon raise up for us some great statesman who shall see these things and enter into effectual measures, if not now too late, for extricating and preserving us.

Public banks are, undoubtedly, attended with great conveniencies. But they also do great harm, and, if their emissions are not restrained and conducted with great wisdom, they may prove the most pernicious of all institutions, not only by substituting fictitious for real wealth, by increasing luxury, by raising the prices of provisions, by concealing an unfavourable balance of trade, and by rendering a kingdom incapable of bearing any internal tumults or external attacks without the danger of a dreadful convulsion, but, particularly, by becoming instruments in the hands of ministers of state to increase their influence, to lessen their dependence on the people, and to keep up a delusive shew of public prosperity, when perhaps ruin may be near. There is, in truth, nothing that a government may not do with such a mine at its command as a public bank while it can maintain its credit, nor, therefore, is there any thing more likely to be improperly

and dangerously used. But to return to what may be more applicable
to our own state at present.

Among the causes that may produce a failure of paper-credit there
are two which the present quarrel with America calls upon us particularly to consider. The first is 'an unfavourable balance of trade'. This,
in proportion to the degree in which it takes place, must turn the
course of foreign exchange against us, raise the price of bullion, and
carry off our specie. The danger to which this would expose us is
obvious, and it has been much increased by the new coinage of the
gold specie which begun in 1773. Before this coinage, the greatest
part of our gold coin being light, but the same in currency as if it had
been heavy, always remained in the kingdom. But, being now nearly
of full weight, whenever a wrong balance of foreign trade alters the
course of exchange, and gold in coin becomes of less value than in
bullion, there is reason to fear that it will be melted down in such
great quantities and exported so fast as in a little time to leave none
behind. The consequence of which must prove that the whole
superstructure of paper-credit, now supported by it, will break down.
The only remedy, in such circumstances, is an increase of coinage at
the mint. But this will operate too slowly, and, by raising the price of
bullion, will only increase the evil. It is the Bank that at such a time
must be the immediate sufferer, for it is from thence that those who
want coin for any purpose will always draw it.

For many years before 1773 the price of gold in bullion had been
from 2 or 3 or 4 per cent higher than in coin. This was a temptation to
melt down and export the coin which could not be resisted. Hence
arose a demand for it on the Bank, and, consequently, the necessity of
purchasing bullion at a loss for a new coinage. But the more coin the
Bank procured in this way, the lower its price became in comparison
with that of bullion, and the faster it vanished, and, consequently, the
more necessary it became to coin again, and the greater loss fell upon
the Bank. Had things continued much longer in this train, the consequences might have proved very serious. I am by no means sufficiently informed to be able to assign the causes which have produced
the change that happened in 1772. But, without doubt, the state of
things that took place before that year must be expected to return.
The fluctuations of trade, in its best state, render this unavoidable.
But the contest with our Colonies has a tendency to bring it on soon
and to increase unspeakably the distress attending it. All know that

the balance of trade with them is greatly in our favour, and that this balance is paid partly by direct remittances of bullion and partly by circuitous remittances through Spain, Portugal, Italy, etc. which diminish the balance against us with these countries. During the last year they have been employed in paying their debts without adding to them, and their exportations and remittances for that purpose have contributed to render the general balance of trade more favourable to us, and also (in conjunction with the late operations of the Bank) to keep up our funds. These remittances are now ceased and a few years will determine, if this contest goes on, how far we can sustain such a loss without suffering the consequences I have described.

The second event, ruinous to our paper circulation, which may arise from our rupture with America, is a deficiency in the revenue. As a failure of our paper would destroy the revenue, so a failure of the revenue, or any considerable diminution of it, would destroy our paper. The Bank is the support of our paper and the support of the Bank is the credit of government. Its principal securities are a capital of eleven millions lent to government and money continually advanced to a vast amount on the land-tax and malt-tax, sinking fund, exchequer bills, navy bills, etc. Should, therefore, deficiencies in the revenue bring government under any difficulties, all these securities would lose their value, and the Bank and Government, and all private and public credit, would fail together. Let any one here imagine what would probably follow were it but suspected by the public in general that the taxes were so fallen as not to produce enough to pay the interest of the public debts, besides bearing the ordinary expences of the nation, and that, in order to supply the deficiency and to hide the calamity, it had been necessary in any one year to anticipate the taxes and to borrow of the Bank. In such circumstances I can scarcely doubt but an alarm would spread of the most dangerous tendency. The next foreign war, should it prove half as expensive as the last, will probably occasion such a deficiency and bring our affairs to that crisis towards which they have been long tending. But the war with America has a greater tendency to do this, and the reason is that it affects our resources more and is attended more with the danger of internal disturbances.

Some have made the proportion of our trade depending on North America to be near one half. A moderate computation makes it a third. Let it, however, be supposed to be only a fourth. I will venture to say this is a proportion of our foreign trade the loss of which, when it comes to be felt, will be found insupportable. In the article of tobacco alone it will cause a deduction from the customs of at least £300,000 per ann., including the duties paid on foreign commodities purchased by the exportation of tobacco. Let the whole deduction from the revenue be supposed to be only half a million. This alone is more than the kingdom can at present bear, without having recourse to lotteries and the land-tax at 4 shillings in order to defray the common and necessary expences of peace. But to this must be added a deduction from the produce of the excises in consequence of the increase of the poor, of the difficulties of our merchants and manufacturers, of less national wealth, and a retrenchment of luxury. There is no possibility of knowing to what these deductions may amount. When the evils producing them begin, they will proceed rapidly and they may end in a general wreck before we are aware of any danger.

In order to give a clearer view of the subject, I will in an Appendix, state particularly the national expenditure and income for eleven years, from 1764 to 1774. From that account it will appear that the money drawn every year from the public by the taxes does not fall greatly short of a sum equal to the whole specie of the kingdom, and that, notwithstanding the late increase in the productiveness of the taxes, the whole surplus of the national income has not exceeded £338,759 per ann. This is a surplus so inconsiderable as to be scarcely sufficient to guard against the deficiencies arising from the common fluctuations of foreign trade and of home consumption. It is nothing when considered as the only fund we have for paying off a debt near 140 millions. Had we continued in a state of profound peace, it could not have admitted of any diminution. What then must follow, when one of the most profitable branches of our trade is destroyed, when a third of the Empire is lost, when an addition of many millions is made to the public debt, and when, at the same time perhaps some millions are taken away from the revenue? I shudder at this prospect. A kingdom on an edge so perilous should think of nothing but a retreat.

Sect. IV
*Of the Honour of the Nation as affected
by the War with America*

One of the pleas for continuing the contest with America is, 'that our honour is engaged, and that we cannot now recede without the most humiliating concessions'.

With respect to this it is proper to observe that a distinction should be made between the nation and its rulers. It is melancholy that there should be ever any reason for making such a distinction. A government is, or ought to be, nothing but an institution for collecting and carrying into execution the will of the people. But so far is this from being in general the fact that the measures of government and the sense of the people are sometimes in direct opposition to one another; nor does it often happen that any certain conclusion can be drawn from the one to the other. I will not pretend to determine whether, in the present instance, the dishonour attending a retreat would belong to the nation at large or only to the persons in power who guide its affairs. Be this as it will, no good argument can be drawn from it against receding. The disgrace which may be implied in making concessions is nothing to that of being the aggressors in an unrighteous quarrel, and dignity, in such circumstances, consists in retracting freely and speedily. For (to adopt, on this occasion, words which I have heard applied to this very purpose, in a great assembly, by a peer to whom this kingdom has often looked as its deliverer, and whose ill state of health at this awful moment of public danger every friend to Britain must deplore) to adopt, I say, the words of this great man, 'Rectitude is dignity, oppression only is meanness, and justice, honour.'

I will add that prudence, no less than true honour, requires us to retract. For the time may come when, if it is not done voluntarily, we may be obliged to do it and find ourselves under a necessity of granting that to our distresses which we now deny to equity and humanity and the prayers of America. The possibility of this appears plainly from the preceding pages; and should it happen, it will bring upon us disgrace indeed, disgrace greater than the worst rancour can wish to see accumulated on a kingdom already too much dishonoured. Let the reader think here what we are doing. A nation, once the protector of liberty in distant countries and the scourge of tyranny, exchanged into an enemy to liberty, engaged in endeavouring to reduce to servitude its own brethren. A great and enlightened nation, not content with a controuling power over millions of people which gave it every reasonable advantage, insisting upon such a supremacy over them as would leave them nothing they could call their own, and carrying desolation and death among them for disputing it. What can be more ignominious? How have we felt for the brave Corsicans in their struggle with the Genoese, and afterwards with the French government? Did Genoa or France want more than an absolute command over their property and legislations or the power of binding them in all cases whatsoever? The Genoese, finding it difficult to keep them in subjection, ceded them to the French. All such cessions of one people by another are disgraceful to human nature. But if our claims are just, may not we also, if we please, cede the Colonies to France? There is, in truth, no other difference between these two cases than that the Corsicans were not descended from the people who governed them but that the Americans are.

There are some who seem to be sensible that the authority of one country over another cannot be distinguished from the servitude of one country to another, and that unless different communities, as well as different parts of the same community, are united by an equal representation, all such authority is inconsistent with the principles of civil liberty. But they except the case of the Colonies and Great Britain because the Colonies are communities which have branched forth from, and which therefore, as they think, belong to Britain. Had the colonies been communities of foreigners, over whom we wanted to acquire dominion or even to extend a dominion before acquired, they are ready to admit that their resistance would have been just. In my opinion this is the same with saying that the Colonies ought to be worse off than the rest of mankind because they are our own brethren.

Again, the United Provinces of Holland were once subject to the Spanish monarchy; but, provoked by a violation of their charters, by levies of money without their consent, by the introduction of Spanish troops among them, by innovations in their antient modes of government, and the rejection of their petitions they were driven to that resistance which we and all the world have ever since admired, and which has given birth to one of the greatest and happiest republics that ever existed. Let any one read also the history of the war which the Athenians, from a thirst of empire, made on the Syracusans in

Sicily, a people derived from the same origin with them, and let him, if he can, avoid rejoicing in the defeat of the Athenians.

Let him, likewise, read the account of the social war among the Romans. The allied states of Italy had fought the battles of Rome, and contributed by their valour and treasure to its conquests and grandeur. They claimed, therefore, the rights of Roman citizens, and a share with them in legislation. The Romans, disdaining to make those their fellow-citizens whom they had always looked upon as their subjects, would not comply and a war followed, the most horrible in the annals of mankind, which ended in the ruin of the Roman Republic. The feelings of every Briton in this case must force him to approve the conduct of the Allies and to condemn the proud and ungrateful Romans.

But not only is the present contest with America thus disgraceful to us, because inconsistent with our own feelings in similar cases, but also because condemned by our own practice in former times. The Colonies are persuaded that they are fighting for liberty. We see them sacrificing to this persuasion every private advantage. If mistaken, and though guilty of irregularities, they should be pardoned by a people whose ancestors have given them so many examples of similar conduct, England should venerate the attachment to liberty amidst all its excesses, and, instead of indignation or scorn, it would be most becoming them, in the present instance, to declare their applause and to say to the Colonies, 'We excuse your mistakes. We admire your spirit. It is the spirit that has more than once saved ourselves. We aspire to no dominion over you. We understand the rights of men too well to think of taking from you the inestimable privilege of governing yourselves, and, instead of employing our power for any such purpose, we offer it to you as a friendly and guardian power to be a mediator in your quarrels, a protection against your enemies, and an aid to you in establishing a plan of liberty that shall make you great and happy. In return, we ask nothing but your gratitude and your commerce.'

This would be a language worthy of a brave and enlightened nation. But alas! it often happens in the political world as it does in religion, that the people who cry out most vehemently for liberty to themselves are the most unwilling to grant it to others.

But farther, this war is disgraceful on account of the persuasion which led to it and under which it has been undertaken. The general cry was last winter that the people of New-England were a body of cowards who would at once be reduced to submission by a hostile look from our troops. In this light were they held up to public derision in both Houses of Parliament, and it was this persuasion that, probably, induced a Nobleman of the first weight in the state to recommend at the passing of the Boston Port Bill, coercive measures, hinting, at the same time, that the appearance of hostilities would be sufficient, and that all would soon be over, *sine clade*. Indeed no one can doubt but that had it been believed some time ago that the people of America were brave, more care would have been taken not to provoke them.

Again, the manner in which this war has been hitherto conducted renders it still more disgraceful. English valour being thought insufficient to subdue the Colonies, the laws and religion of France were established in Canada on purpose to obtain the power of bringing upon them from thence an army of French Papists. The wild Indians and their own slaves have been instigated to attack them, and attempts have been made to gain the assistance of a large body of Russians. With like views, German troops have been hired and the defence of our forts and garrisons trusted in their hands.

These are measures which need no comment. The last of them, in particular, having been carried into execution without the consent of parliament, threatens us with imminent danger and shews that we are in the way to lose even the forms of the constitution. If, indeed, our ministers can at any time, without leave, not only send away the national troops, but introduce foreign troops in their room, we lie entirely at mercy and we have everything to dread.

Sect. V
Of the Probability of Succeeding in the War with America

Let us next consider how far there is a probability of succeeding in the present war.

Our own people, being unwilling to enlist, and the attempts to procure armies of Russians, Indians, and Canadians having miscarried, the utmost force we can employ, including foreigners, does not exceed, if I am rightly informed, 40,000 effective men. This is the force that is to conquer half a million at least, of determined men fighting on their own ground, within sight of their houses and families, and for that sacred blessing of liberty, without which man is a beast and government a curse. All history proves that in such a situation, a handful is a match for millions.

In the Netherlands a few states, thus circumstanced, withstood, for a long course of years the whole force of the Spanish monarchy when at its zenith; and at last humbled its pride and emancipated themselves from its tyranny. The citizens of Syracuse also, thus circumstanced, withstood the whole power of the Athenians and almost ruined them. The same happened in the contest between the house of Austria, and the cantons of Switzerland. There is in this case an infinite difference between attacking and being attacked, between fighting to destroy and fighting to preserve or acquire liberty. Were we, therefore, capable of employing a land force against America equal to its own there would be little probability of success. But to think of conquering that whole continent with 30,000 or 40,000 men to be transported across the Atlantic and fed from hence and incapable of being recruited after any defeat. This is indeed a folly so great that language does not afford a name for it.

With respect to our naval force, could it sail at land as it does at sea, much might be done with it, but as that is impossible, little or nothing can be done with it which will not hurt ourselves more than the colonists. Such of their maritime towns as they cannot guard against our fleets and have not been already destroyed, they are determined either to give up to our resentment or destroy themselves. The consequence of which will be that these towns will be rebuilt in safer situations, and that we shall lose some of the principal pledges by which we have hitherto held them in subjection. As to their trade, having all the necessaries and chief conveniencies of life within themselves they have no dependence upon it, and the loss of it will do them unspeakable good, by preserving them from the evils of luxury and the temptations of wealth and keeping them in that state of virtuous simplicity which is the greatest happiness. I know that I am now speaking the sense of some of the wisest men in America. It has long been their wish that Britain would shut up all their ports. They will rejoice, particularly, in the last restraining act.[n] It might have happened that the people would have grown weary of their agreements not to export or import. But this act will oblige them to keep these

---

[n] The American Prohibitory Act (1776), 16 Geo. III c. 5.

agreements and confirm their unanimity and zeal. It will also furnish them with a reason for confiscating the estates of all the friends of our government among them and for employing their sailors, who would have been otherwise idle, in making reprisals on British property. Their ships, before useless, and consisting of many hundreds, will be turned into ships of war and that attention, which they have hitherto confined to trade, will be employed in fitting out a naval force for their own defence and thus the way will be prepared for their becoming, much sooner than they would otherwise have been, a great maritime power. This act of parliament, therefore, crowns the folly of all our late measures. None who know me can believe me to be disposed to superstition. Perhaps, however, I am not in the present instance free from this weakness. I fancy I see in these measures something that cannot be accounted for merely by human ignorance. I am inclined to think that the hand of Providence is in them working to bring about some great ends. But this leads me to one consideration more which I cannot help offering to the public and which appears to me in the highest degree important.

In this hour of tremendous danger it would become us to turn our thoughts to Heaven. This is what our brethren in the Colonies are doing. From one end of North-America to the other they are fasting and praying. But what are we doing? We are ridiculing them as fanatics, and scoffing at religion, We are running wild after pleasure and forgetting every thing serious and decent at masquerades. We are trafficking for boroughs, perjuring ourselves at elections, and selling ourselves for places. Which side then is Providence likely to favour?

In America we see a number of rising states in the vigour of youth, inspired by the noblest of all passions, the passion for being free, and animated by piety. Here we see an old state, great indeed, but inflated and irreligious, enervated by luxury, encumbered with debts, and hanging by a thread. Can any one look without pain to the issue? May we not expect calamities that shall recover to reflection (perhaps to devotion) our libertines and atheists?

Is our cause such as gives us reason to ask God to bless it? Can we in the face of Heaven declare, 'that we are not the aggressors in this war; and that we mean by it, not to acquire or even preserve dominion for its own sake, not conquest, or empire, or the gratification of resentment, but solely to deliver ourselves from oppression, to gain reparation for injury; and to defend ourselves against men who would plunder or kill us?' Remember, reader, whoever thou art, that there are no other just causes of war and that blood spilled with any other views must some time or other be accounted for. But not to expose myself by saying more in this way, I will now beg leave to recapitulate some of the arguments I have used and to deliver the feelings of my heart in a brief but earnest address to my countrymen.

I am hearing it continually urged, 'Are they not our subjects?' The plain answer is that they are not your subjects. The people of America are no more the subjects of the people of Britain than the people of Yorkshire are the subjects of the people of Middlesex. They are your fellow-subjects.

'But we are taxed, and why should they not be taxed?' You are taxed by yourselves. They insist on the same privilege. They are taxed to support their own governments and they help also to pay your taxes by purchasing your manufactures and giving you a monopoly of their trade. Must they maintain two governments? Must they submit to be triple taxed? Has your moderation in taxing yourselves been such as encourages them to trust you with the power of taxing them?

'But they will not obey the Parliament and the laws.' Say rather, they will not obey your parliament and your laws. Their reason is, they have no voice in your parliament. They have no share in making your laws.[5] 'Neither have most of us.' Then you so far want liberty and your language is, 'We are not free, 'Why should they be free?' But many of you have a voice in parliament. None of them have. All your freehold land is represented. But not a foot of their land is represented. At worst, therefore, you are only enslaved partially. Were they to submit they would be enslaved totally. They are governed by parliaments chosen by themselves and by legislatures similar to yours. Why will you disturb them in the enjoyment of a blessing so invaluable? Is it reasonable to insist that your discretion alone shall be their law, that they shall have no constitutions of government, except such as you shall be pleased to give them, and no property except such as your

---

[5] 'I have no other notion of slavery, but being bound by a law to which I do not consent.' See the case of Ireland's being bound by acts of Parliament in England, stated by William Molyneux, ... [William Molyneux, *The Case of Ireland's being bound by Acts of Parliament in England, Stated* (Dublin, 1698; London, 1770)]. In arguing against the authority of Communities, and all people not incorporated, over one another; I have confined my views to taxation and internal legislation. Mr. Molyneux carried his views much farther, and denied the right of England to make any laws, even to regulate the trade of Ireland.

parliament shall be pleased to leave them? – What is your parliament? Is there not a growing intercourse between it and the court? Does it awe ministers of state as it once did? Instead of contending for a controuling power over the government of America, should you not think more of watching and reforming your own? Suppose the worst. Suppose, in opposition to all their own declarations that the colonists are now aiming at independence. 'If they can subsist without you', is it to be wondered at? Did there ever exist a community, or even an individual, that would not do the same? 'If they cannot subsist without you', let them alone. They will soon come back. 'If you cannot subsist without them', reclaim them by kindness; engage them by moderation and equity. It is madness to resolve to butcher them. This will make them detest and avoid you for ever. Freemen are not to be governed by force, or dragooned into compliance. If capable of bearing to be so ill treated, it is a disgrace to be connected with them.

'If they can subsist without you and also you without them', the attempt to subjugate them by confiscating their effects, burning their towns, and ravaging their territories, is a wanton exertion of cruel ambition which, however common it has been among mankind, deserves to be called by harder names than I chuse to apply to it. Suppose such an attempt was to be succeeded. Would it not be a fatal preparation for subduing yourselves? Would not the disposal of American places and the distribution of an American revenue render that influence of the crown irresistible which has already stabbed your liberties?

Turn your eyes to India. There more has been done than is now attempted in America. There Englishmen, actuated by the love of plunder and the spirit of conquest, have depopulated whole kingdoms and ruined millions of innocent people by the most infamous oppression and rapacity. The justice of the nation has slept over these enormities. Will the justice of heaven sleep? Are we not now execrated on both sides of the globe?

With respect to the Colonists, it would be folly to pretend they are faultless. They were running fast into our vices. But this quarrel gives them a salutary check and it may be permitted on purpose to favour them, and in them the rest of mankind; by making way for establishing, in an extensive country possessed of every advantage, a plan of government and a growing power that will astonish the world and under which every subject of human enquiry shall be open to free discussion, and the friends of liberty in every quarter of the globe find a safe retreat from civil and spiritual tyranny. I hope, therefore, our brethren in America will forgive their oppressors. It is certain they know not what they are doing.

Conclusion

Having said so much of the war with America, and particularly of the danger with which it threatens us, it may be expected that I should propose some method of escaping from this danger, and of restoring this once happy Empire to a state of peace and security. Various plans of pacification have been proposed and some of them by persons so distinguished by their rank and merit as to be above my applause. But till there is more of a disposition to attend to such plans they cannot, I am afraid, be of any great service. And there is too much reason to apprehend that nothing but calamity will bring us to repentance and wisdom. In order, however, to complete my design in these observations, I will take the liberty to lay before the public the following sketch of one of the plans just referred to, as it was opened before the holidays to the house of Lords by the Earl of Shelburne, who while he held the seals of the Southern Department, with the business of the colonies annexed, possessed their confidence, without ever compromising the authority of this country, a confidence which discovered itself by peace among themselves, and duty and submission to the mother-country. I hope I shall not take an unwarranted liberty if, on this occasion, I use his Lordship's own words as nearly as I have been able to collect them.[*o*]

> Meet the Colonies on their own ground, in the last petition from Congress to the king. The surest as well as the most dignified mode of proceeding for this country – Suspend all hostilities. Repeal the acts which immediately distress America, namely, the last restraining act, the charter act, the act for the more impartial administration of justice, and the Quebec act. All the other acts (the custom house act, the post office act, etc.) leave to a temperate revisal. There will be found much matter which both

---

[*o*] Shelburne's speech to the House of Lords was delivered on 10 November 1775, *Parl. Hist.*, 18, 920–7. As he had summarized Shelburne's proposals in the 'Conclusion' to his pamphlet, Price submitted that part of it to Shelburne for verification. Price to Shelburne, 6 January and 22 January 1776, *Correspondence*, I, pp. 237–9.

countries may wish repealed. Some which can never be given up, the principle being that regulation of trade for the common good of the Empire, which forms our palladium. Other matter which is fair subject of mutual accommodation. Prescribe[p] the most explicit acknowledgement of your right of regulating commerce in its most extensive sense if the petition and other public acts of the Colonies have not already by their declaration and acknowledgements left it upon a sufficiently secure foundation. Besides the power of regulating the general commerce of the Empire, something further might be expected, provided a due and tender regard were had to the means and abilities of the several provinces, as well as to those fundamental, unalienable rights of Englishmen, which no father can surrender on the part of his son, no representative on the part of his elector, no generation on the part of the succeeding one: the right of judging not only of the mode of raising, but the quantum, and the appropriation of such aids as they shall grant. To be more explicit, the debt of England, without entering into invidious distinctions how it came to be contracted, might be acknowledged, the debt of every individual part of the whole Empire, Asia, as well as America, included. Provided, that full security were held forth to them that such free aids, together with the Sinking Fund (Great Britain contributing her superior share), should not be left as the privy purse of the minister, but be unalienably appropriated to the original intention of that fund, the discharge of the debt, and that by an honest application of the whole fund, the taxes might in time be lessened, and the price of our manufactures consequently reduced, so that every contributory part might feel the returning benefit – always supposing the laws of trade duly observed and enforced. The time was, I am confident, and perhaps is, when these points might be obtained upon the easy, the constitutional, and, therefore, the indispensible terms of an exemption from parliamentary taxation, and an admission of the sacredness of their charters instead of sacrificing their good humour, their affection, their effectual aids, and the act of Navigation itself (which you are now

[p] As his letter to Shelburne of 22 January 1776 makes clear, Price would have preferred to substitute some other word for 'prescribe' in this place, as this was of 'a higher tone' than was 'agreeable' to his 'sentiments'. Price doubtless felt that the claim that the Imperial Parliament as then constituted had the right to *prescribe* to the colonies conflicted with his own view that the colonists had the right to govern themselves understood both as a right to determine their own affairs and as a right to participate on equal terms with other colonies and the home country in an Imperial Parliament responsible for the common concerns of the whole empire. See *Correspondence*, I, p. 238.

in the direct road to do) for a commercial quit-rent, or a barren metaphysical chimaera. How long these ends may continue attainable, no man can tell. But if no words are to be relied on except such as make against the Colonies, if nothing is acceptable, except what is attainable by force, it only remains to apply, what has been so often remarked of unhappy periods, Quos deus vult, etc.

These are sentiments and proposals of the last importance and I am very happy in being able to give them to the public from so respectable an authority as that of the distinguished peer I have mentioned, to whom, I know, this kingdom, as well as America, is much indebted for his zeal to promote those grand public points on which the preservation of liberty among us depends, and for the firm opposition, which, jointly with many others (noblemen and commoners of the first character and abilities) he has made to the present measures.

Had such a plan as that now proposed been adopted a few months ago, I have little doubt that a pacification would have taken place on terms highly advantageous to this kingdom. In particular, it is probable that the Colonies would have consented to grant an annual supply, which, increased by a saving of the money now spent in maintaining troops among them and by contributions which might have been gained from other parts of the Empire, would have formed a fund considerable enough, if unalienably applied, to redeem the public debt; in consequence of which, agreeably to Lord Shelburne's ideas, some of our worst taxes might be taken off, and the Colonies would receive our manufactures cheaper, our paper-currency might be restrained, our whole force would be free to meet at any time foreign danger, the influence of the Crown would be reduced, our Parliament would become less dependent, and the kingdom might, perhaps, be restored to a situation of permanent safety and prosperity.

To conclude. An important revolution in the affairs of this kingdom seems to be approaching. If ruin is not to be our lot, all that has been lately done must be undone and new measures adopted. At that period, an opportunity (never perhaps to be recovered, if lost) will offer itself for serving essentially this country, as well as America, by putting the national debt into a fixed course of payment, by subjecting to new regulations the administration of the finances, and by establishing measures for exterminating corruption and restoring the constitution. For my own part, if this is not to be the consequence of any future changes in the ministry, and the system of corruption, lately so much improved, is to go on, I think it totally indifferent to the kingdom who are in, or who are out of power.

The following fact is of so much importance that I cannot satisfy myself without laying it before the public. In a Committee of the American Congress, in June 1775, a declaration was drawn up containing an offer to Great Britain, 'that the Colonies would not only continue to grant extraordinary aids in time of war, but also, if allowed a free commerce, pay into the Sinking-Fund such a sum annually for one hundred years, as should be more than sufficient in that time, if faithfully applied, to extinguish all the present debts of Britain. Or, provided this was not accepted, that, to remove the groundless jealousy of Britain that the Colonies aimed at Independence and an abolition of the Navigation Act, which, in truth, they had never intended, and also, to avoid all future disputes about the right of making that and other acts for regulating their commerce for the general benefit, they would enter into a covenant with Britain that she should fully possess and exercise that right for one hundred years to come'.

At the end of the preceding tract I have had the honour of laying before the public the Earl of Shelburne's plan of pacification with the Colonies. In that plan it is particularly proposed that the Colonies should grant an annual supply to be carried to the Sinking Fund and unalienably appropriated to the discharge of the public debt. It must give this excellent peer great pleasure to learn, from this resolution, that even this part of his plan, as well as all the other parts, would, most probably, have been accepted by the Colonies. For though the resolution only offers the alternative of either a free trade with extraordinary aids and an annual supply, or an exclusive trade confirmed and extended, yet there can be little reason to doubt but that to avoid the calamities of the present contest, both would have been consented to, particularly, if, on our part, such a revisal of the laws of trade had been offered as was proposed in Lord Shelburne's plan.

The preceding resolution was, I have said, drawn up in a Committee of the Congress. But it was not entered in their minutes, a severe act of Parliament happening to arrive at that time,[q] which determined them not to give the sum proposed in it.

---

[q] An Act to restrain the trade and commerce of Massachusetts Bay, 15 Geo. III c. 10.

Additional Observations
(1777)
Additional Observations on the Nature and Value of Civil Liberty, and the War with America
(1777)

Sect. I
Of the Nature of Civil Liberty, and the Essentials of a Free Government

With respect to Liberty in general there are two questions to be considered:

First, what it is? and secondly, how far it is of value? There is no difficulty in answering the first of these questions. To be free, is 'to be able to act or forbear acting, as we think best' or 'to be masters of our own resolutions and conduct'. It may be pretended that it is not desirable to be thus free, but, without doubt, this it is to be free, and this is what all mean when they say of themselves or others that they are free.

I have observed that all the different kinds of liberty run up into the general idea of self-government. The liberty of men as agents is that power of self-determination which all agents, as such, possess. Their liberty as moral agents is their power of self-government in their moral conduct. Their liberty as religious agents is their power of self-government in religion. And their liberty as members of communities associated for the purposes of civil government is their power of self-government in all their civil concerns. It is liberty in the last of these views of it that is the subject of my present enquiry, and it may, in other words, be defined to be 'the power of a state to govern itself by its own will'. In order, therefore, to determine whether a state is free, no more is necessary than to determine whether there is any will, different from its own, to which it is subject.

When we speak of a state, we mean the whole state and not any part of it, and the will of the state, therefore, is the will of the whole. There are two ways in which this will may be expressed. First, by the suffrages of all the members given in person. Or secondly, by the suffrages of a body of representatives, in appointing whom all the members have voices. A state governed by its own will in the first of these ways enjoys the most complete and perfect liberty, but such a government being impracticable, except in very small states, it is necessary that civil communities in general should satisfy themselves with that degree of liberty which can be obtained in the last of these ways, and liberty so obtained may be sufficiently ample and at the same time is capable of being extended to the largest states.

But here, before I proceed, I must desire, that an observation may be attended to which appears to me of considerable consequence. A distinction should be made between the liberty of a state, and its not suffering oppression, or between a free government and a government under which freedom is enjoyed. Under the most despotic government liberty may happen to be enjoyed. But being derived from a will over which the state has no controul, and not from its own will, or from an accidental mildness in the administration, and not from a constitution of government, it is nothing but an indulgence of a precarious nature and of little importance. Individuals in private life, while held under the power of masters, cannot be denominated free however equitably and kindly they may be treated. This is strictly true of communities as well as of individuals. Civil liberty (it should be remembered) must be enjoyed as a right derived from the Author of nature only or it cannot be the blessing which merits this name. If there is any human power which is considered as giving it, on which it depends, and which can invade or recall it at pleasure, it changes its nature and becomes a species of slavery.

But to return, the force superseding self-government in a state, or the power destroying its liberty, is of two kinds. It may be either a power without itself, or a power within itself. The former constitutes what may be properly called external, and the latter internal slavery. Were there any distant state which had acquired a sovereignty over this country and exercised the power of making its laws and disposing its property, we should be in the first kind of slavery; and, if not totally depraved by a habit of subjection to such a power, we should think ourselves in a miserable condition; and an advocate for such a power would be considered as insulting us, who should attempt to reconcile us to it by telling us, that we were one community with that distant state, though destitute of a single voice in its legislature, and, on this ground, should maintain that all resistance to it was no less criminal than any resistance within a state to the authority of that state. In short, every state not incorporated with another by an equal representation, and yet subject to its dominion, is enslaved in this sense. Such was the slavery of the provinces subject to antient Rome, and such is the slavery of every community, as far as any other community is master of it, or as far as, in respect of taxation and internal legislation, it is not independent of every other community. Nor does it make any difference to such a community that it enjoys within itself a free constitution of government, if that constitution is itself liable to be altered, suspended or over-ruled at the discretion of the state which possesses the sovereignty over it.

But the slavery most prevalent in the world has been internal slavery. In order better to explain this, it is proper to observe that all civil government being either the government of a whole by itself, or of a whole by a power extraneous to it, or of a whole by a part; the first alone is liberty, and the two last are tyranny, producing the two sorts of slavery which I have mentioned. Internal slavery, therefore, takes place wherever a whole community is governed by a part, and this, perhaps, is the most concise and comprehensive account that can be given of it. The part that governs may be either a single man, as in absolute monarchies; or, a body of grandees, as in aristocracies. In both these cases the powers of government are commonly held for life without delegation, and descend from father to son; and the people governed are in the same situation with cattle upon an estate, which descends by inheritance from one owner to another. But farther, a community may be governed by a body of delegates and yet be enslaved. Though government by representation alone is free, unless when carried on by the personal suffrages of all the members of a state, yet all such government is by no means free. In order to render it so, the following requisites are necessary.

First, the representation must be complete. No state, a part of which only is represented in the Legislature that governs it, is self-governed. Had Scotland no representatives in the Parliament of Britain, it would not be free, nor would it be proper to call Britain free, though England, its other part, were adequately represented. The like is true, in general, of every country subject to a legislature in which some of its parts, or some classes of men in it, are represented and others not.

Secondly, the representatives of a free state must be freely chosen. If this is not the case, they are not at all representatives; and government by them degenerates into government by a junto of men in the community who happen to have power or wealth enough to command or purchase their offices.

Thirdly, after being freely chosen they must be themselves free. If there is any higher will which directs their resolutions, and on which they are dependent, they become the instruments of that will; and it is that will alone that in reality governs the state.

Fourthly, they must be chosen for short terms and, in all their acts, be accountable to their constituents. Without this a people will have no controul over their representatives and, in chusing them, they will give up entirely their liberty and only enjoy the poor privilege of naming, at certain intervals, a set of men whom they are to serve, and who are to dispose, at their discretion, of their property and lives.

The causes of internal slavery now mentioned prevail, some of them more and others less, in different communities. With respect, in particular, to a government by representation, it is evident that it deviates more or less from liberty in proportion as the representation is more or less imperfect. And, if imperfect in every one of the instances I have recited, that is, if inadequate and partial, subject to no controul from the people, corruptly chosen for long terms, and, after being chosen, venal and dependent – in these circumstances a representation becomes an imposition and a nusance and government by it is as inconsistent with true liberty as the most arbitrary and despotic government.

I have been so much misunderstood on this subject that it is necessary I should particularly observe here that my intention in this account has been merely to shew what is requisite to constitute a state or a government free, and not at all to define the best form of government. These are two very different points. The first is attended with few difficulties. A free state is a state self-governed in the manner I have described. But it may be free and yet not enjoy the best constitution of government. Liberty, though the most essential requisite in government, is not the only one. Wisdom, union, dispatch, secrecy, and vigour are likewise requisite, and that is the best form of government which best unites all these qualities or which, to an equal and perfect liberty adds the greatest wisdom in deliberating and resolving, and the greatest union, force and expedition in executing.

In short, my whole meaning is that the will of the community alone ought to govern, but that there are different methods of obtaining and executing this will, of which those are the best which collect into it most of the knowledge and experience of the community, and at the same time carry it into execution with most dispatch and vigour.

It has been the employment of the wisest men in all ages to contrive plans for this purpose, and the happiness of society depends so much on civil government, that it is not possible the human understanding should be better employed.

I have said in the *Observations on civil liberty*, that 'in a free state every man is his own legislator'. I have been happy in since finding the same assertion in Montesquieu, and also in Mr. Justice Blackstone's Commentaries.[6] It expresses the fundamental principle of our constitution; and the meaning of it is plainly that every independent agent in a free state ought to have a share in the government of it, either by himself personally, or by a body of representatives in chusing whom he has a free vote, and therefore all the concern and weight which are possible and consistent with the equal rights of every other member of the state. But though the meaning of this assertion is so obvious, and the truth of it undeniable, it has been much exclaimed against, and occasioned no small part of the opposition which has been made to the principles advanced in the *Observations on civil liberty*. One even of the most candid as well as the ablest of my opponents (whose difference of opinion from me I sincerely lament) has intimated that it implies that, in a free state thieves and pick-pockets have a right to make laws for themselves.[7] The public will not, I hope, wonder that I chuse to take little notice of such objections.

It has been said that the liberty for which I have pleaded, is 'a right or power in every one to act as he likes without any restraint'. However unfairly this representation has been given of my account of liberty, I am ready to adopt it, provided it is understood with a few

---

[6] *De l'esprit des lois*, Bk. XI, ch. vi; [Sir William] Blackstone, *Commentaries on the laws of England* [(Oxford, 1765–9)], I, 158.

[7] [Adam Ferguson], *Remarks . . . on a pamphlet published by Dr. Price . . .* [London, 1776].

limitations. Moral liberty, in particular, cannot be better defined than by calling it 'a power in every one to do as he likes'. My opponents in general seem to be greatly puzzled with this, and I am afraid it will signify little to attempt explaining it to them by saying that every man's will, if perfectly free from restraint, would carry him invariably to rectitude and virtue and that no one who acts wickedly acts as he likes, but is conscious of a tyranny within him overpowering his judgment and carrying him into a conduct for which he condemns and hates himself. *The things that he would he does not, and the things that he would not, those he does.* He is, therefore, a slave in the properest sense.

Religious liberty, likewise, is a power of acting as we like in religion, or of professing and practising that mode of religious worship which we think most acceptable to the Deity. But here the limitation to which I have referred must be attended to. All have the same unalienable right to this liberty, and, consequently, no one has a right to such a use of it as shall take it from others. Within this limit, or as far as he does not encroach on the equal liberty of others, everyone has a right to do as he pleases in religion. That the right to religious liberty goes as far as this every one must allow who is not a friend to persecution; and that it cannot go farther is self-evident; for if it did, there would be a contradiction in the nature of things, and it would be true that every one had a right to enjoy what every one had a right to destroy. If, therefore, the religious faith of any person leads him to hurt another because he professes a different faith, or if it carries him, in any instances, to intolerance, liberty itself requires he should be restrained and that, in such instances, he should lose his liberty.

All this is equally applicable to the liberty of man in his civil capacity; and it is a maxim true universally, 'that as far as any one does not molest others, others ought not to molest him'. All have a right to the free and undisturbed possession of their good names, properties and lives, and it is the right all have to this that gives the right to establish civil government, which is or ought to be nothing but an institution (by laws and provisions made with common consent) for guarding this right against invasion, for giving to every one, in temporals and spirituals, the power of commanding his own conduct, or of acting as he pleases and going where he will, provided he does not run foul of others. Just government, therefore, does not infringe liberty, but establishes it. It does not take away the rights of mankind but protect and confirm them. I will add that it does not even create any new subordinations of particular men to one another, but only gives security in those several stations, whether of authority and pre-eminence, or of subordination and dependence, which nature has established and which must have arisen among mankind whether civil government had been instituted or not. But this goes beyond my purpose in this place and more will be said of it presently.

To sum up the whole, our ideas of civil liberty will be rendered more distinct by considering it under the three following views: the liberty of the citizen, the liberty of the government, and the liberty of the community. A citizen is free when the power of commanding his own conduct and the quiet possession of his life, person, property and good name are secured to him by being his own legislator in the sense explained in page 80. A government is free when constituted in such a manner as to give this security. And the freedom of the community or nation is the same among nations that the freedom of a citizen is among his fellow-citizens. It is not, therefore, as observed on page 77, the mere possession of liberty that denominates a citizen or a community free, but that security for the possession of it which arises from such a free government as I have described, and which takes place, when there exists no power that can take it away.

It is in the same sense that the mere performance of virtuous actions is not what denominates an agent virtuous, but the temper and habits from whence they spring, or that inward constitution, and right balance of the affections, which secure the practice of virtue, produce stability of conduct, and constitute a character.

I cannot imagine how it can be disputed whether this is a just account of the nature of liberty. It has been already given more briefly in the *Observations on civil liberty* and it is with reluctance I have repeated so much of what has been there said. But the wrong apprehensions which have been entertained of my sentiments have rendered this necessary. And, for the same reason, I am obliged to go on to the subject of the next section.

Sect. II
Of the Value of Liberty, and the Excellence
of a Free Government

Having drawn in the preceding section what liberty is, the next question to be considered is, how far it is valuable.

Nothing need be said to shew the value of the three kinds of liberty which I have distinguished under the names of physical, moral, and religious liberty. They are, without doubt, the foundation of all the happiness and dignity of men as reasonable and moral agents and the subjects of the Deity. It is, in like manner, true of civil liberty that it is the foundation of the whole happiness and dignity of men as members of civil society and the subjects of civil government.

First, it is civil liberty, or such free government as I have described, that alone can give just security against oppression. One government is better than another in proportion as it gives more of this security. It is, on this account, that the supreme government of the Deity is perfect. There is not a possibility of being oppressed or aggrieved by it. Subjection to it is the same with complete freedom.

Were there any men on whose superior wisdom and goodness we might absolutely depend, they could not possess too much power and the love of liberty itself would engage us to fly to them and to put ourselves under their direction. But such are the principles that govern human nature, such the weakness and folly of men, such their love of domination, selfishness, and depravity, that none of them can be raised to an elevation above others without the utmost danger. The constant experience of the world has verified this and proved that nothing intoxicates the human mind so much as power, and that men, when they have got possession of it, have seldom failed to employ it in grinding their fellow-men and gratifying the vilest passions. In the establishment, therefore, of civil government it would be preposterous to rely on the discretion of any men. If a people would obtain security against oppression, they must seek it in themselves and never part with the powers of government out of their own hands. It is there only they can be safe. A people will never oppress themselves or invade their own rights. But if they trust the arbitrary will of any body or succession of men, they trust enemies and it may be depended on that the worst evils will follow.

It follows from hence that a free government is the only government which is consistent with the ends of government. Men combine into communities and institute government to obtain the peaceable enjoyment of their rights and to defend themselves against injustice and violence; and when they endeavour to secure these ends by such a free government as I have described, improved by such arrangements as may have a tendency to preserve it from confusion and to concentrate in it as much as possible of the wisdom and force of the community, in this case, it is a most rational and important institution. But when the contrary is done and the benefits of government are sought by establishing a government of men, and not of laws made with common consent, it becomes a most absurd institution. It is seeking a remedy for oppression in one quarter by establishing it in another, and avoiding the outrages of little plunderers by constituting a set of great plunderers. It is, in short, the folly of giving up liberty in order to maintain liberty, and, in the very act of endeavouring to secure the most valuable rights, to arm a body of enemies with power to destroy them.

I can easily believe that mankind in the first and rude state of society might act thus irrationally. Absolute governments, being the simplest forms of government, might be the first that were established. A people having experienced the happy effects of the wisdom or the valour of particular men, might be led to trust them with unlimited power as their rulers and legislators. But they would soon find reason to repent. And the time, I hope, may come when mankind in general, taught by long and dear experience, and weary of the abuses of power under slavish governments, will learn to detest them, and never to give up that self-government which, whether we consider men in their private or collective capacities, is the first of all the blessings they can possess.

Again, free governments are the only governments which give scope to the exertion of the powers of men and are favourable to their improvement. The members of free states, knowing their rights to be secure and that they shall enjoy without molestation the fruits of every acquisition they can make, are encouraged and incited to industry. Being at liberty to push their researches as far as they can into all subjects, and to guide themselves by their own judgments in all their religious and civil concerns, while they allow others to do the same, error and superstition must lose ground. Conscious of being their own governors, bound to obey no laws except such as they have given their consent to, and subject to no controul from the arbitrary will of any of their fellow-citizens, they possess an elevation and force of mind which must make them great and happy. How different is the situation of the vassals of despotic power? Like cattle inured to the yoke, they are driven on in one track, afraid of speaking or even thinking on the most interesting points, looking up continually to a poor creature who is their master, their powers fettered, and some of the noblest springs of action in human nature rendered useless within them. There is nothing indeed more humiliating than that debasement of mankind which takes place in such situations.

It has been observed of free governments that they are often torn by violent contests which render them dreadful scenes of distress and anarchy. But it ought to be considered that this has not been owing to the nature of such governments, but to their having been ill-modelled and wanting those arrangements and supplemental checks which are necessary to constitute a wise form of government. There is no reason to doubt but that free governments may be so contrived as to exclude the greatest part of the struggles and tumults which have arisen in free states, and, as far as they cannot be excluded, they will do more good than harm. They will occasion the display of powers and produce exertions which can never be seen in the still scenes of life. They are the active efforts of health and vigour and always tend to preserve and purify. Whereas, on the contrary, the quiet which prevails under slavish governments and which may seem to be a recommendation of them, proceeds from an ignominious tameness, and stagnation of the human faculties. It is the same with the stillness of midnight, or the silence and torpor of death.

Further, free governments are the only governments which are consistent with the natural equality of mankind. This is a principle which, in my opinion, has been assumed with the greatest reason by some of the best writers on government. But the meaning of it is not that all the subordinations in human life owe their existence to the institution of civil government. The superiorities and distinctions arising from the relation of parents to their children, from the differences in the personal qualities and abilities of men, and from servitudes founded on voluntary compacts, must have existed in a state of nature and would now take place were all men so virtuous as to leave no occasion for civil government. – The maxim, therefore, 'that all men are naturally equal' refers to their state when grown up to maturity and become independent agents, capable of acquiring property, and of directing their own conduct. And the sense of it is that no one of them is constituted by the author of nature the vassal or subject of another, or has any right to give law to him, or, without his consent, to take away any part of his property, or to abridge him of his liberty. In a state of nature one man may have received benefits from another, and this would lay the person obliged under an obligation of gratitude, but it would not make his benefactor his master, or give him a right to judge for him what grateful returns he ought to make and to extort them from him. In a state of nature, also, one man may possess more strength, or more knowledge, or more property than another, and this would give him weight and influence, but it would not give him any degree of authority. There would not be one human being who would be bound to obey him. A person, likewise in a state of nature, might let out his labour or give up to another, on certain stipulated terms, the direction of his conduct, and this would so far bring him into that station of a servant, but being done by himself, and on such terms only as he chuses to consent to, it is an instance of his liberty, and he will always have it in his power to quit the service he has chosen or to enter into another.

This equality or independence of men is one of their essential rights. It is the same with that equality or independence which now actually takes place among the different states or kingdoms of the world with respect to one another. Mankind came with this right from the hands of their maker. But all governments which are not free are totally inconsistent with it. They imply that there are some of mankind who are born with an inherent right of dominion, and that the rest are born under an obligation to subjection, and that civil government, instead of being founded on any compact, is nothing but the exercise of this right. Some such sentiments seem to be now reviving in this country and even to be growing fashionable. Most of the writers against *Observations on civil liberty* argue on the supposition of a right in the few to govern the many, independently of their own choice. Some of these writers have gone so far as to assert, in plain language, that civil governors derive their power immediately from the Deity, and are his agents or representatives, accountable to him only. And one courtly writer, in particular, has honoured them with the appellation of our political gods. Probably, this is the idea of civil governors entertained by the author [i.e. John Lind] of the *Remarks on the Acts of the Thirteenth Parliament of Great Britain*; for it is not easy to imagine on what other ground he can assert, that property and civil rights are derived from civil governors and their gifts to mankind.

If these sentiments are just, civil governors are indeed an awful order of beings, and it becomes us to enquire with anxiety who they are and how we may distinguish them from the rest of mankind. Shall we take for such all, whether men or women, whom we find in actual possession of civil power, whatever may be their characters or however they may have acquired their power? This is too extravagant to be asserted. It would legalize the American Congress. There must be some pretenders among civil governors, and it is necessary we should know how to discover them. It is incredible that the Deity should not have made this easy to us by some particular marks and distinctions which point out to our notice his real viceregents, just as he has pointed out man, by his figure and superior powers, to be the governor of the lower creatures. In particular, these persons must be possessed of wisdom and goodness superior to those of the rest of mankind for, without this, a grant of the powers they are supposed to possess would be nothing but a grant of power to injure and oppress, without remedy and without bounds. But this is a test by which they cannot be tryed. It would leave but few of them in possession of the places they hold and the rights they claim. It is not in the high ranks of life, or among the great and mighty, that we are to seek wisdom and goodness. These love the shade and fly from observation. They are to be found chiefly in the middle ranks of life and among the contemplative and philosophical who decline public employments and look down with pity on the scramble for power among mankind and the restlessness and misery of ambition. It is proper to add that it has never been hitherto understood that any superiority in intellectual and moral qualifications lays the foundation of a claim to dominion.

It is not then, by their superior endowments that the Deity intended to point out to us the few whom he has destined to command the many. But in what other manner could they be distinguished? Must we embrace Sir Robert Filmer's Patriarchal scheme? One would have thought, that Mr. Locke has said more than enough to expose this stupid scheme. One of my opponents, however, has adopted it, and the necessary inference from it is that, as there is but now one lineal descendant from Adam's eldest son, there can be but one rightful monarch of the world. But I will not abuse my reader's patience by saying more on this subject. I am sorry that in this country there should be any occasion for taking notice of principles so absurd and at the same time so pernicious. I say *pernicious* for they imply, that King James the Second was deposed at the Revolution unlawfully and impiously, that the present King is an usurper, and that the present government, being derived from rebellion and treason, has no right to our allegiance.

Without all doubt, it is the choice of the people that makes civil governors. The people are the spring of all civil power and they have a right to modify it as they please.

Mankind being naturally equal according to the foregoing explanation, civil government, in its genuine intention, is an institution for maintaining that equality by defending it against the encroachments of violence and tyranny. All the subordinations and distinctions in society previous to its establishment, it leaves as it found them, only confirming and protecting them. It makes no man master of another. It elevates no person above his fellow citizens. On the contrary, it levels all by fixing all in a state of subjection to one common authority. The authority of the laws. The will of the community. Taxes are given, not imposed. Laws are regulations of common choice, not injunctions of superior power. The authority of magistrates is the authority of the state, and their salaries are wages paid by the state for executing its will and doing its business. They do not govern the state. It is the state governs them, and had they just ideas of their own stations they would consider themselves as no less properly servants of the public than the labourers who work upon its roads or the soldiers who fight its battles. A king, in particular, is only the first executive officer, the creature of the law, and as much accountable and subject to the law as the meanest peasant. And were kings properly attentive to their duty, and as anxious as they should be about performing it, they could not easily avoid sinking under the weight of their charge.

The account now given is, I am fully persuaded, in every particular, a true account of what civil government ought to be, and it teaches us plainly the great importance and excellence of free government. It is this only that answers the description I have given of government, that secures against oppression, that gives room for that elevation of spirit and that exertion of the human powers which is necessary to human improvement, or that is consistent with the ends of government, with the rights of mankind, and their natural equality and independence. Free government, therefore, only, is just and legitimate government.

It follows farther from the preceding account that no people can lawfully surrender or cede their liberty. This must appear to anyone who will consider that when a people make such a cession and the extensive powers of government are trusted to the discretion of any man or body of men, they part with the powers of life and death and give themselves up a prey to oppression, that they make themselves the instruments of any injustice in which their rulers may chuse to employ them, by arming them against neighbouring states, and also, that they do this not only for themselves, but for their posterity. I will add that if such a cession has been made, or if through any causes a people have lost their liberty, they must have a right to emancipate themselves as soon as they can. In attempting this, indeed, they ought to consider the sufferings which may attend the struggle, and the evils which may arise from a defeat.

But at the same time it will be proper to consider that the sufferings attending such a struggle must be temporary, whereas the evils to be avoided are permanent, and that liberty is a blessing so inestimable, 'that whenever there appears any probability of covering it, a people should be willing to run many hazards, and even not to repine at the greatest expence of blood or treasure'.

I am very sensible that civil government, as it actually exists in the world, by no means answers to the account I have given of it. Instead of being an institution for guarding the weak against the strong, we find an institution which makes the strong yet stronger and gives them a systematical power of oppressing. Instead of promoting virtue and restraining vice, encouraging free enquiry, establishing liberty, and protecting alike all peaceable persons in the enjoyment of their civil and religious rights, we see a savage despotism, under its name, laying waste the earth, unreasonably elevating some and depressing others, discouraging improvement, and trampling upon every human right. That force of states which ought to be applied only to their own defence, we see continually applied to the purpose of attack and used to extend dominion by conquering neighbouring communities. Civil governors consider not themselves as servants but as masters. Their stations they think they hold in their own right. The people they reckon their property and their possessions a common stock from which they have a right to take what they will, and of which no more belongs to any individual than they are pleased to leave him.

What a miserable perversion is this of a most important institution? What a grievance is government so degenerated? But this perversion furnishes no just argument against the truth of the account I have given. Similar degeneracies have prevailed in other instances of no less importance.

Reason in man, like the will of the community in the political world, was intended to give law to his whole conduct, and to be the supreme controuling power within him. The passions are subordinate powers, or an executive force under the direction of reason, kindly given to be, as it were, wind and tide to the vessel of life in its course through this world to future honour and felicity. How different from this is the actual state of man? Those powers which were destined to govern are made to serve, and those powers which were destined to serve are allowed to govern. Passion guides human life and most men make no other use of their reason than to justify whatever their interest or their inclinations determine them to do.

Religion likewise (the perfection of reason) is, in its true nature, the inspirer of humanity and joy and the spring of all that can be great and worthy in a character, and were we to see its genuine effects among mankind, we should see nothing but peace and hope and justice and kindness, founded on that regard to God and to his will which is the noblest principle of action. But how different an aspect does religion actually wear? What is it, too generally, in the practice of mankind, but a gloomy and cruel superstition, rendering them severe and sour, teaching them to compound for wickedness by punctuality in religious forms, and prompting them to harrass, persecute and exterminate one another?

The same perversion has taken place still more remarkably in Christianity; the perfection of religion. Jesus Christ has established among Christians an absolute equality. He has declared that they have but one master, even himself, and that they are all brethren, and, therefore, has commanded them not to be called masters and, instead of assuming authority over one another, to be ready to wash one another's feet.

The princes of the Gentiles, he says, exercise lordship over them and are flattered with high titles; but he has ordained that it shall not be so amongst his followers, and that if any one of them would be chief, he must be the servant of all. The clergy in his church are, by his appointment, no more than a body of men, chosen by the different societies of Christians, to conduct their worship and to promote their spiritual improvement without any other powers than those of persuasion and instruction. It is expressly directed that they shall not make themselves Lords of God's heritage, or exercise dominion over the faith of Christians, but be *helpers of their joy*. Who can, without astonishment, compare these appointments of Christianity with the events which have happened in the Christian church? That religion which thus inculcates humility and forbids all domination, and the end of which was to produce *peace on earth, and good will among men*, has been turned into an occasion of animosities the most dreadful and of ambition the most destructive. Notwithstanding its mildness and benignity and the tendency it has to extinguish in the human breast pride and malevolence, it has been the means of arming the spirits of men with unrelenting fury against one another. Instead of peace, it has brought a sword, and its professors, instead of washing one another's feet, have endeavoured to tread on one another's necks. The ministers, in particular, of Christianity, became, soon after its establishment, an independent body of spiritual rulers, nominating one another in perpetual succession, claiming, by divine right, the highest powers and forming a hierarchy which by degrees produced a despotism more extravagant than any that ever before existed on this earth.

A considerate person must find difficulties in enquiring into the causes and reasons of that depravity of human nature which has produced these evils and rendered the best institutions liable to be so corrupted. This enquiry is much the same with the enquiry into the origin of moral evil which has in all ages puzzled human wisdom. I have at present nothing to do with it. It is enough for my purpose in these observations that the facts I have mentioned prove undeniably that the state of civil government in the world affords no reason for concluding that I have not given a just account of its true nature and origin.

I have shewn at the beginning of this section that it is free government alone that can preserve from oppression, give security to the rights of a people, and answer the ends of government. It is necessary I should here observe that I would not be understood to mean that there can be no kind or degree of security for the rights of a people under any government which cannot be denominated free. Even under an absolute monarchy or an aristocracy there may be laws and customs which, having gained sacredness by time, may restrain oppression and afford some important securities. Under government by representation there must be still greater checks on oppression provided the representation, though partial, is uncorrupt and also frequently changed. In these circumstances there may be so much of a common interest between the body of representatives and the people, and they may stand so much on one ground, that there will be no temptations to oppression. The taxes which the representative body impose they will be obliged themselves to pay, and the laws they make, they will make with the prospect of soon returning to the situation of those for whom they make them, and of being themselves governed by them.

It seems particularly worth notice here that as far as there are any such checks under any government they are the consequence of its partaking so far of liberty, and that the security attending them is more or less in proportion as a government partakes more or less of liberty. If, under an absolute government, fundamental laws and long established institutions give security in any instances, it is because they are held so sacred that a despot is afraid to violate them, or, in other words, because a people, not being completely subdued, have still some controul over the government. The like is more evidently true under mixed governments of which a house of representatives, fairly chosen and freely deliberating and resolving, forms a part, and it is one of the highest recommendations of such governments that, even when the representation is most imperfect, they have a tendency to give more security than any other governments. Under other governments it is the fear of exciting insurrections by contradicting established maxims that restrains oppression. But, as, in general, a people will bear much, and are seldom driven to resistance till grievances become intolerable, their rulers can venture far without danger, and, therefore, under such governments are very imperfectly restrained. On the contrary, if there is an honest representation, vested with powers like to those of our House of Commons, the redress of grievances, as soon as they appear, will be always easily attainable, and the rulers of a state will be under a necessity of regarding the first beginnings of discontent. Such, and greater than can be easily described, are the advantages of even an imperfect representation in a government.

How great then must be the blessing of a complete representation?[8] It is this only gives full security and that can properly denominate a people free.

It deserves to be added here, that as there can be no private character so abandoned as to want all virtue, so there can be no government so slavish as to exclude every restraint upon oppression. The most slavish and, therefore, the worst governments are those under which there is nothing to set bounds to oppression besides the discretion and humanity of those who govern. Of this kind are the following governments.

First, all governments purely despotic. These may be either monarchical or aristocratical. The latter are the worst, agreeably to a common observation, that it is better to have one master than many. The appetites of a single despot may be easily satiated, but this may be impossible where there is a multitude.

Secondly, all provincial governments. The history of mankind proves these to be the worst of all governments and that no oppression is equal to that which one people are capable of practising towards another . . . Bodies of men do not feel for one another as individuals do. The odium of a cruel action, when shared among many, is not regarded. The master of slaves working on a plantation, though he may keep them down to prevent their becoming strong enough to emancipate themselves, yet is led by interest, as well as humanity, to govern them with such moderations as to preserve their use. But these causes will produce more of this good effect when the slaves are under the eye of their proprietor and form a part of his family than when they are settled on a distant plantation where he can know little of them and is obliged to trust them to the management of rapacious servants.

It is particularly observable here that free governments, though happier in themselves, are more oppressive to their provinces than despotic governments. Or, in other words, that the subjects of free states are worse slaves than the objects of slaves not free. This is one

---

[8] He who wants to be convinced of the practicability, even in this country, of a complete representation should read a pamphlet lately published, *Take your Choice* [John Cartwright, *The Legislative Rights of the Commonalty Vindicated; or, Take your Choice!* (London, 1777)].

of the observations which Mr. Hume represents as an universal axiom in politicks.[9] 'Though', says he, 'free governments have been commonly the most happy for those who partake of their freedom, yet are they the most oppressive and ruinous to their provinces, and this observation may be fixed as an universal axiom in politics. What cruel tyrants were the Romans over the world during the time of their commonwealth? After the dissolution of the commonwealth the Roman yoke became easier upon the provinces, as Tacitus informs us, and it may be observed, that many of the worst Emperors (Domitian, for instance) were very careful to prevent all oppression of the provinces. The oppression and tyranny of the Carthaginians over their future states in Africa went so far as we learn from Polybius . . . that not content with exacting the half of all the produce of the ground, which of itself was a very high rent, they also loaded them with many other taxes. If we pass from antient to modern times we shall always find the observation to hold. The provinces of absolute monarchies are always better treated than those of free states.'

Thirdly, among the worst sorts of governments I reckon all governments by a corrupt representation. There is no instance in which the trite observation is more true than in this, 'that the best things when corrupted become the worst'. A corrupt representation is so far from being any defence against oppression that it is a support to it. Long established customs, in this case, afford no security because, under the sanction of such a representation, they may be easily undermined or counteracted, nor is there any injury to a people which, with the help of such an instrument, may not be committed with safety. It is not, however, every degree of corruption that will destroy the use of a representation and turn it into an evil so dreadful. In order to this, corruption must pass a certain limit. But every degree of it tends to this, saps the foundation of liberty and poisons the fountain of legislation. And when it gets to its last stage and has proceeded its utmost length, when, in particular, the means by which candidates get themselves chosen are such as admit the worst, but exclude the best men, a House of Representatives becomes little better than a sink into which is collected all that is most worthless and vile in a kingdom. There cannot be a greater calamity than such a government. It is impossible there should be a condition more wretched than that of a nation, once free, so degenerated.

[9] [*Essays and Treatises* (London, 1788), I, pp. 28–30.]

Conclusion

It is time to dismiss this subject. But I cannot take a final leave of it, (and probably of all subjects of this kind) without adding the following reflections on our own state in this kingdom.

It is well known, that Montesquieu has paid the highest compliment to this country by describing its constitution of government in giving an account of a perfect government, and by drawing the character of its inhabitants, in giving an account of the manners and characters of a free people. 'All (he says) having, in free states, a share in government, and the laws not being made more for some than others they consider themselves as monarchs, and are more properly confederates than fellow-subjects. No one citizen being subject to another, each sets a greater value on his liberty than on the glory of any of his fellow-citizens. Being independent, they are proud for the pride of kings is founded on their independence. They are in a constant ferment and believe themselves in danger, even in those moments when they are most safe. They reason, but it is indifferent whether they reason well or ill. It is sufficient that they do reason. Hence springs that liberty which is their security. This state, however, will lose its liberty. It will perish, when the legislative power shall become more corrupt than the executive.'[10]

Such is the account which this great writer gave, many years ago, of the British constitution and people. We may learn from it that we have nothing to fear from that disposition to examine every public measure, to censure ministers of state, and to be restless and clamorous which has hitherto characterized us. On the contrary, we shall have every thing to fear when this disposition is lost. As soon as a people grow secure and cease to be quick in taking alarms they are undone. A free constitution of government cannot be preserved without an earnest and unremitting jealousy. Our constitution, in particular, is so excellent, that it is the properest object of such jealousy. For my own part, I admire so much the general frame and principles of it that I could be almost satisfied with that representation of the kingdom which forms the most important part of it, had I no other objection to this representation than its inadequateness. Did it consist of a body of men, fairly elected for a short term, by a number of independent persons, of all orders in every part of the kingdom, equal to the

[10] *De l'esprit des lois*, Bk. xix, ch. 27.

95

number of the present voters and were it, after being elected, under no undue influence, it would be a security of such importance that I should be less disposed to complain of the injustice done by its own inadequateness, to the greatest part of the kingdom by depriving them of one of their natural and unalienable rights. To such a body of representatives we might commit, with confidence, the guardianship of our rights knowing that, having one interest with the rest of the state, they could not violate them or that if they ever did, a little time would bring the power of gaining redress without tumult or violence. Happy the people so blessed. If wise, they will endeavour, by every possible method, to preserve the purity of their representation and, should it have degenerated, they will lose no time in effecting a reformation of it. But if, unhappily, infection should have pervaded the whole mass of the state and there should be no room to hope for any reformation, it will be still some consolation to reflect, that slavery, in all its rigour, will not immediately follow. Between the time in which the securities of liberty are undermined and its final subversion there is commonly a flattering interval during which the enjoyment of liberty may be continued in consequence of fundamental laws and rooted habits which cannot be at once exterminated. And this interval is longer or shorter according as the progress of corruption is more or less rapid and men in power more or less attentive to improve favourable opportunities. The government of this country, in particular, is so well balanced, and the institutions of our common law are so admirable and have taken such deep root, that we can bear much decay before our liberties fall. Fall, however, they must, if our public affairs do not soon take a new turn. That very evil which, according to the great writer I have quoted, is to produce our ruin, we see working every where and increasing every day. The following facts, among many others, shew too plainly whither we are tending and how far we are advanced.

First, it seems to me that a general indifference is gaining ground fast among us. This is the necessary effect of increasing luxury and dissipation, but there is another cause of it which I think of with particular regret. In consequence of having been often duped by false patriots and found that the leaders of opposition, when they get into places, forget all their former declarations, the nation has been led to a conviction that all patriotism is an imposture and all opposition to the measures of government nothing but a struggle for power and its emoluments. The honest and independent part of the nation entertain at present most of this conviction and, therefore, having few public men to whom they can look with confidence, they give up all zeal, and sink into inactivity and despondence.

Secondly, at the Revolution, the House of Commons acquired its just weight in the constitution. And, for some years afterwards, it was often giving much trouble to men in power. Of late, it is well known that means have been tryed and a system adopted for quieting it. I will not say with what success. But I must say that the men whose policy this has been have struck at the very heart of public liberty and are the worst traitors this kingdom ever saw. 'If ever (says Judge Blackstone) it should happen, that the independency of any one of the three branches of our legislature should be lost, or that it should become subservient to the views of either of the other two, there would soon be an end of our constitution. The legislature would be changed from that which was originally set up by the general consent and fundamental act of the society, and such a change, however effected, is according to Mr. Locke (who perhaps carries his theory too far) at once an entire dissolution of the bonds of government, and the people are thereby reduced to a state of anarchy, with liberty to constitute themselves a new legislative power.'[11]

Thirdly, soon after the Revolution, bills for triennial parliaments passed both Houses, in opposition to the court. At the Accession, septennial parliaments were established. Since this last period many attempts have been made by the friends of the constitution to restore triennial parliaments and, formerly, it was not without difficulty that the ministry were able to defeat these attempts. The division in the House of Commons in 1735 on a bill for this purpose was 247 to 184. I need not say that now all such attempts drop of themselves. So much are the sentiments of our representatives changed in this instance that the motion for such a bill, annually made by a worthy member of the House of Commons [John Sawbridge], can scarcely produce a serious debate, or gain the least attention. For several years, at the beginning of the last reign, the House of Commons constantly passed pension and place bills which were as constantly rejected by the House of Lords. At present, no one is so romantic as ever to think of introducing any such bills into the House of Commons.

---

[11] *Commentaries*, I, p. 48.

Fourthly, standing armies have in all ages been destructive to the liberties of the states into which they have been admitted. Montesquieu observes that the preservation of liberty in England requires that it should have no land forces. Dr. Ferguson calls the establishment of standing armies 'a fatal refinement in the present state of civil government.' Mr. Hume pronounces 'our standing army a moral distemper in the British constitution, of which it must inevitably perish.' Formerly the nation was apprehensive of this danger and the standing army was a constant subject of warm debate in both Houses of Parliament. The principal reason then assigned for continuing it was the security of the House of Hanover against the friends of the Pretender. This is a reason which now exists no more, the House of Hanover being so well established as not to want any such security. The standing army also is now more numerous and formidable than ever, and yet all opposition to it is lost and it is become in a manner a part of the constitution.

Fifthly, for many years after the accession the national debt was thought an evil so alarming that the reduction of it was recommended every year from the throne to the attention of Parliament as an object of the last importance. The fund appropriated to this purpose was called the only hope of the kingdom and when the practice of alienating it begun, it was reckoned a kind of sacrilege and zealously opposed in the House of Commons and protested against in the House of Lords. But now, though the debt is almost tripled, we sit under it with perfect indifference and the sacred fund which repeated laws had ordered to be applied to no other purposes than the redemption of it, is always alienated of course and become a constant part of the current supplies and much more an encouragement to dissipation than a preservative from bankruptcy.

Sixthly, nothing is more the duty of the representatives of a nation than to keep a strict eye over the expenditure of the money granted for public services. In the reign of King William the House of Commons passed almost every year bills for appointing commissioners for taking, stating and examining the public accounts and, particularly, the army and navy debts and contracts. In the reign of Queen Ann such bills became less frequent. But since the Accession, only two motions have been made for such bills, one in 1715, and the other in 1741, and both were rejected.

Seventhly, I hope I may add that there was a time when the kingdom could not have been brought to acquiesce in what was done in the case of the Middlesex election. This is a precedent which, by giving the House of Commons the power of excluding its members at discretion and of introducing others in their room on a minority of votes, has a tendency to make it a self-created House and to destroy entirely the right of representation. And a few more such precedents would completely overthrow the constitution.

Lastly, I cannot help mentioning here the addition which has been lately made to the power of the Crown by throwing into its hands the East-India Company. Nothing more unfavourable to the security of public liberty has been done since the Revolution. And should our statesmen, thus strengthened by the patronage of the East, be farther strengthened by the conquest and patronage of the West, they will indeed have no small reason for triumph and there will be little left to protect us against the encroachments and usurpations of power. Rome sunk into slavery in consequence of enlarging its territories and becoming the center of the wealth of conquered provinces, and the seat of universal empire. It seems the appointment of Providence that free states, when, not contented with self-government and prompted by the love of dominion, they make themselves masters of other states shall lose liberty at the same time that they take it away and, by subduing, be themselves subdued. Distant and dependent provinces can be governed only by a military force. And a military force which governs abroad will soon govern at home. The Romans were so sensible of this that they made it treason for any of their generals to march their armies over the Rubicon into Italy. Caesar, therefore, when he came to this river, hesitated; but he passed it, and enslaved his country.

'Among the circumstances (says Dr. Ferguson) which in the event of national prosperity and in the result of commercial arts, lead to the establishment of despotism, there is none perhaps that arrives at this termination with so sure an aim as the perpetual enlargement of territory. In every state the freedom of its members depends on the balance and adjustment of its interior parts, and the existence of any such freedom among mankind depends on the balance of nations. In the progress of conquest those who are subdued are said to have lost their liberties. But, from the history of mankind, to conquer or to be conquered has appeared in effect the same.'[12]

Many more facts of this kind might easily be enumerated, but these

---

[12] *An essay on the history of civil society.* 6th edn. (Edinburgh, 1793), 454–455.

are sufficient. They shew with sad evidence how fast we have, for some time, been advancing towards the greatest of all public calamities.

We may also infer from the preceding observations that there is only one way in which our deliverance is possible, and that is, by restoring our grand national security. This is the object which our great men in opposition ought to hold forth to the kingdom and to bind themselves by some decisive tests to do all they can to obtain. That patriotism must be spurious which does not carry its views principally to this. Without it, nothing is of great importance to the kingdom and even an accommodation with America would only preserve a limb and save from present danger, while a gangrene was left to consume the vitals.

But probably we are gone too far and corruption has struck its roots too deep to leave us much room for hope. Mr. Hume has observed that as the affairs of this country are not likely to take a turn favourable to the establishment of a perfect plan of liberty, 'an absolute monarchy is the easiest death, the true euthanasia of the British constitution.'[13] If this observation is just our constitution (should no great calamity intervene) is likely, in some future period, to receive a very quiet dissolution. At present, however, it must be acknowledged, that we enjoy a degree of liberty, civil and religious, which has seldom been paralleled among mankind. We ought to rejoice in this happiness and to be grateful to that benevolent disposer of all events who blesses us with it. But, at the same time, our hearts must bleed when we reflect that, the supports of it having given way, it is little more than a sufferance which we owe to the temper of the times, the lenity of our governors, and some awe in which the friends of despotism are still held, by the voice and spirit of the uncorrupted part of the kingdom. May these causes, if no better securities can be hoped for, long delay our fate.

It must not be forgotten that all I have now said is meant on the supposition that our affairs will proceed smoothly till, by a common and natural progress, we have gone the round of other nations once free, and are brought to their end. But it is possible this may not happen. Our circumstances are singular and give us reason to fear that we have before us a death which will not be easy or common.

---

[13] [*Essays and treatises*], I, 53–54.

A Fast Sermon
(1781)

A Discourse
addressed to a Congregation at Hackney,
on February 21, 1781
Being the day appointed for a Public Fast.
(1781)

2 Pet. I. 11
For so an entrance shall be ministered to you
abundantly into the everlasting kingdom of our Lord and
Saviour Jesus Christ.

2 Pet. III. 13.
Nevertheless we, according to his promise,
look for new heavens and a new earth, wherein dwelleth
righteousness.

Numberless are the calamities to which we are liable in this world.
There are few of us who have not some share of trouble allotted us,
either in our persons, or families, or fortunes. But, if happily
exempted from troubles of this kind, there are troubles of a public
nature which are very shocking and which at present throw a dark
cloud over all our views and hopes. In such circumstances we are
necessarily led to look out for consolation. It would be dreadful to
suffer under present evils and to be under a necessity perhaps of
looking forward to future greater evils, without any considerations
that have a tendency to abate anxiety and mitigate pain. But this is not
our condition. There are many springs of comfort to which in the

worst circumstances we may have recourse, and which will help to reconcile us to our lot, and to give us patience and fortitude. Most of them, however, are of little moment compared with the two following; I mean, 'the consideration of the perfect government of the deity', and 'the prospect of a future better state'. These are the grand springs of consolation amidst the evils of life and wretched is the person who, either from scepticism, or inattention, or viciousness of character, loses the hope and satisfaction which they are fitted to afford. Were the course of events under no wise and good direction, or were the present scene of trial and tumult the whole we are to enjoy of existence, were the universe forlorn and fatherless, did joy and grief, defeat and success, prosperity and adversity, arise fortuitously, without any superintendency from a righteous and benevolent power; or, were we, after being witnesses to the scramble among the children of men, and making our way through this distracted world, to close our eyes for ever, and to sink to rise no more; were, I say, this our state, we might well lose all spirit and give up ourselves to bitter sorrow and despondence. But, on the contrary, if there is a perfect order established in nature, and infinite wisdom and goodness govern all things, and if also the scene will mend hereafter, and we are to sink in death only to rise to new heavens and a *new earth wherein dwelleth righteousness*, and to have *an entrance* ministered to us into an everlasting kingdom of peace and virtue; if, I say, this is our true situation we have abundant reason for comfort. The lot appointed us is glorious. We may contemplate the course of events with pleasure. We may look forward with triumph, and make ourselves easy and happy at all times.

My present design is to endeavour to engage your attention to the second of these sources of consolation, or to that future better state for which we are destined. In doing this I shall, first, just mention some of the evidences of such a state; secondly, I shall make some observations on the nature of it as a happy community or kingdom, contrasting at the same time the peace and order which we have reason to expect in it with the disorders and troubles which take place among the kingdoms and under the corrupted governments of this world. After which my intention is to make an improvement of the whole for our relief in the present circumstances of this kingdom.

The evidence for a future state is such as leaves no doubt in my mind. However threatening the stroke of death appears, and whatever interruption it may possibly produce in the exercise of our powers, there is no reason for thinking that it will destroy us. The soul is a simple and, therefore, does not admit of that separation of parts which produces corruption and dissolution. The body is a machine by which the soul perceives and acts, and the destruction of the one no more infers the destruction of the other than the destruction of a weapon infers the destruction of the hand that uses it, or the destruction of a telescope the destruction of the eye that looks through it. If, therefore, death annihilates us, it cannot be by destroying our bodies but by a positive exertion of the power of the Creator to put us then out of being. And such an exertion being improbable, the just conclusion is that we shall go on to exist and, at some period subsequent to death, recover our active powers and become again embodied spirits. Our capacity of existing forever is alone a reason for believing that we are intended for such an existence, and this capacity we possess in a manner which cannot be considered without astonishment. For such are our powers that we are capable not only of existing, but of improving for ever. Is it credible that such beings were designed for nothing but this short life? Are they led to carry their views to an immortality which they cannot enjoy, and to entertain hopes which cannot be gratified? After being shewn *a house not made with hands eternal in the heavens*, and being put in the way to it, are they to be cut off at the threshold? Can it be imagined that the Deity should thus mock his reasonable offspring, or that such inconsistencies should be established in the constitution of nature?

But this is by no means the best evidence we have on this subject. The character of the Deity as the moral governor of the world affords another argument for a future state of irresistible force. There is, evidently in this life, a scheme of moral government begun, but if there is no other life it is left imperfect and unfinished. Virtue, though in general our present interest, is not followed with an adequate reward, nor is vice followed with an adequate punishment. That righteousness of practice which is our nearest resemblance to the Deity, is sometimes the object of oppression and insult, and that wickedness which turns men into demons and would, were it to prevail, turn the world into a chaos, is sometimes successful and prosperous. The man who devotes his life to save his country loses, by that very action, all possibility of any present reward; and, on the contrary, the man who acquires power and wealth by spoiling or betraying his country, secures himself against any present punishment by the enormity of his villainy. It is impossible that irregularities so inconsistent with our ideas of distributive justice should be suffered to pass without redress under the divine government. Since the present world is not the seat of adequate retribution, it must be reserved for another, and a future state appears to be as certain as the existence of a wise and righteous Deity. We may be assured that no one shall finally be a loser by his virtue, or a gainer by his wickedness. He who now sacrifices his life in any good cause shall find it again, and he who saves his life by falshood and treachery or any wrong means, shall lose a better life. This is our Saviour's meaning, when he says ... that *whosoever will save his life shall lose it, and that whosoever will lose his life shall find it.*

But this leads me to observe farther on this head that the doctrine of a future state is confirmed by the promise of God in the christian revelation. We expect, my text says, according to his promise, *new heavens and a new earth wherein dwelleth righteousness. This is the promise,* St John says, *which he hath promised, even eternal life, and this life is in his Son.* The gospel has abolished death, and brought life and immortality to the clearest light. It not only acquaints us that there will be a resurrection from death through the power of Christ, but sets before us a particular demonstration of it from fact. Christ rose himself from the dead and thus has shewn to our senses the path of life, and become the *first-fruits of all that sleep.* One of the ends of his appearance among mankind was to ascertain to us a future state and, by discovering to us our own dignity as heirs of a glorious immortality, to engage us to raise our views above this world.

But it is time to hasten to the account which I have proposed to give you of the nature of the future state of reward as a kingdom or community into which we are to be hereafter admitted. This is the view which the Scriptures give us of it. Thus, in Rev. xxii. 24, it is said that those are blessed who keep the commandments of God, because *they shall enter through the gates into the city,* and in Mark x. 24, that it is hard for those who *trust in riches to enter into the kingdom of God,* and in Matth. vii. 21. that not every one who says to Christ, *Lord, Lord, shall enter into the kingdom of heaven, but he that doeth the will of God,* and, in the passages which I have chosen for my text, that we *look for new heavens and a new earth wherein dwelleth righteousness,* and that an *entrance is to be ministered to us abundantly into the everlasting kingdom of our Lord and Saviour.* These are representations which plainly lead us to consider the future heavenly state as a happy society or community, and reason concurs with revelation in leading us to this view of it.

We find ourselves so made that we necessarily seek society and cannot exist happily out of it. There is reason to think this must be the case with all intelligent creatures, for it is not to be conceived that any of them can want social affections or be entirely indifferent to all social connections and intercourse. An existence absolutely solitary must, one would think, be dreary and melancholy. But whatever in this respect may be true of intelligent creatures in general, we know that what I am observing is true of ourselves. The principles of our natures lead us to unite and to form ourselves into societies. In consequence of this we gain many pleasures and advantages which we could not otherwise enjoy. Some of our noblest affections, which would otherwise lie dormant, are drawn forth into exercise and the strength of a whole community is employed in the defence and protection of every particular member of it.

The forms of association among mankind have been very different in different ages and countries, and it has been at all times one of the chief employments of human wisdom to contrive such forms of association as should be most likely to produce security, peace and comfort. At first these forms were simple and rude. As mankind encreased they became more complicated, and legislation and government were gradually enlarged and improved. But with improvement entered also corruption and debasement. Powerful kingdoms and empires arose which established themselves by usurpation and conquest, and which were no better than detestable conspiracies against the happiness of the world. The regulations necessary to the support of civil society laid the foundation of oppression. Government degenerated into tyranny, and subjection to legal authority into slavery. The best institutions for the purpose of government are extremely imperfect, and attended with many dangers. But some have grown up in the world which are so absurd and so incompatible with the rights of mankind as to be intolerable nuisances. How abject and wretched is a kingdom under despotism? What a disgrace is it to human nature that the lives and property of millions should be subject (as they are in most nations) to the disposal of one man, meaner perhaps than the meanest of the people he governs, whose will is their law and from whom they are to descend like a herd of cattle, by hereditary right, to the next plunderer, libertine or madman that may happen to come in succession. When I think of such governments, I am almost ashamed that I am a man. But when I think of the mischiefs they occasion, I feel more painful emotions. A free government, as distinguished from a despotic government, is the dominion of men over themselves in opposition to the dominion of men over other men, or a government by laws made with common consent, in opposition to a government by will; but the power of executing laws must be lodged in the hands of men deputed for that purpose, and this is a power which seldom fails to be dreadfully perverted. All civil governors are trustees for the people governed, and when they abuse their trust they forfeit their authority. But instead of attending to this, they generally forget both the source and the end of their authority, and look upon the people whose servants they are, as their property, which they may dispose of as they please.

Such are the evils to which human society is at present subject, and I have given you this account of them as a preparation for engaging your attention to that better state of things which will take place in the future everlasting kingdom of Jesus Christ. In this world there is no such thing as a kingdom free from tumult, or a government of perfect virtue, but we expect one to come. The heavens we now see are often overcast with frightful clouds and convulsed with storms, and the earth we now inhabit is almost every where the seat of violence, rapine and injustice. But we look for heavens which will enjoy a constant sunshine, and for an earth wherein righteousness and peace will take up their abode for ever.

This is a reviving prospect. Let us dwell upon it and consider,

First, that the heavens and the earth we expect are to be, as St. Peter speaks, new heavens and a new earth, that is, totally different in their nature and constitution from our present heavens and earth which, according to the same Apostle, are reserved for the fire of the last day. This world in its present state is by no means fitted to be the seat of complete happiness or of a perfect government, and, therefore, we have been described as having in view a better, that is, an heavenly country. Our citizenship, St. Paul says, is in heaven from whence we look for the Saviour the Lord Jesus Christ, who is hereafter to appear in glory to judge the world, and to put down all rule, authority and power, in order to establish in their room that kingdom of his Father for which this world is a preparation.

Secondly, from this kingdom there will be an exclusion of all the workers of iniquity. We are assured that, previously to the establishment of it, there will be a general discrimination of mankind according to their works. The wicked will be severed from the just and placed by themselves to suffer the punishment of their crimes. As *tares are gathered and burnt in the fire, so shall it be at the end of this world. The son of man will gather out of his kingdom all things that offend, and them who do iniquity, and shall cast them into a furnace of fire to be destroyed. Then shall the righteous shine forth as the sun in the kingdom of their father.* To the same purpose we are told in Rev. xxi. 8, that into the *heavenly city shall be brought the glory and honour of the nations, and that there shall in no wise enter into it any thing that defileth, or that loveth and maketh a lye.* But that *all the vicious and deceitful shall be cast into that lake of fire and brimstone, which is the second death.* This extermination of the wicked is a circumstance of the last importance. Were they to be admitted into the future kingdom of Christ, it could not be a quiet and happy kingdom.

Further, it requires your particular notice that this kingdom is called the *kingdom of our Lord and Saviour Jesus Christ.* The foundation of it was laid by him. The great end of his descent from heaven was to provide subjects for it and to obtain the power of raising mankind to life, in order to put the virtuous part of them into the possession of it. He has now a kingdom in the world over which he exercises an invisible government. The seat of it will hereafter be transferred to another world, where it will be established in its full glory. Christ will, we are told, hereafter gather his elect (that is, all the faithful and worthy) from the four corners of the earth. He will publicly declare his approbation of their charity and piety and take them with him, as his brethren and joint-heirs, to inherit the kingdom that had been prepared for them from the foundations of the world. There they shall live with him and be advanced to a participation of the honour and dignity to which he has risen.

The Scriptures promise a more happy state of Christ's kingdom even in this world. They foretell a period when his church shall be cleared from the corruptions which have been introduced into it, when a general amendment shall take place in human affairs, the nations learn war no more, and the kingdoms of the earth become *the kingdoms of the Lord and of his Christ.* But this happy state of Christ's kingdom will be succeeded by a state of it infinitely more happy in the heavens. There the nations of those that are saved will enjoy perfect felicity and nothing remain of the evil we now see.

It follows from these particulars that this kingdom will be a kingdom of perfect order and tranquility. No malignant passions will there produce confusion. Religious bigotry will not persecute. The lust of power will not oppress. Envy will not defame or pride and malice torment, but the joy of every individual will be augmented by the joy of all around him. *The wicked will there cease from troubling, and the weary be at rest.*

But there is one farther circumstance relating to this kingdom which is of the greatest consequence. It will be an everlasting kingdom of our Lord and Saviour Jesus Christ. In the Epistle to the Hebrews, ch. xii. and 28th verse, it is called *a kingdom that cannot be moved,* and in the xith chap. *a city which hath foundations, whose builder and maker is God.* This is the circumstance that crowns the future happiness. It will never come to an end. All earthly governments have in them the seeds of decay and dissolution. The mightiest empires have fallen and the best formed societies, after enjoying liberty and prosperity for a time, have been ruined either by foreign violence, or the more slow operations of internal corruption; nor is any thing more melancholy than the reflection on the revolutions of this kind which have taken place among mankind. But that future government in the heavens, under which the virtuous are to be happy, will be subject to no calamitous revolutions. It will preserve for ever its order and dignity without the possibility of being disturbed by any tumults, or shaken by any convulsions. In short, I can scarcely better describe to you this state than in the figurative language of St. John, in the xxist and xxiid chapters of the Revelations. *I saw new heavens and a new earth, and the holy city, the new Jerusalem, descending from God. And I heard a loud voice saying, Behold the tabernacle of God is with men, and he will dwell with them, and wipe away all tears from their eyes. They shall hunger no more, neither thirst any more, neither shall the sun smite on them any more. In the midst of the streets of the city shall be the tree of life, and they shall reign with Christ for ever and ever.* What a happiness will this be! To get out of this polluted world and, after seeing the wickedness that abounds in it and passing through its trials, to become members of a quiet and joyful community, to join superior beings and all the worthy of the earth, to see and know the eternal Deity, and to dwell with him to complain and suffer no more, and to die no more.

But it is time to proceed to the main point I have had all along in view, or the use we ought to make of this subject for our comfort under the evils which prevail among the kingdoms of this world. Let me press you to make this use of what I have been saying. Withdraw your minds from temporal objects and amidst the devastations, the slaughters and cruelties around you, look forward to a better state. I pity from my heart those whose principles will not allow them to do this, who, believing they are made only to struggle and fret for a short time on this earth, can look no higher. Men who think thus meanly of themselves must be proportionably mean in their dispositions and pursuits. They must think meanly of the divine administration. They must want the strongest motives to noble exertions, and can have nothing to preserve them from despondence when they reflect on the present state of civil society and government. No reflection can be more painful to a reasonable person. The occasion for civil government is derived from the wickedness of mankind, and the end of it is to provide securities for our person, property and liberty. But it is a very insufficient security and often proves the cause of intolerable distresses, by arming the ambitious with power and enabling them to trample on their fellow-creatures. General experience has proved this and the history of the world is but little more than a recital of the oppressions and rapines of men entrusted with the powers of government, and the calamities occasioned by the endeavours of mankind to defend themselves against them. This is particularly exemplified in the history of our own country, the annals of which are full of accounts of hard struggles between liberty and tyranny.

Free governments are the only equitable governments, but how few of them are there in the world and what seats of contention do we often find them? This contention is even necessary to their existence, for all governments tend to despotism and will end in it if no opposition checks them. Nothing corrupts more than power. Nothing is more encroaching and, therefore, nothing requires more to be watched and restrained. The safety of a free people depends entirely on their maintaining a constant and suspicious vigilance, and as soon as they cease to be quick at taking alarms, they are undone. But the vigilance and jealousy necessary to the security of free governments have been the occasion of dreadful convulsions. They are apt to degenerate into faction and licentiousness, and an impatience of all controul; and very often exertions apparently the most ardent in favour of public liberty, have proved to be nothing but the turbulence of ambitious men and a vile struggle for places and the emoluments of power.

I make these observations to render you more sensible of the imperfection of all earthly governments. If they are free they are subject to intestine broils which keep them in a constant ferment and sometimes end in insurrections and civil wars. If they are slavish they may be indeed more quiet, but that quiet is founded on a depression of the human mind, which is the greatest of all calamities.

How then can it be possible to consider them without pain? What a theatre of confusion and tumult is this world? On one hand the lust of power invading the rights of mankind. On the other fierce defiance and resistance. In one country a haughty despot ordering a general carnage to gratify his avarice or pride. In another a wicked incendiary fomenting discord and disgracing patriotism. Here, a body of crouching slaves looking up to a king as a god, and bowing down that he may go over them. There a nation of freemen enraged by oppression, flying to arms and in the conflict giving their oppressors blood to drink. Here, a Caesar, at the head of his legions, returning from the slaughter of millions, crossing the Rubicon and overturning the liberties of his country. There, a Brutus, at the head of a band of conspirators, striking a poniard into his breast. Such are the spectacles which this world presents to us. These are spectacles which are indeed enough to make us sick of human affairs. Turn your eyes from them to brighter scenes, from the din of arms and the triumphs of tyranny, from the shouts of warriors, and the cries of plundered citizens, from the insolence of power, the hypocrisy of courts, and the pride of princes; transfer your views to the tranquility and order of Christ's everlasting kingdom. Let the confusion and disasters to which you are now witnesses engage you to secure a place there. Remember that you have before you *Mount Zion and the city of the living God,* and that you are soon to be united *to the general assembly and church of the first-born whose names are written in heaven, to the spirits of just men made perfect, to an innumerable company of angels, to Jesus the mediator of the new covenant, and God the judge of all.* Oh, happy state! Here shelter yourselves from the storms of this world. Make this your retreat when assaulted by adversity or vexed by oppression. Blessed be the God and Father of our Lord Jesus Christ for such a hope. It is enough to warm and elevate our minds, and to prevent us from sinking under any public or private calamities.

But lastly, let us on this subject take care not to forget that the happiness I have described will be the happiness only of virtuous men. All I have said has supposed this and my text plainly expresses it. For so (that is, by adding to faith, fortitude, prudence, temperance, patience, godliness, brotherly kindness and charity) *an entrance shall be ministered to you abundantly into the everlasting kingdom of our Lord and Saviour Jesus Christ, for if ye do these things ye shall never fall.* The wicked are nuisances and pests and there can be no happiness where they are. *Know ye not,* says St. Paul, *that the unrighteous cannot inherit the kingdom of God. Be not deceived. Neither fornicators, nor adulterers, nor thieves, nor covetous, nor drunkards, nor revilers, nor extortioners, shall inherit the kingdom of God.* Christ, by taking upon him our natures, acquired power to raise us from death and to gather together all the virtuous into a state of future existence where, with him at their head, they are to be formed into one joyful society, and to be exalted to the highest honours under a government of peace and righteousness which shall never be destroyed. This is the doctrine which the Scriptures teach us, but the same Scriptures teach us, with respect to the vicious part of mankind, that after being raised up from death they are to be consigned to a state of punishment, where they will suffer a *second death,* from which there will be no redemption.

What remains then but that we now resolve to avoid every evil way and devote all that is to come of our lives to the practice of righteousness. This must be your resolution if you wish to get to the kingdom of heaven. And let me, on the present occasion, desire you particularly to consider that in the practice of righteousness is included the faithful discharge of all your duties as members of civil society. The conversation of a christian is not so in heaven as to render him indifferent to what passes on earth. He that expects to be a citizen of the heavenly Jerusalem ought to be the best citizen of this world. He who hopes for a place under a government of eternal peace and virtue will make the best subject to any earthly government under which his lot is cast. He will be the warmest friend to liberty and the most ready to spend his substance, or to pour out his blood in defence of the rights of his country. Act, fellow-christians under the influence of these sentiments and, while others think of nothing but making their way in the world, do you strive to make your way through the world, exhibiting always in your tempers and conduct, a zeal for virtue, and a conscious dignity becoming those who expect honour and glory, greater than this world can bestow, *in the everlasting kingdom of Jesus Christ.*

We have at present in this country particular reason for making these resolutions, and for recurring to that source of consolation which I have been pointing out to you. The aspect of public affairs continues darker than I can describe. We see this nation (lately the first upon earth) reduced to a state of deep humiliation. Our glory departed – fallen from our high station among the powers of the world – devastation and bloodshed extending themselves round us – without colonies – without allies – some of the best branches of our trade lost – a monstrous burden weighing us down – and at war with America, with France, with Spain, with Holland, and in danger of being soon at war with all Europe. In these tremendous circumstances what can we do? Shall we exclaim against our governors? That would be unavailing and vain. It is not possible they should have meant to ruin the kingdom. Shall we accuse Providence? That would be ungrateful and impious. We are too corrupt to deserve the favour of Providence. Let us then accuse ourselves. Had we been a more virtuous people, or as really a nation of christians as we are so nominally, we could not have been brought into this situation. It is fit that having become more irreligious than perhaps any civilized people that ever existed, and lost that vigilant, jealous, and enlightened spirit of liberty which once characterized us, it is fit, I say, that having thus degenerated we should be degraded. Let us then acknowledge the justice of Heaven in our correction and prepare to meet those sharper corrections which this kingdom may have still before it, remembering for our encouragement that better state on which I have been discoursing, and at the same time making it our constant business to fit ourselves for it, by discharging every duty of life and godliness and, particularly, by acting the part of faithful members of the community to which we belong. If we see our country threatened with calamity, let us warn it. If we see our countrymen proud and insensible to the rights of mankind, let us admonish them. If the demon of corruption is poisoning the springs of legislation and converting the securities of public liberty into instruments of slavery, let us point out to them the shocking mischief, and endeavour to recover them to a sense of their danger. It is true we may be able to do but little in this way. But in this case every little is of unspeakable consequence, and if no one would neglect the little in his power much might be done.

Will you on this occasion bear with me if I say that it has been my study to form my own conduct agreeably to this exhortation. My life has been hitherto spent in such endeavours as I am capable of to promote all the best interests of my country and of mankind. I can, in particular, reflect with pleasure on the part I have taken in that dispute with the colonies which has for some years made us the derision of Europe and to which we owe all our present difficulties. Convinced that our claim of a right to dispose of their property and to alter their governments without their consent, was an unjust claim, and, in general, that provincial governments are the most rapacious and oppressive of all governments, and that the subjection of countries to one another has always been and must always be the worst sort of slavery. Convinced, I say, of this and believing also that a war with our colonies, supposing it just, was in the highest degree impolitic, I could not avoid publishing my sentiments in a pamphlet to which few of you can be strangers. This pamphlet was published five years ago at the commencement of our present troubles. I endeavoured to explain in it the nature of civil liberty and legitimate government, and to set forth particularly the danger to which the war with America would expose us. I argued in it freely against the war. But I only argued. I did not enter into personal invectives or speak disrespectfully of any particular men, and a kingdom ceases to be free as soon as the members of it cease to enjoy the liberty of canvassing in this manner public measures.

It was not possible that I should have any indirect view in this publication. I was led to it by no kind of advice or sollicitation. It was extorted from me entirely by my judgment and feelings in opposition to my inclinations. So true is this and so conscious am I of having acted, in this instance, from pure motives that it has ever since laid the foundation of a comfort in my own mind which has made me perfectly insensible to all censures. Nor would I now for any emoluments part with the satisfaction I feel when I recollect my attempts, by that publication and the publications that followed it, to serve my country, and to propagate just notions of government and a zeal for that liberty on which the happiness of man essentially depends and without which he is a creature scarcely superior to a beast. I was far from having reason to expect that any thing I could write would influence the managers of our affairs. I must say, however, that had they been influenced by it this kingdom, instead of being on the brink of ruin, would now have been enjoying its former prosperity.

I cannot help reminding you here that I insisted strongly, in the publications I have mentioned, on a peculiarity in the state of this kingdom which made any war, but more especially such a war as that with America, dreadfully hazardous, and that I represented particularly the danger there was that the colonies would be driven to form an alliance with France, that this jealous rival would seize the opportunity to ruin us, that a general war would be kindled, and that a catastrophe might follow in this country never before known among nations. These representations when written were apprehensions only. A great part of them may be now read as history. When I say this I do not mean to boast of any sagacity. It was easy to foresee these consequences and there are many distinguished and excellent persons, in every respect my superiors, who entertained the same apprehensions and who have given the same warnings. But though I am only one and one of the least of many who have stood forth on this occasion, yet it has happened that no one has fallen under a greater load of abuse. You will be sensible how improper an object of abuse I have been if you will consider,

First, that detesting all abuse in political as well as religious discussions I have myself always avoided it.

Secondly, that I have done no more than what it is in a particular manner the duty of a Minister of the Gospel of peace to do; I mean, endeavoured to prevent the carnage of war and to promote peace and righteousness.

Thirdly, what most of all justifies me is that events have proved that I was right in my opinion of the pernicious tendency of the measures against which I wrote.

Upon the whole, I must repeat to you that there is nothing in the course of my life that I can think of with more satisfaction than the testimony I have borne and the attempts I have made to serve the cause of general liberty and justice, and the particular interest of this country at the present period. A period big with events of unspeakable consequences and perhaps one of the most momentous in the annals of mankind.

But I have detained you too long and talked too much of myself. You are my friends and know me, I hope, too well to question the uprightness of my views. May you be blest with every comfort this world can give and with eternal happiness in that country beyond the grave which is now the hope and will soon be the refuge of the virtuous. In that country alone I wish for honour and there God of his infinite mercy grant that we may all at last meet!

Observations on the Importance of the American Revolution (1785)

Observations
on the
Importance
of the
American Revolution
and
The Means of making it a Benefit to
the World
(1785)

Advertisement

Having reason to hope I should be attended to in the American States and thinking I saw an opening there favourable to the improvement and best interests of mankind, I have been induced to convey thither the sentiments and advice contained in the following Observations. They were, therefore, originally intended only for America. The danger of a spurious edition has now obliged me to publish them in my own country.

I should be inexcusable did I not take this opportunity to express my gratitude to a distinguished writer (the Count de Mirabeau) for his translation of these Observations into French, and for the support and kind civility with which it has been accompanied . . .

I think it necessary to add that I have expressed myself in some respects too strongly in the conclusion of the following Observations.

By accounts from persons the best informed, I have lately been assured that no such dissentions exist among the American States as have been given out in this country, that the new governments are in general well settled, and the people happy under them, and that, in particular, a conviction is becoming universal of the necessity of giving more strength to that power which forms and which is to conduct and maintain their union.
March, 1785.

Of the Importance of the Revolution which has Established the Independence of the United States

Having, from pure conviction, taken a warm part in favour of the British colonies (now the United States of America) during the late war and been exposed, in consequence of this, to much abuse and some danger, it must be supposed that I have been waiting for the issue with anxiety. I am thankful that my anxiety is removed and that I have been spared to be a witness to that very issue of the war which has been all along the object of my wishes. With heartfelt satisfaction I see the revolution in favour of universal liberty which has taken place in America, a revolution which opens a new prospect in human affairs and begins a new aera in the history of mankind, a revolution by which Britons themselves will be the greatest gainers, if wise enough to improve properly the check that has been given to the despotism of their ministers, and to catch the flame of virtuous liberty which has saved their American brethren.

The late war, in its commencement and progress, did great good by disseminating just sentiments of the rights of mankind and the nature of legitimate government, by exciting a spirit of resistance to tyranny which has emancipated one European country and is likely to emancipate others, and by occasioning the establishment in America of forms of government more equitable and more liberal than any that the world has yet known. But, in its termination, the war has done still greater good by preserving the new governments from that destruction in which they must have been involved, had Britain conquered, by providing, in a sequestrated continent possessed of many singular advantages, a place of refuge for opprest men in every region of the world, and by laying the foundation there of an empire which may be the seat of liberty, science and virtue, and from whence there is reason to hope these sacred blessings will spread till they become universal and the time arrives when kings and priests shall have no more power to oppress, and that ignominious slavery which has hitherto debased the world exterminated. I therefore think I see the hand of Providence in the late war working for the general good.

Reason, as well as tradition and revelation, lead us to expect that a more improved and happy state of human affairs will take place before the consummation of all things. The world has hitherto been gradually improving. Light and knowledge have been gaining ground, and human life at present, compared with what it once was, is much the same that a youth approaching to manhood is compared with an infant.

Such are the natures of things that this progress must continue. During particular intervals it may be interrupted, but it cannot be destroy'd. Every present advance prepares the way for farther advances, and a single experiment or discovery may sometimes give rise to so many more as suddenly to raise the species higher and to resemble the effects of opening a new sense or of the fall of a spark on a train that springs a mine. For this reason mankind may at last arrive at degrees of improvement which we cannot now even suspect to be possible. A dark age may follow an enlightened age but, in this case, the light, after being smothered for a time, will break out again with a brighter lustre. The present age of increased light, considered as succeeding the ages of Greece and Rome and an intermediate period of thick darkness, furnishes a proof of the truth of this observation. There are certain kinds of improvement which, when once made, cannot be entirely lost. During the dark ages the improvements made in the ages that preceded them remained so far as to be recovered immediately at the resurrection of letters, and to produce afterwards that more rapid progress in improvement which has distinguished modern times.

There can scarcely be a more pleasing and encouraging object of reflection than this. An accidental observation of the effects of gravity in a garden has been the means of discovering the laws that govern the solar system, and of enabling us to look down with pity on the ignorance of the most enlightened times among the antients. What new dignity has been given to man, and what additions have been made to his powers, by the invention of optical glasses, printing, gunpowder, etc., and by the late discoveries in navigation, mathematics, natural philosophy, etc.!

But among the events in modern times tending to the elevation of mankind, there are none probably of so much consequence as the recent one which occasions these observations. Perhaps I do not go too far when I say that, next to the introduction of Christianity among mankind, the American revolution may prove the most important step in the progressive course of improvement. It is an event which may produce a general diffusion of the principles of humanity, and become the means of setting free mankind from the shackles of superstition and tyranny, by leading them to see and know 'that nothing is fundamental but impartial enquiry, an honest mind, and virtuous practice, that state policy ought not to be applied to the support of speculative opinions and formularies of faith'. 'That the members of a civil community are *confederates* not *subjects*, and their rulers, *servants* not *masters*. And that all legitimate government consists in the dominion of equal laws made with common consent, that is, in the dominion of men over *themselves*, and not in the dominion of communities over communities, or of any men over other men.'[14]

Happy will the world be when these truths shall be every where acknowledged and practised upon. Religious bigotry, that cruel demon, will be then laid asleep. Slavish governments and slavish hierarchies will then sink and the old prophecies be verified, 'that the last universal empire upon earth shall be the empire of reason and virtue, under which the gospel of peace (better understood) *shall have free course and be glorified, many will run to and fro and knowledge be increased, the wolf dwell with the lamb and the leopard with the kid, and nation no more lift up a sword against nation.*'

It is a conviction I cannot resist that the independence of the English colonies in America is one of the steps ordained by Providence to introduce these times and I can scarcely be deceived in this conviction if the United States should escape some dangers which threaten them and will take proper care to throw themselves open to future improvements and to make the most of the advantages of their present situation. Should this happen, it will be true of them as it was of the people of the Jews, that *in them all the families of the earth shall be*

---

[14] These are the words of Montesquieu.

blessed. It is scarcely possible they should think too highly of their own consequence. Perhaps there never existed a people on whose wisdom and virtue more depended or to whom a station of more importance in the plan of Providence has been assigned. They have begun nobly. They have fought with success for themselves and the world, and, in the midst of invasion and carnage, established forms of government favourable in the highest degree to the rights of mankind. But they have much more to do, more indeed than it is possible properly to represent. In this address my design is only to take notice of a few great points which seem particularly to require their attention in order to render them permanently happy in themselves and useful to mankind. On these points I shall deliver my sentiments with freedom, conscious I mean well, but, at the same time, with real diffidence, conscious of my own liableness to error.

Of the Means of Promoting Human Improvement and Happiness in the United States. And first, of Public Debts

It seems evident that what first requires the attention of the United States is the redemption of their debts and making compensation to that army which has carried them through the war. They have an infant credit to cherish and rear which, if this is not done, must perish, and with it their character and honour for ever. Nor is it conceivable they should meet with any great difficulty in doing this. They have a vast resource peculiar to themselves in a continent of unlocated lands possessing every advantage of soil and climate. The settlement of these lands will be rapid, the consequence of which must be a rapid increase of their value. By disposing of them to the army and to emigrants, the greatest part of the debts of the United States may probably be sunk immediately. But had they no such resource, they are very capable of bearing taxes sufficient for the purpose of a gradual redemption. Supposing their debts to amount to nine millions sterling carrying interest at $5\frac{1}{2}$ per cent, taxes producing a revenue of a million per ann. would pay the interest and at the same time leave a surplus of half a million per ann. for a sinking fund which would discharge the principal in thirteen years. A surplus of a quarter of a million would do the same in 20½ years. After discharging the principal, the appropriated revenue being no longer wanted, might be abolished and the states eased of the burthen of it. But it would be imprudent to abolish it entirely. £100,000 per ann. reserved and faithfully laid out in clearing unlocated lands and other improvements, would in a short time increase to a treasure (or continental patrimony) which would defray the whole expenditure of the union, and keep the states free from debts and taxes for ever.

Such a reserve would (supposing it improved so as to produce a profit of 5 per cent.) increase to a capital of three millions in 19 years, 30 millions in 57 years and 261 millions in 100 years. But supposing it capable of being improved so as to produce a profit of 10 per cent. it would increase to five millions in 19 years, 100 millions in 49 years, and 10,000 millions in 97 years.

It is wonderful that no state has yet thought of taking this method to make itself great and rich. The smallest appropriation in a sinking fund, never diverted, operates in cancelling debts, just as money increases at compound interest and is, therefore, omnipotent. But, if diverted, it loses all its power. Britain affords a striking proof of this. Its sinking fund (once the hope of the kingdom) has, by the practice of alienating it, been rendered impotent and useless. Had it been inviolably applied to the purpose for which it was intended, there would, in the year 1775, have been a surplus in the revenue of more than five millions per ann. But instead of this, we were then encumbered with a debt of 137 millions, carrying an interest of near 4½ millions, and leaving no surplus of any consequence. This debt has been since increased to 280 millions, carrying an interest (including expences of management) of nine millions and a half. A monstrous bubble, and if no very strong measures are soon taken to reduce it within the limits of safety, it must produce a dreadful convulsion. Let the United States take warning. Their debts at present are moderate. A sinking fund, guarded against misapplication, may soon extinguish them and prove a resource in all events of the greatest importance.

I must not, however, forget that there is one of their debts on which no sinking fund can have any effect and which it is impossible for them to discharge, A debt, greater, perhaps, than has been ever due from any country and which will be deeply felt by their latest posterity. But it is a debt of gratitude only – of gratitude to that General, who has been raised up by Providence to make them free and independent, and whose name must shine among the first in the future annals of the benefactors of mankind.

The measures now proposed may preserve America for ever from too great an accumulation of debts and, consequently of taxes – – an evil which is likely to be the ruin not only of Britain, but of other European states. But there are measures of yet greater consequence which I wish ardently to recommend and inculcate.

For the sake of mankind I wish to see every measure adopted that can have a tendency to preserve peace in America and to make it an open and fair stage for discussion and the seat of perfect liberty.

Of peace.
And the Means of Perpetuating it

Civil government is an expedient for collecting the wisdom and force of a community or confederacy in order to preserve its peace and liberty against every hostile invasion, whether from within or from without. In the latter of these respects the United States are happily secured, but they are far from being equally happy in the former respect. Having now, in consequence of their successful resistance of the invasion of Britain, united in their remoteness from Europe, no external enemy to fear, they are in danger of fighting with one another. This is their greatest danger and providing securities against it is their hardest work. Should they fail in this, America may some time or other be turned into a scene of blood and, instead of being the hope and refuge of the world, may become a terror to it.

When a dispute arises among individuals in a state, an appeal is made to a court of law, that is, to the wisdom and justice of the state. The court decides. The losing party acquiesces or, if he does not, the power of the state forces him to submission, and thus the effects of contention are suppress and peace is maintained. In a way similar to this, peace may be maintained between any number of confederate states and I can almost imagine that it is not impossible but that by such means universal peace may be produced and all war excluded from the world. Why may we not hope to see this begun in America? The articles of confederation make considerable advances towards it. When a dispute arises between any of the states they order an appeal to Congress, an enquiry by Congress, a hearing, and a decision. But here they stop. What is most of all necessary is omitted. No provision is made for enforcing the decisions of Congress, and this renders them inefficient and futile. I am by no means qualified to point out the best method of removing this defect. Much must be given up for this purpose, nor is it easy to give up too much. Without all doubt the powers of Congress must be enlarged. In particular, a power must be given it to collect, on certain emergencies, the force of the confederacy and to employ it in carrying its decisions into execution. A state against which a decision is made will yield of course when it knows that such a force exists and that it allows no hope from resistance.

By this force I do not mean a standing army. God forbid that standing armies should ever find an establishment in America. They are every where the grand supports of arbitrary power and the chief causes of the depression of mankind. No wise people will trust their defence out of their own hands, or consent to hold their rights at the mercy of armed slaves. Free states ought to be bodies of armed citizens, well regulated and well disciplined, and always ready to turn out, when properly called upon, to execute the laws, to quell riots, and to keep the peace. Such, if I am rightly informed, are the citizens of America. Why then may not Congress be furnished with a power of calling out from the confederated states quotas of militias sufficient to force at once the compliance of any state which may shew an inclination to break the union by resisting its decisions?

I am very sensible that it will be difficult to guard such a power against abuse, and, perhaps, better means of answering this end are discoverable. In human affairs, however, the choice generally offered us is 'of two evils to take the least'. We chuse the restraint of civil government because a less evil than anarchy and, in like manner, in the present instance, the danger of the abuse of power and of its being employed sometimes to enforce wrong decisions, must be submitted to, because a less evil than the misery of intestine wars. Much, however, may be done to lessen this danger. Such regulations as those in the ninth of the Articles of Confederation will, in a great measure, prevent hasty and partial decisions. The rotation established by the fifth article will prevent that corruption of character which seldom fails to be produced by the long possession of power, and the right reserved to every state of recalling its delegates when dissatisfied with them, will keep them constantly responsible and cautious.

The observations now made must be extended to money transactions. Congress must be trusted with a power of procuring supplies for defraying the expences of the confederation, of contracting debts, and providing funds for discharging them, and this power must not be capable of being defeated by the opposition of any minority in the states.

In short, the credit of the United States, their strength, their respectableness abroad, their liberty at home, and even their existence, depend on the preservation of a firm political union; and such an union cannot be preserved without giving all possible weight and energy to the authority of that delegation which constitutes the union.

Would it not be proper to take periodical surveys of the different states, their numbers of both sexes in every stage of life, their condition, occupations, property, etc.? Would not such surveys, in conjunction with accurate registers of births, marriages and deaths at all ages, afford much important instruction by shewing what laws govern human mortality and what situations, employments, and civil institutions are most favourable to the health and happiness of mankind? Would they not keep constantly in view the progress of population in the states, and the increase or decline of their resources? But more especially, are they not the only means of procuring the necessary information for determining accurately and equitably the proportions of men and money to be contributed by each state for supporting and strengthening the confederation?

Of Liberty

The next point I would insist on, as an object of supreme importance, is the establishment of such a system of perfect liberty, religious as well as civil, in America as shall render it a country where truth and reason shall have fair play and the human powers find full scope for exerting themselves and for shewing how far they can carry human improvement.

The faculties of man have hitherto, in all countries, been more or less cramped by the interference of civil authority in matters of speculation, by tyrannical laws against heresy and schism, and by slavish hierarchies and religious establishments. It is above all things desirable that no such fetters on reason should be admitted into America. I observe, with inexpressible satisfaction, that at present they have no existence there. In this respect the governments of the United States are liberal to a degree that is unparalleled. They have the distinguished honour of being the first states under heaven in which forms of government have been established favourable to universal liberty. They have been thus distinguished in their infancy. What then will they be in a more advanced state, when time and experience, and the concurring assistance of the wise and virtuous in every part of the earth shall have introduced into the new governments, corrections and amendments which will render them still more friendly to liberty, and more the means of promoting human happiness and dignity? May we not see the dawning of brighter days on earth and a new creation rising. But I must check myself. I am in danger of being carried too far by the ardor of my hopes.

The liberty I mean includes in it liberty of conduct in all civil matters, liberty of discussion in all speculative matters, and liberty of conscience in all religious matters. And it is then perfect, when under no restraint except when used to injure any one in his person, property, or good name, that is, except when used to destroy itself.

In liberty of discussion, I include the liberty of examining all public measures and the conduct of all public men, and of writing and publishing on all speculative and doctrinal points.

Of Liberty of Discussion

It is a common opinion that there are some doctrines so sacred, and others of so bad a tendency, that no public discussion of them ought to be allowed. Were this a right opinion all the persecution that has ever been practised would be justified. For, if it is a part of the duty of civil magistrates to prevent the discussion of such doctrines, they must, in doing this, act on their own judgments of the nature and tendency of doctrines, and, consequently, they must have a right to prevent the discussion of all doctrines which they think to be too sacred for discussion, or too dangerous in their tendency, and this right they must exercise in the only way in which civil power is capable of exercising it, 'by inflicting penalties on all who oppose sacred doctrines, or who maintain pernicious opinions'. In Mahometan countries, therefore, civil magistrates have a right to silence and punish all who oppose the divine mission of Mahomet, a doctrine there reckoned of the most sacred nature. The like is true of the doctrines of substantiation, worship of the Virgin Mary, etc. in Popish countries, and of the doctrines of the Trinity, satisfaction, etc. in Protestant countries. In England itself this principle has been acted upon and produced the laws which subject to severe penalties all who write or speak against the supreme divinity of Christ, the Book of Common Prayer, and the Church Articles of Faith. All such laws are right if the opinion I have mentioned is right. But in reality, civil power has nothing to do with any such matters, and civil governors go miserably out of their proper province whenever they take upon them the care of truth or the support of any doctrinal points. They are not judges of truth and if they pretend to decide about it, they will decide wrong. This all the countries under heaven think of the application of civil power to doctrinal points in every country but their own. It is, indeed, superstition, idolatry, and nonsense, that civil power at present supports almost everywhere under the idea of supporting sacred truth and opposing dangerous error. Would not, therefore, its perfect neutrality be the greatest blessing? Would not the interest of truth gain unspeakably were all the rulers of states to aim at nothing but keeping the peace, or did they consider themselves as bound to take care, not of the future, but the present interest of men, not of their souls and their faith but of their persons and property, not of any ecclesiastical, but secular matters only? All the experience of past time proves that the consequence of allowing civil power to judge of the nature and tendency of doctrines must be making it a hindrance to the progress of truth and an enemy to the improvement of the world. Anaxagoras was condemned in Greece for teaching that the sun and stars were not Deities, but masses of corruptible matter. Accusations of a like kind contributed to the death of Socrates. The threats of bigots and the fear of persecution prevented Copernicus from publishing, during his whole life time, his discovery of the true system of the world. Galileo was obliged to renounce the doctrine of the motion of the earth, and suffered a year's imprisonment for having asserted it. And so lately as the year 1742, the best commentary on the first production of human genius (Newton's *Principia*) was not allowed to be printed at Rome because it asserted this doctrine, and the learned commentators were obliged to prefix to their work a declaration that on this point they submitted to the decisions of the supreme Pontiffs. Such have been and such (while men continue blind and ignorant) will always be the consequence of the interposition of civil governments in matters of speculation.

When men associate for the purpose of civil government, they do it, not to defend truth or to support formularies of faith and speculative opinions, but to defend their civil rights and to protect one another on the free exercise of their mental and corporeal powers. The interference, therefore, of civil authority in such cases is directly contrary to the end of its institution. The way in which it can best promote the interest and dignity of mankind (as far as they can be promoted by the discovery of truth) is by encouraging them to search for truth wherever they can find it, and by protecting them in doing this against the attacks of malevolence and bigotry. Should any attempt be made by contending sects to injure one another, its power will come in properly to crush the attempt and to maintain for all sects equal liberty by punishing every encroachment upon it. The conduct of a civil magistrate, on such an occasion, should be that of Gallio the wise Roman proconsul who, on receiving an accusation of the apostle Paul, would not listen to it, but drove from his presence the accusers who had laid violent hands upon him, after giving them the following admonition, *If it were a matter of wrong or wicked lewdness, reason would require that I should bear with you. But if it be a question of words and names and the law, look you to it. For I will be no judge of such matters.* How much happier would the world have been had all magistrates acted in this manner? Let America learn this important lesson and profit by the experience of past times. A dissent from established opinions and doctrines has indeed often miserably disturbed society and produced mischief and bloodshed. But it should be remembered that this has been owing to the establishment of the points dissented from, and the use of civil power to enforce the reception of them. Had civil government done its duty, left all free, and employed itself in procuring instead of restraining fair discussion, all mischief would have been avoided and mankind would have been raised higher than they are in knowledge and improvement.

When Christianity, that first and best of all the means of human improvement, was first preached it was charged with turning the world upside down. The leaders of Jewish and Pagan establishments were alarmed and by opposing the propagation of it, converted a religion of peace and love into an occasion of violence and slaughter and thus verified our Lord's prophecy that he was come *not to send peace, but a sword on earth.* All this was the effect of the misapplication of the powers of government. Instead of creating, they should have been employed in preventing such mischief and been active only in causing the Christian cause to receive a fair hearing and guarding the propagators of it against insult. The like observation may be made concerning the first reformers. What we all see would have been right in pagan and popish governments with respect to Christianity and the Reformation, would it not be now right in Christian or Protestant governments, were any attempts made to propagate a new religion or any doctrines advanced opposite to those now held sacred? Such attempts, if unsupported by reason and evidence, would soon come to nothing. An imposture cannot stand the test of fair and open examination. On the contrary, the cause of truth will certainly be served by it. Mahometanism would have sunk as soon as it rose, had no other force than that of evidence been employed to propagate it; and it is an unspeakable recommendation of Christianity that it made its way till it became the religion of the world in one of its most enlightened periods, by evidence only, in opposition to the strongest exertions of civil power. There cannot be a more striking proof that nothing but fair discussion is necessary to suppress error and to propagate truth. I am grieved, indeed, whenever I find any Christians shewing a disposition to call in the aid of civil power to defend their religion. Nothing can be more disgraceful to it. If it wants such aid it cannot be of God. Its corruption and debasement took place from the moment that civil power took it under its patronage, and this corruption and debasement increased till at last it was converted into a system of absurdity and superstition more gross and more barbarous than Paganism itself. The religion of Christ disclaims all connexion with the civil establishments of the world. It has suffered infinitely by their friendship. Instead of silencing its opponents, let them be encouraged to produce their strongest arguments against it. The experience of Britain has lately shewn that this will only cause it to be better understood and more firmly believed.

I would extend these observations to all points of faith, however sacred they may be deemed. Nothing reasonable can suffer by discussion. All doctrines really sacred must be clear and incapable of being opposed with success. If civil authority interposes it will be to support some misconception or abuse of them.

That immoral tendency of doctrines which has been urged as a reason against allowing the public discussion of them must be either avowed and direct, or only a consequence with which they are charged. If it is avowed and direct, such doctrines certainly will not spread. The principles rooted in human nature will resist them and the advocates of them will be soon disgraced. If, on the contrary, it is only a consequence with which a doctrine is charged, it should be considered how apt all parties are to charge the doctrines they oppose with bad tendencies. It is well known, that Calvinists and Arminians, Trinitarians and Socinians, Fatalists and Free-willers, are continually exclaiming against one another's opinions as dangerous and licentious. Even Christianity itself could not, at its first introduction, escape this accusation. The professors of it were considered as atheists, because they opposed pagan idolatry, and their religion was on this account reckoned a destructive and pernicious enthusiasm. If, therefore, the rulers of a state are to prohibit the propagation of all doctrines in which they apprehend immoral tendencies, an opening will be made, as I have before observed, for every species of persecution. There will be no doctrine, however true or important, the avowal of which will not in some country or other be subjected to civil penalties. Undoubtedly, there are doctrines which have such tendencies. But the tendencies of speculative opinions have often very little effect on practice. The Author of nature has planted in the human mind principles and feelings which will operate in opposition to any theories that may seem to contradict them. Every sect, whatever may be its tenets, has some salvo for the necessity of virtue. The philosophers who hold that matter and motion have no existence except in our own ideas are capable of believing this only in their closets. The same is true of the philosophers who hold that nothing exists but matter and motion, and at the same time teach that man has no self-determining power; that an unalterable fate governs all things; and that no one is any thing that he can avoid being, or does any thing that he can avoid doing. These philosophers when they come out into the world act as other men do. Common sense never fails to get the better of their theories, and I know that many of them are some of the best as well as the ablest men in the world and the warmest friends to the true interests of society. Though their doctrine may seem to furnish an apology for vice, their practice is an exhibition of virtue and a government which would silence them would greatly injure itself.

Only overt acts of injustice, violence or defamation, come properly under the cognizance of civil power. Were a person now to go about London teaching that 'property is founded in grace', I should, were I a magistrate, let him alone while he did nothing but teach, without being under any other apprehension than that he would soon find a lodging in Bedlam. But were he to attempt to carry his doctrine into its consequences by actually stealing, under the pretence of his right as a saint to the property of his neighbours, I should think it my duty to lay hold of him as a felon, without regarding the opinion from which he acted.

I am persuaded that few or no inconveniencies would arise from such a liberty. If the magistrates will do their duty as soon as violence begins or any overt acts which break the peace are committed, no great harm will arise from their keeping themselves neutral till then. Let, however, the contrary be supposed. Let it be granted that civil authority will in this case often be too late in its exertions, the just inference will be, not that the liberty I plead for ought not to be allowed, but that there will be two evils between which an option must be made, and the least of which must be preferred. One is the evil just mentioned. The other includes in it every evil which can arise from making the rulers of states judges of the tendency of doctrines, subjecting freedom of enquiry to the controul of their ignorance and perpetuating darkness, intolerance and slavery. I need not say which of these evils is least.

Of Liberty of Conscience and Civil Establishment of Religion

In liberty of conscience I include much more than toleration. Jesus Christ has established a perfect equality among his followers. His command is, that they shall assume no jurisdiction over one another and acknowledge no master besides himself. It is, therefore, presumption in any of them to claim a right to any superiority or pre-eminence over their brethren. Such a claim is implied whenever any of them pretend to tolerate the rest. Not only all Christians but all men of all religions ought to be considered by a state as equally entitled to its protection as far as they demean themselves honestly and peacably. Toleration can take place only where there is a civil establishment of a particular mode of religion, that is, where a predominant sect enjoys exclusive advantages, and makes the encouragement of its own mode of faith and worship a part of the constitution of the state, but at the same time thinks fit to suffer the exercise of other modes of faith and worship. Thanks be to God, the new American States are at present strangers to such establishments. In this respect, as well as many others, they have shewn, in framing their constitutions a degree of wisdom and liberality which is above all praise.

Civil establishments of formularies of faith and worship are inconsistent with the rights of private judgment. They engender strife. They turn religion into a trade. They shoar up error. They produce hypocrisy and prevarication. They lay an undue byass on the human mind in its enquiries, and obstruct the progress of truth. Genuine religion is a concern that lies entirely between God and our own souls. It is incapable of receiving any aid from human laws. It is contaminated as soon as worldly motives and sanctions mix their influence with it. Statesmen should countenance it only by exhibiting in their own example a conscientious regard to it in those forms which are most agreeable to their own judgments, and by encouraging their fellow-citizens in doing the same. They cannot as public men give it any other assistance. All besides that has been called a public leading in religion, has done it an essential injury, and produced some of the worst consequences.

The Church Establishment in England is one of the mildest and best sort. But even here what a snare has it been to integrity? And what a check to free enquiry? What dispositions favourable to despotism has it fostered? What a turn to pride and narrowness and domination has it given the clerical character? What struggles has it produced in its members to accommodate their opinions to the subscriptions and tests which it imposes? What a perversion of learning has it occasioned to defend obsolete creeds and absurdities? What a burthen is it on the consciences of some of its best clergy who, in consequence of being bound down to a system they do not approve, and having no support except that which they derive from conforming to it, find themselves under the hard necessity of either prevaricating or starving? No one doubts but that the English clergy in general could with more truth declare that they do not, than that they do, given their unfeigned assent to all and everything contained in the Thirty-nine Articles and the Book of Common-Prayer; and yet, with a solemn declaration to this purpose, are they obliged to enter upon an office which above all offices requires those who exercise it to be examples of simplicity and sincerity. Who can help execrating the cause of such an evil?

But what I wish most to urge is the tendency of religious establishments to impede the improvement of the world. They are boundaries prescribed by human folly to human investigation, and inclosures which intercept the light and confine the exertions of reason. Let any one imagine to himself what effects similar establishments would have in philosophy, navigation, metaphysicks, medicine or mathematicks. Something like this took place in logick and philosophy while the *ipse dixit* of Aristotle and the nonsense of the schools maintained an authority like that of the creeds of churchmen. And the effect was a longer continuance of the world in the ignorance and barbarity of the dark ages. But civil establishments of religion are more pernicious. So apt are mankind to misrepresent the character of the Deity and connect his favour with particular modes of faith, that it must be expected that a religion so settled will be what it has hitherto been – a gloomy and cruel superstition bearing the name of religion.

It has been long a subject of dispute, which is worse in its effects on society, such a religion or speculative atheism. For my own part, I could almost give the preference to the latter. Atheism is so repugnant to every principle of common sense that it is not possible it should ever gain much ground or become very prevalent. On the contrary, there is a particular proneness in the human mind to superstition, and nothing is more likely to become prevalent. Atheism leaves us to the full influence of most of our natural feelings and social principles and these are so strong in their operation that in general they are a sufficient guard to the order of society. But superstition counteracts these principles by holding forth men to one another as objects of divine hatred, and by putting them on harassing, silencing, imprisoning and burning one another in order to do God service. Atheism is a sanctuary for vice by taking away the motives to virtue arising from the will of God and the fear of a future judgment. But superstition is more a sanctuary for vice by teaching men ways of pleasing God without moral virtue and by leading them even to compound for wickedness by ritual services, by bodily penances and mortifications, by adorning shrines, doing pilgrimages, saying many prayers, receiving absolution from the priest, exterminating heretics, etc. Atheism destroys the sacredness and obligation of an oath. But has there not been also a religion (so called) which has done this, by leading its professors to a persuasion that there exists a power on earth which can dispense with the obligation of oaths, that pious frauds are right and that faith is not to be kept with heretics?

It is indeed only a rational and liberal religion, a religion founded on just notions of the Deity as a being who regards equally every sincere worshipper, and by whom all are alike favoured as far as they act up to the light they enjoy, a religion which consists in the imitation of the moral perfections of an almighty but benevolent governor of nature, who directs for the best all events, in confidence in the care of his providence, in resignation to his will, and in the faithful discharge of every duty of piety and morality from a regard to his authority and the apprehension of a future righteous retribution. It is only this religion (the inspiring principle of every thing fair and worthy and joyful and which in truth is nothing but the love of God and man and virtue warming the heart and directing the conduct) – it is only this kind of religion that can bless the world or be an advantage to society. This is the religion that every enlightened friend to mankind will be zealous to promote. But it is a religion that the powers of the world know little of and which will always be best promoted by being left free and open.

I cannot help adding here that such in particular is the Christian religion. Christianity teaches us that there is none good but one, that is, God, that he willeth all men to be saved, and will punish nothing but wickedness, that he desires mercy and not sacrifice (benevolence rather than rituals), that loving him with all our hearts, and loving our neighbour as ourselves, is the whole of our duty, and that in every nation he that feareth him and worketh righteousness is accepted of him. It rests its authority on the power of God, not of man, refers itself entirely to the understandings of men, makes us the subjects of a kingdom that is not of this world, and requires us to elevate our minds above temporal emoluments and to look forwards to a state beyond the grave where a government of perfect virtue will be erected under that Messiah who has *tasted death for every man*. What have the powers of the world to do with such a religion? It disclaims all connexion with them, it made its way at first in opposition to them, and, as far as it is now upheld by them, it is dishonoured and vilified.

The injury which civil establishments do to Christianity may be learnt from the following considerations.

First, the spirit of religious establishments is opposite to the spirit of Christianity. It is a spirit of pride and tyranny in opposition to the Christian lowly spirit, a contracted and selfish spirit, in opposition to the Christian enlarged and benevolent spirit, the spirit of the world in opposition to the Christian heavenly spirit.

Secondly, religious establishments are founded on a claim of authority in the Christian church which overthrows Christ's authority. He has in the Scriptures given his followers a code of laws to which he requires them to adhere as their only guide. But the language of the framers of church establishments is 'We have authority in controversies of faith and power to decree rites and ceremonies. We are the deputies of Christ upon earth who have been commissioned by him to interpret his laws, and to rule his church. You must therefore follow us. The Scriptures are insufficient. Our interpretations you must receive as Christ's laws, our creeds as his doctrine, our inventions as his institutions.'

It is evident, as the excellent Hoadly has shewn, that these claims turn Christ out of the government of his own kingdom and place usurpers on his throne. They are therefore derogatory to his honour and a submission to them is a breach of the allegiance due to him. They have been almost fatal to true Christianity and attempts to enforce them by civil penalties have watered the Christian world with the blood of saints and martyrs.

Thirdly, the difficulty of introducing alterations into church establishments after they have been once formed is another objection to them. Hence it happens that they remain always the same amidst all changes of public manners and opinions and that a kingdom even of Christians may go on for ages in idolatrous worship after a general conviction may have taken place that there is but one being who is the proper object of religious adoration and that this one being is that one only living and true God who sent Christ into the world and who is his, no less than he is our God and father. What a sad scene of religious hypocrisy must such a discordance between public conviction and the public forms produce?

At this day in some European countries the absurdity and slavishness of their hierarchies are seen and acknowledged but, being incorporated with the state, it is scarcely possible to get rid of them.

What can be more striking than the state of England in this respect? The system of faith and worship established in it was formed above two hundred years ago, when Europe was just emerging from darkness and barbarity. The times have ever since been growing more enlightened, but without any effect on the establishment. Not a ray of the increasing light has penetrated it. Not one imperfection, however gross, has been removed.

The same articles of faith are subscribed. The same ritual of devotion is practised. There is reason to fear that the absolution of the sick, which forms a part of this ritual, is often resorted to as a passport to heaven after a wicked life and yet it is continued. Perhaps nothing more shocking to reason and humanity ever made a part of a religious system than the damning clauses in the Athanasian creed and yet the obligation of the clergy to declare assent to this creed, and to read it as a part of the public devotion, remains.

The necessary consequence of such a state of things, is, that, fourthly, Christianity itself is disgraced and that all religion comes to be considered as a state trick and a barbarous mummery. It is well known that in some Popish countries there are few Christians among the higher ranks of men, the religion of the state being in those countries mistaken for the religion of the Gospel. This indeed shows a criminal inattention in those who fall into such a mistake, for they ought to consider that Christianity has been grievously corrupted and that their ideas of it should be taken from the New Testament only. It is, however, so natural to reckon Christianity to be that which it is held out to be in all establishments of it, that it cannot but happen that such an error will take place and produce some of the worst consequences. There is probably a greater number of rational Christians (that is, of Christians upon enquiry) in England, than in all Popish countries. The reason is that the religious establishment here is Popery reformed, and that a considerable body dissent from it and are often inculcating the necessity of distinguishing between the Christianity established by law and that which is taught in the Bible. Certain it is that, till this distinction is made, Christianity can never recover its just credit and usefulness.

Such then are the effects of civil establishments of religion. May heaven soon put an end to them. The world will never be generally wise or virtuous or happy till these enemies to its peace and improvement are demolished. Thanks be to God they are giving way before increasing light. Let them never shew themselves in America. Let no such monster be known there as human authority in matters of religion. Let every honest and peaceable man, whatever is his faith, be protected there and find an effectual defence against the attacks of bigotry and intolerance. In the united States may religion flourish. They cannot be very great and happy if it does not. But let it be a better religion than most of those which have been hitherto professed in the world. Let it be a religion which enforces moral obligations, not a religion which relaxes and evades them. A tolerant and catholic religion, not a rage for proselitism. A religion of peace and charity, not a religion that persecutes, curses and damns. In a word, let it be the genuine gospel of peace, lifting above the world, warming the heart with the love of God and his creatures, and sustaining the fortitude of good men by the assured hope of a future deliverance from death, and an infinite reward in the everlasting kingdom of our Lord and Saviour.

From the preceding observations it may be concluded that it is impossible I should not admire the following article in the declaration of rights which forms the foundation of the Massachusett's constitution:

'In this state every denomination of Christians demeaning themselves peaceably and as good subjects of the commonwealth shall be equally under the protection of the law, and no subordination of any one sect or denomination to another shall ever be established by law.'

This is liberal beyond all example. I should, however, have admired it more had it been more liberal, and the words, *all men of all religions* been substituted for the words, *every denomination of Christians*.

It appears farther from the preceding observations that I cannot but dislike the religious tests which make a part of several of the American constitutions. In the Massachusett's constitution it is ordered that all who take seats in the House of Representatives or Senate shall declare 'their firm persuasion of the truth of the Christian religion'. The same is required by the Maryland constitution, as a condition of being admitted into *any* places of profit or trust. In Pensylvania every member of the House of Representatives is required to declare that he 'acknowledges the Scriptures of the Old and New Testament to be given by divine inspiration'. In the state of Delaware, that 'he believes in God the Father, and in Jesus Christ his only Son, and in the Holy Ghost, one God blessed for evermore'. All this is more than is required even in England where, though every person however debauched or atheistical is required to receive the sacrament as a qualification for inferior places, no other religious test is imposed on members of parliament than a declaration against Popery. It is an observation no less just than common that such tests exclude only honest men. The dishonest never scruple them.

Montesquieu probably was not a Christian. Newton and Locke were not Trinitarians and therefore not Christians according to the commonly received ideas of Christianity. Would the United States, for this reason, deny such men, were they living, all places of trust and power among them?

Of Education

Such is the state of things which I wish to take place in the united American states. In order to introduce and perpetuate it, and at the same time to give it the greatest effect on the improvement of the world, nothing is more necessary than the establishment of a wise and liberal plan of Education. It is impossible properly to represent the importance of this. So much is left by the author of nature to depend on the turn given to the mind in early life, and the impressions then made, that I have often thought there may be a secret remaining to be discovered in education which will cause future generations to grow up virtuous and happy and accelerate human improvement to a greater degree than can at present be imagined.

The end of education is to direct the powers of the mind in unfolding themselves and to assist them in gaining their just bent and force. And, in order to this, its business should be to teach how to think, rather than what to think, or to lead into the best way of searching for truth, rather than to instruct in truth itself. As for the latter, who is qualified for it? There are many indeed who are eager to undertake this office. All parties and sects think they have discovered truth and are confident that they alone are its advocates and friends. But the very different and inconsistent accounts they give of it demonstrate they are utter strangers to it and that it is better to teach nothing than to teach what they hold out for truth. The greater their confidence, the greater is the reason for distrusting them. We generally see the warmest zeal, where the object of it is the greatest nonsense.

Such observations have a particular tendency to shew that education ought to be an initiation into candour, rather than into systems of faith, and that it should form a habit of cool and patient investigation, rather than an attachment to any opinions.

But hitherto education has been conducted on a contrary plan. It has been a contraction, not an enlargement, of the intellectual faculties, an injection of false principles hardening them in error, not a discipline enlightening and improving them. Instead of opening and strengthening them, and teaching to think freely, it hath cramped and enslaved them, and qualified for thinking only in one track. Instead of instilling humility, charity, and liberality, and thus preparing for an easier discovery and a readier admission of truth, it has inflated with conceit, and stuffed the human mind with wretched prejudices.

The more has been learnt from such education, the more it becomes necessary to unlearn. The more has been taught in this way, of so much the more must the mind be emptied before true wisdom can enter. Such was education in the time of the first teachers of Christianity. By furnishing with skill in the arts of disputation and sophistry, and producing an attachment to established systems, it turned the minds of men from truth, and rendered them more determined to resist evidence and more capable of evading it. Hence it happened that this heavenly instruction, when first communicated was to the Jews a stumbling block, and to the Greeks foolishness, and that, in spite of miracles themselves, the persons who rejected it with most disdain, and who opposed it with most violence, were those who had been educated in colleges and were best versed in the false learning of the times. And had it taught the true philosophy instead of the true religion, the effect would have been the same. The doctrine 'that the sun stood still, and that the earth moved round it', would have been reckoned no less absurd and incredible, than the doctrine of a crucified Messiah. And the men who would have treated such an instruction with most contempt would have been the wise and the prudent, that is, the proud sophists and learned doctors of the times who had studied the Ptolemaick system of the world and learnt, by cycles and epicycles, to account for all the motions of the heavenly bodies.

In like manner, when the improvement of logick in Mr. Locke's

Essay on the Human Understanding was first published in Britain the persons readiest to attend to it and to receive it were those who had never been trained in colleges and whose minds, therefore, had never been perverted by an instruction in the jargon of the schools.

To the deep professors of the time, it appeared (like the doctrine taught in his book on the reasonableness of Christianity) to be a dangerous novelty and heresy, and the University of Oxford, in particular, condemned and reprobated the author. The like happened when Sir Isaac Newton's discoveries were first published. A romance (that is, the philosophy of Descartes) was in possession of the philosophical world. Education had rivetted it in the mind of the learned, and it was twenty-seven years before Newton's *Principia* could gain sufficient credit to bring it to a second edition. Such are the prejudices which have generally prevailed against new lights. Such the impediments which have been thrown in the way of improvement by a narrow plan of education. Even now the principal object of education (especially in divinity) is to teach established systems as certain truths, and to qualify for successfully defending them against opponents and thus to arm the mind against conviction and render it impenetrable to farther light. Indeed, were it offered to my option which I would have, the plain sense of a common and untutored man, or the deep erudition of the proud scholars and professors in most universities, I should eagerly prefer the former, from a persuasion that it would leave me at a less distance from real wisdom. An unoccupied and simple mind is infinitely preferable to a mind warped by systems, and the entire want of learning better than a learning such as most of that is which hitherto has been sought and admired. A learning which puffs up, while in reality it is nothing but profounder ignorance and more inveterate prejudice.

It may be worth adding here that a narrow education (should it ever happen not to produce the evils now mentioned) will probably produce equal evils of a contrary nature. I mean, that there will be danger when persons so educated come to see the absurdity of some of the opinions in which they have been educated, that they will become prejudiced against them all and, consequently, throw them all away and run wild into scepticism and infidelity. At present, in this part of the world this is a very common event.

I am by no means qualified to give a just account of the particular method in which education ought to be conducted so as to avoid these evils, that is, so as to render the mind free and unfettered, quick in discerning evidence, and prepared to follow it from whatever quarter and in whatever manner it may offer itself. But certain it is that the best mode of education is that which does this most effectually, which guards best against silly prejudices, which enflames most with the love of truth, which disposes most to ingenuity and fairness, and leaves the mind most sensible of its own need of farther information. Had this always been the aim of education, mankind would now have been further advanced. It supposes, however, an improved state of mankind, and when once it has taken place it will quicken the progress of improvement.

I have in these observations expressed a dislike of systems, but I have meant only to condemn that attachment to them as standards of truth which has been too prevalent. It may be necessary in education to make use of them or of books explaining them. But they should be used only as guides and helps to enquiry. Instruction in them should be attended with a fair exhibition of the evidence on both sides of every question, and care should be taken to induce, as far as possible, a habit of believing only on an overbalance of evidence, and of proportioning assent in every case to the degree of that overbalance, without regarding authority, antiquity, singularity, novelty, or any of the prejudices which too commonly influence assent. Nothing is so well fitted to produce this habit as the study of mathematics. In these sciences no one ever thinks of giving his assent to a proposition till he can clearly understand it and see it proved by a fair deduction from propositions previously understood and proved. In these sciences the mind is inured to close and patient attention, shewn the nature of just reasoning, and taught to form distinct ideas and to expect clear evidence in all cases before belief. They furnish, therefore, the best exercise for the intellectual powers and the best defence against that credulity and precipitation and confusion of ideas which are the common sources of error.

There is, however, a danger even here to be avoided. Mathematical studies may absorb the attention too much, and when they do they contract the mind by rendering it incapable of thinking at large by disqualifying it for judging of any evidence except mathematical and, consequently, disposing it to an unreasonable scepticism on all subjects which admit not of such evidence. There have been many instances of this narrowness in mathematicians.

But to return from this digression, I cannot help observing on this occasion, with respect to Christianity in particular, that education ought to lead to a habit of judging of it as it is in the code itself of Christianity, that the doctrines it reveals should be learnt only from a critical and fair enquiry into the sense of this code, and that all instruction in it should be a preparation for making this enquiry and a communication of assistance in examining into the proofs of its divine original, and in determining to what degree of evidence the proofs amount, after allowing every difficulty its just weight. This has never yet been the practice among Christians. The New Testament has been reckoned hitherto an insufficient standard of Christian Divinity and, therefore, formularies of human invention pretending to explain and define it (but in reality misrepresenting and dishonouring it) have been substituted in its room, and teaching these has been called teaching Christianity. And it is very remarkable that in the English Universities lectures in the New Testament are seldom or ever read, and that, through all Christendom, it is much less an object of attention than the systems and creeds which have been fathered upon it.

I will only add on this subject that it is above all things necessary, while instruction is conveyed, to convey with it a sense of the imbecility of the human mind and of its great proneness to error, and also a disposition even on points which seem the most clear, to listen to objections, and to consider nothing as involving in it our final interest but an honest heart.

Nature has so made us that an attachment must take place within us to opinions once formed, and it was proper that we should be so made, in order to prevent that levity and desultoriness of mind which must have been the consequence had we been ready to give up our opinions too easily and hastily. But this natural tendency, however wisely given us, is apt to exceed its proper limits and to render us unreasonably tenacious. It ought, therefore, like all our other natural propensities, to be carefully watched and guarded, and education should put us upon doing this. An observation before made should, in particular, be inculcated, 'that all mankind have hitherto been most tenacious when most in the wrong, and reckoned themselves most enlightened when most in the dark'. This is indeed, a very mortifying fact but attention to it is necessary to cure that miserable pride and dogmaticalness which are some of the worst enemies to improvement. Who is there that does not remember the time when he was entirely satisfied about points which deeper reflexion has shewn to be above his comprehension? Who, for instance, does not remember a time when he would have wondered at the question, 'Why does water run down hill?' What ignorant man is there who is not persuaded that he understands this perfectly? But every improved man knows it to be a question he cannot answer, and what distinguishes him in this instance from the less improved part of mankind is his knowing this. The like is true in numberless other instances. One of the best proofs of wisdom is a sense of our want of wisdom, and he who knows most possesses most of this sense.

In thinking of myself I derive some encouragement from this reflexion. I now see that I do not understand many points which once appeared to me very clear. The more I have inquired, the more sensible I have been growing of my own darkness, and a part of the history of my life is that which follows.

In early life I was struck with Bishop Butler's *Analogy of religion natural and revealed to the constitution and course of nature.* I reckon it happy for me that this book was one of the first that fell into my hands. It taught me the proper method of reasoning on moral and religious subjects, and particularly the importance of paying a due regard to the imperfection of human knowledge. His sermons also, I then thought, and do still think, excellent. Next to his works, I have always been an admirer of the writings of Dr. Clark[e]. And I cannot help adding, however strange it may seem, that I owe much to the philosophical writings of Mr. Hume, which I likewise studied in early life. Though an enemy to his scepticism, I have profited by it. By attacking, with great ability, every principle of truth and reason, he put me upon examining the ground upon which I stood and taught me not hastily to take any thing for granted. The first fruits of my reading and studies were laid before the public in a treatise entitled *A review of the principal questions and difficulties in morals.* This publication has been followed by many others on various subjects. And now, in the evening of a life devoted to enquiry and spent in endeavours (weak indeed and feeble) to serve the best interests, present and future, of mankind, I am waiting for the great teacher, convinced that the order of nature is perfect, that infinite wisdom and goodness govern all things, and that Christianity comes from God. But at the same time puzzled by many difficulties, anxious for more light, and resting with full and constant assurance only on this one truth; that the practice of virtue is the duty and dignity of man and, in all events, his wisest and safest course.

Of the Dangers to which the American States are exposed

In the preceding observations I have aimed at pointing out the means of promoting the progress of improvement in the united states of America. I have insisted, particularly, on the importance of a just settlement of the Federal Union and the establishment of a well-guarded and perfect liberty in speculation, in government,[15] in education, and in religion. The united states are now setting out, and all depends on the care and foresight with which a plan is begun, which hereafter will require only to be strengthened and ripened. This is, therefore, the time for giving them advice, and mean advice (like the present) may suggest some useful hints. In this country when any improvements are proposed or any corrections are attempted of abuses so gross as to make our boasts of liberty ridiculous, a clamour immediately arises against innovation, and an alarm spreads lest the attempt to repair should destroy. In America no such prejudices can operate. These abuses have not yet gained sacredness by time. There the way is open to social dignity and happiness, and reason may utter her voice with confidence and success.

Of Debts and Internal Wars

I have observed in the introduction to this address that the American states have many dangers to shun. In what follows I shall give a brief recital of some of the chief of these dangers.

The danger from an endless increase of public debts has been already sufficiently noticed.

Particular notice has been likewise taken of the danger from internal wars. Again and again, I would urge the necessity of pursuing every measure and using every precaution which can guard against

---

[15] It was proposed to the convention for settling the Massachusett's constitution that one of the two houses which constitute the general court of that state should be a representation of persons, and the other a representation of property, and that the body of the people should appoint only the electors of their representatives. By such regulations corruption in the choice of representatives would be rendered less practicable, and it seems the best method of concentering in the legislature as much as possible of the virtue and ability of the state, and of making its voice always an expression of the will and best sense of the people. On this plan also the number of members constituting a legislature might be much lessened. This is a circumstance of particular consequence, to which the united states, in some future period of their increase, will find it necessary to attend. It has been often justly observed, that a legislative body very numerous is little better than a mob.

this danger. It will be shocking to see in the new world a repetition of all the evils which have hitherto laid waste the old world. War raging where peace and liberty were thought to have taken their abodes. The points of bayonets and the mouths of cannon settling disputes, instead of the collected wisdom of the confederation – and perhaps one restless and ambitious state rising by bloody conquest above the rest, and becoming a sovereign state, claiming impiously (as Britain once did), 'full authority to make laws that shall bind its sister states in all cases whatever', and drawing to itself all advantages at their expence. I deprecate this calamity. I shudder when I consider how possible it is and hope those persons are mistaken who think that such are the jealousies which govern human nature, and such the imperfections of the best human arrangements, that it is not within the reach of any wisdom to discover any effectual means of preventing it without encroaching too much on the liberty and independence of the states. I have mentioned an enlargement of the powers of Congress. Others have proposed a consolidation of the powers of government in one parliament representing all the states and superseding the particular parliaments by which they are now separately governed. But it is obvious that this will be attended with greater inconveniencies and encroach more on the liberty of the states than the enlargement I have proposed of the powers of Congress. If such a parliament is not to supersede any of the other parliaments, it will be the same with Congress as at present constituted.

Of an Unequal Distribution of Property

It is a trite observation 'that dominion is founded on property'. Most free states have manifested their sense of the truth of this observation by studying to find out means of preventing too great an inequality in the distribution of property. What tumults were occasioned at Rome, in its best times, by attempts to carry into execution the Agrarian law? Among the people of Israel, by the direction of heaven, all estates which had been alienated during the course of fifty years returned to their original owners at the end of that term. One of the circumstances that has been most favourable to the American states in forming their new constitutions of government has been the equality which subsists among them.

The happiest state of man is the middle state between the savage and the refined, or between the wild and the luxurious state. Such is the state of society in Connecticut and some others of the American provinces where the inhabitants consist, if I am rightly informed, of an independent and hardy yeomanry, all nearly on a level, trained to arms, instructed in their rights, cloathed in homespun, of simple manners, strangers to luxury, drawing plenty from the ground, and that plenty, gathered easily by the hand of industry and giving rise to early marriages, a numerous progeny, length of days, and a rapid increase – the rich and the poor, the haughty grandee and the creeping sycophant, equally unknown – protected by laws which (being their own will) cannot oppress, and by an equal government which, wanting lucrative places, cannot create corrupt canvassings and ambitious intrigue. O distinguished people! May you continue long thus happy, and may the happiness you enjoy spread over the face of the whole earth! But I am forgetting myself. There is danger that a state of society so happy will not be of long duration, that simplicity and virtue will give way to depravity, that equality will in time be lost, the cursed lust of domineering shew itself, liberty languish, and civil government gradually degenerate into an instrument in the hands of the few to oppress and plunder the many. Such has hitherto been the progress of evil in human affairs. In order to give them a better turn, some great men (Plato, Sir Thomas More, Mr. Wallace, etc.) have proposed plans which, by establishing a community of goods and annihilating property, would make it impossible for any one member of a state to think of enslaving the rest, or to consider himself as having any interest distinct from that of his fellow-citizens. Such theories are in speculation pleasing, nor perhaps are they wholly impracticable. Some approaches to them may hereafter be made and schemes of government may take place which shall leave so little, besides personal merit, to be a means of distinction as to exclude from society most of the causes of evil. But be this as it will, it is out of doubt that there is an equality in society which is essential to liberty and which every state that would continue virtuous and happy ought as far as possible to maintain. It is not in my power to describe the best method of doing this. I will only observe that there are three enemies to equality against which America ought to guard.

First, granting hereditary honours and titles of nobility. Persons thus distinguished, though perhaps meaner than the meanest of their dependents, are apt to consider themselves as belonging to a higher order of beings, and made for power and government. Their birth and rank necessarily dispose them to be hostile to general liberty, and when they are not so, and discover a just zeal for the rights of mankind, it is always a triumph of good sense and virtue over the temptations of their situation. It is, therefore, with peculiar satisfaction that I have found in the Articles of Confederation an order that no titles of nobility shall be ever granted by the united states. Let there be honours to encourage merit, but let them die with the men who have earned them. Let them not descend to posterity to foster a spirit of domination and to produce a proud and tyrannical aristocracy. In a word, let the united states continue for ever what it is now their glory to be – a confederation of states prosperous and happy, without lords, without bishops[16] and without kings.

Secondly, the right of primogeniture. The tendency of this to produce an improper inequality is very obvious. The disposition to raise a name by accumulating property in one branch of a family is a vanity no less unjust and cruel than dangerous to the interest of liberty and no wise state will encourage or tolerate it.

Thirdly, foreign trade is another of the enemies against which I wish to caution the united states. But this operates unfavourably to a state in so many more ways than by destroying that equality which is the basis of liberty that it will be proper to take more particular notice of it.

Of Trade, Banks, and Paper Credit

Foreign trade has, in some respects, the most useful tendency. By creating an intercourse between distant kingdoms it extends benevolence, removes local prejudices, leads every man to consider himself more as a citizen of the world than of any particular state, and, consequently, checks the excesses of that love of our country[17] which

---

[16] I do not mean by 'bishops' any officers among Christians merely spiritual, but lords spiritual, as distinct from lords temporal, or clergymen raised to pre-eminence and invested with civil honours and authority by a state establishment. I must add that by what is here said I do not mean to express a general preference of a republican constitution of government. There is a degree of political degeneracy which unfits for such a constitution. Britain, in particular, consists too much of the high and the low, (of scum and dregs) to admit of it. Nor will it suit America should it ever become equally corrupt.

[17] The love of our country is then only a noble passion when it engages us to promote the internal happiness of our country and to defend its rights and liberties against domestic

146

has been applauded as one of the noblest, but which, really, is one of the most destructive principles in human nature. Trade also, by enabling every country to draw from other countries conveniencies and advantages which it cannot find within itself, produces among nations a sense of mutual dependence, and promotes the general improvement. But there is no part of mankind to which these uses of trade are of less consequence than the American states. They are spread over a great continent and make a world within themselves. The country they inhabit includes soils and climates of all sorts, producing not only every necessary, but every convenience of life. And the vast rivers and widespread lakes which intersect it create such an inland communication between the different parts as is unknown in any other region of the earth. They possess then within themselves the best means of the most profitable traffic, and the amplest scope for it. Why should they look much farther? What occasion have they for being anxious about pushing foreign trade, or even about raising a great naval force? Britain, indeed, consisting as it does of unarmed inhabitants, and threatened as it is by ambitious and powerful neighbours, cannot hope to maintain its existence long after becoming open to invasion by losing its naval superiority. But this is not the case with the American states. They have no powerful neighbours to dread. The vast Atlantic must be crossed before they can be attacked. They are all a well trained militia, and the successful resistance which, in their infancy and without a naval force, they have made to the invasion of the first European power, will probably discourage and prevent all future invasions. Thus singularly happy, why should they seek connexions with Europe and expose themselves to the danger of being involved in its quarrels? What have they to do with its politics? Is there any thing

and foreign invasion, maintaining at the same time an equal regard to the rights and liberties of other countries. But this has not been its most common effects. On the contrary, it has in general been nothing but a spirit of rivalship between different communities, producing contention and a thirst for conquest and dominion. What is his country to a Russian, a Turk, a Spaniard, etc. but a spot where he enjoys no right, and is disposed of by owners as if he was a beast? And what is his love to his country but an attachment to degradation and slavery? What was the love of their country among the Jews but a wretched partiality for themselves and a proud contempt for other nations? Among the Romans also what was it, however great in many of its exertions, but a principle holding together a band of robbers in their attempts to crush all liberty but their own? Christianity has wisely omitted to recommend this principle. Had it done this, it would have countenanced a vice among mankind. It has done what is infinitely better. It has recommended universal benevolence.

very important to them which they can draw from thence except infection? Indeed, I tremble when I think of the rage for trade which is likely to prevail among them. It may do them infinite mischief. All nations are spreading snares for them and courting them to a dangerous intercourse. Their best interest requires them to guard themselves by all proper means, and, particularly, by laying heavy duties on importations. But in no case will any means succeed unless aided by manners. In this instance, particularly, there is reason to fear that an increasing passion for foreign frippery will render all the best regulations ineffectual. And should this happen, that simplicity of character, that manliness of spirit, that disdain of tinsel in which true dignity consists, will disappear. Effeminacy, servility, and venality will enter, and liberty and virtue be swallowed up in the gulph of corruption. Such may be the course of events in the American states. Better infinitely will it be for them to consist of bodies of plain and honest farmers, than of opulent and splendid merchants. Where in these states do the purest manners prevail? Where do the inhabitants live most on an equality and most at their ease? Is it not in those inland parts where agriculture gives health and plenty, and trade is scarcely known? Where, on the contrary, are the inhabitants most selfish, luxurious, loose, and vicious, and at the same time most unhappy? Is it not along the sea coasts and in the great towns where trade flourishes and merchants abound? So striking is the effect of these different situations on the vigour and happiness of human life, that in the one, population would languish did it receive no aid from emigration, while in the other, it increases to a degree scarcely ever before known.

But to proceed to some observations of a different nature. The united States have, I think, particular reason to dread the following effects of foreign trade.

By increasing importation to feed luxury and gratify prodigality, it will carry out their coin and occasion the substitution of a delusive paper currency, the consequence of which will be that ideal wealth will take place of real, and their security come to depend on the strength and duration of a bubble. I am very sensible that paper credit is one of the greatest of all conveniencies, but this makes it likewise one of the greatest of all temptations. A public bank (while it can circulate its bills) facilitates commerce and assists the exertions of a state in proportion to its credit. But when it is not carefully restricted and watched, when its emissions exceed the coin it can command and are carried near the utmost length that the confidence of the public will allow, and when, in consequence of this, its permanence comes to depend on the permanence of public credulity, in these circumstances, a bank, though it may for a time (that is, while a balance of trade too unfavourable does not occasion a run, and no events arise which produce alarm) answer all the ends of a mine from which millions may be drawn in a minute, and, by filling a kingdom with cash, render it capable of sustaining any debts, and give it a kind of omnipotence. In such circumstances, I say, notwithstanding these temporary advantages, a public bank must at last prove a great calamity and a kingdom so supported, at the very time of its greatest exertions, will be only striving more violently to increase the horror of an approaching convulsion.

The united States have already verified some of these observations and felt in some degree the consequences to which I have alluded. They have been carried through the war by an emission of paper which had no solid support and which now has lost all value. It is indeed surprising that, being secured on no fund and incapable of being exchanged for coin, it should ever have obtained a currency, or answered any important purpose.

Unhappily for Britain, it has used the means of giving more stability to its paper-credit and being enabled by it to support expences greater than any that have been yet known, and to contract a debt which now astonishes, and may hereafter produce a catastrophe that will terrify the world. A longer duration of the late war would have brought on this catastrophe immediately. The peace has put it off for the present. God grant, if still possible, that measures may be adopted which shall put it off for ever.

Of Oaths

Oaths are expedients to which all states have had recourse in order to obtain true information and ascertain facts by securing the veracity of witnesses. But I know not how to relish that imprecation which always makes a part of an oath. Perhaps there is no such necessity for it as is commonly imagined. An affirmation solemnly made with laws inflicting severe penalties on falshood when detected, would probably answer all the ends of oaths. I am, therefore, disposed to wish that in the united states imprecatory oaths may be abolished and the same indulgence in this respect granted to all which is now granted to the Quakers. But I am afraid they will think this too dangerous an experiment, and what is of most consequence is to avoid, first, such a multiplicity of oaths as will render them too familiar, and, secondly, a slight manner of administering them. England, in this respect, seems to be sunk to the lowest possible degree of degeneracy. Oaths among us are required on so many occasions and so carelessly administered as to have lost almost all their use and efficacy. It has been asserted that, including oaths of office, oaths at elections, custom-house oaths, etc., there are about a million of perjuries committed in this kingdom annually. This is one of the most atrocious of our national iniquities and it is a wonder if we are not to be visited for it with some of the severest of God's judgments.

Of the Negro Trade and Slavery

The negro trade cannot be censured in language too severe. It is a traffic which, as it has been hitherto carried on, is shocking to humanity, cruel, wicked, and diabolical. I am happy to find that the united states are entering into measures for discountenancing it and for abolishing the odious slavery which it has introduced. Till they have done this, it will not appear they deserve the liberty for which they have been contending. For it is self-evident that if there are any men whom they have a right to hold in slavery, there may be others who have had a right to hold them in slavery. I am sensible, however, that this is a work which they cannot accomplish at once. The emancipation of the negroes must, I suppose, be left in some measure to be the effect of time and of manners. But nothing can excuse the united states if it is not done with as much speed, and at the same time with as much effect, as their particular circumstances and situation will allow. I rejoice that on this occasion I can recommend to them the example of my own country. In Britain, a negro becomes a freeman the moment he sets his foot on British ground.

Conclusion

Such is the advice which I would humbly (but earnestly) offer to the united states of America. Such are the means by which they may become the seats of liberty, science, peace, and virtue, happy within themselves, and a refuge to the world.

Often, while employed in writing these papers, have I wished for a warning voice of more power. The present moment, however auspicious to the united states if wisely improved, is critical and, though apparently the end of all their dangers, may prove the time of their greatest danger. I have, indeed, since finishing this address, been mortified more than I can express by accounts which have led me to fear that I have carried my ideas of them too high and deceived myself with visionary expectations. And should this be true, should the return of peace and the pride of independence lead them to security and dissipation, should they lose those virtuous and simple manners by which alone republics can long subsist, should false refinement, luxury, and irreligion spread among them, excessive jealousy distract their governments, and clashing interests, subject to no strong controul, break the federal union, the consequence will be that the fairest experiment ever tried in human affairs will miscarry and that a revolution which had revived the hopes of good men and promised an opening to better times will become a discouragement to all future efforts in favour of liberty and prove only an opening to a new scene of human degeneracy and misery.

The Evidence for a Future Period of Improvement in the State of Mankind
(1787)

The Evidence for a future period of improvement in the state of Mankind, with the means and duty of promoting it, represented in a discourse delivered on Wednesday the 25th of April, 1787, at the Meeting-House in the Old Jewry, London, to the Supporters of a New Academical Institution among Protestant Dissenters.
(1787)

Matthew vi. 10

Thy Kingdom come. Thy will be done on earth as it is in heaven. These words, being a part of the Lord's prayer, must be perfectly familiar to you. It is evident that by the kingdom mentioned in them is meant, not that absolute dominion of the Deity by which he does *whatever he pleases in the Armies of Heaven and among the inhabitants of the earth*, but that moral kingdom which consists in the voluntary obedience of reasonable beings to his laws and, particularly, that kingdom of the Messiah which our Saviour came to establish.

The same kingdom is undoubtedly here meant with that which we are told in the Gospel history the apostles went about preaching every where and declaring to be at hand, which the Jews at the time this prayer was framed were impatiently expecting, and which in their religious services they were continually praying for in the words, *May his kingdom reign. May the Messiah come, and deliver his people.*

This kingdom is described in the prophecy of Daniel under the character of a kingdom which the God of heaven was to set up in the time of the fourth temporal kingdom upon earth (or the Roman empire) and which was *to be given to the Son of Man, and* to increase gradually *till it broke in pieces all other kingdoms, and filled the whole earth.* In the prophecy of the seventy weeks the very time of the commencement of this kingdom is fixed, and it appears evidently that the phrases, *kingdom of God* and *kingdom of heaven*, which the Jews used to signify the reign of their Messiah and by which it is expressed in the New Testament, were derived from these prophetical representations in Daniel.

This petition, therefore, in our Lord's prayer referred primarily to the introduction of the Christian religion among mankind. His disciples were directed by it and by the petition that follows it (*thy will be done on earth as it is in heaven*) to pray that the advent of his kingdom might be speedy, that the Gospel might soon be established in the world, that the virtue which it was fitted to inspire might take place every where, and mortal men be taught to regard God's will with a submission resembling that of the heavenly spirits. We cannot express before the Deity any desires that are more reasonable and important. The establishment of Christ's kingdom includes in it the enjoyment of the highest blessings that can be communicated to the world. It is a kingdom of light, and peace, and virtue. It is the beginning and foundation of an everlasting kingdom in the heavens. The subjects of it are fellow-citizens with angels and heirs of a glorious immortality. With the utmost ardour then might the apostles and first disciples pray for the coming of this kingdom, and nothing can now be a juster object of the prayers of Christians. For I cannot be of the opinion of those of our dissenting brethren who scruple using this prayer, from an apprehension that the words (*thy kingdom come*) cannot be used with propriety now the kingdom of Christ is come and the grace of the Gospel made known to men. The truth is that there is a kingdom of Christ still to come. You should recollect that there are two comings of Christ's kingdom mentioned in the Scriptures, one partial and the other universal, and that though the former is past, yet we may with the utmost reason pray for the latter, and for that better state of things upon earth which our Lord expresses, by *doing the will of God on earth as it is done in heaven.*

Hitherto, the kingdom of the Messiah has been in its infancy. The most glorious period of it is yet future. His religion is now confined to a few nations. It will hereafter extend itself over all nations. It is now dishonoured by much contention, superstition, and wickedness. Hereafter, it is to be cleared of these evils and to triumph over all false religions. Hitherto, it has caused the will of God to be done but very imperfectly. Hereafter, it will cause the will of God to be done on earth, as it is done in heaven. The light it has hitherto produced has been like the dawn of the morning. It will hereafter produce a bright day over the whole earth. In other words, and to use our Lord's comparison in the parable of the grain of mustard seed, the kingdom of heaven has hitherto resembled a small seed germinating under ground. A period is coming in which it will throw off all that encumbers it, and grow up to a tree large enough for the birds of the air to lodge among its branches.

That such a state of Christianity lies before us between this and the end of time, or, that there is a progressive improvement in human affairs which will terminate in greater degrees of light and virtue and happiness than have been yet known appears to me highly probable and my present business will be to represent to you the nature, the grounds, and the uses of this expectation. In doing this I shall first state the evidence which makes it probable, after which I shall be naturally led to take notice of the means by which it is to be accomplished and the encouragement it gives us in our exertions to promote the improvement of the world and, particularly, in that undertaking which occasions the present service.

The evidence on which the expectation I have mentioned rests is taken, partly from tradition and scripture, and partly from reason and the necessary tendencies of things, confirmed by what we know of the past and see of the present state of the world.

There has been a tradition which has led Jews and Pagans (as well as Christians) to expect that the last ages of the world will be ages of improvement and happiness. This tradition is so ancient and has been so general that there is, I think, some regard due to it. But it is of little consequence compared with the declarations of scripture on this subject. These are clear and decisive. I have just mentioned a parable of our Lord's which directs our views to a future enlargement of his kingdom. To the same purpose is his comparison of his kingdom to a particle of leaven which worked gradually and insensibly in a large quantity of meal till the whole was leavened. St. Paul speaks in very plain language of a time when the *fullness of the Gentiles shall come in, and all Israel be saved.*

Isaiah prophesies that, in the latter days, the mountain of the Lord's house shall be established on the top of the mountains, and all nations flock into it, *and the Lord shall judge among the nations, and they shall beat their swords into plow-shares, and their spears into pruning-hooks. Nation shall not lift up a sword against nation, neither shall they learn war any more.* The same prophet, in the eleventh and sixth chapters, foretells that under the reign of the Messiah the Lord *would create new heavens and a new earth. The people of the Jews should be all righteous, and inhabit their land for ever. The wolf should dwell with the lamb, and the leopard lie down with the kid, and the lion eat straw with the ox, and the earth be filled with the knowledge of the Lord as the waters cover the sea.* Daniel, in a passage already quoted, tells us that the kingdom of the Messiah was *to break in pieces all other kingdoms, and to encrease till it filled the whole earth.* In the seventh chapter he gives a particular account of a tyrannical power which was to appear after the fall of the Roman empire, and which, after continuing a limited time, was to be destroyed and to be succeeded by an universal kingdom which should never be destroyed. This kingdom, according to Daniel's representation, is to be the fifth and last universal monarchy on earth, and he describes it under the character of the reign of the *saints*; that is, of an empire of reason and liberty and virtue which is to follow despotism, ignorance, and wickedness. *I beheld*, says he *till the beast* (that is, the tyrannical power just mentioned) *was destroyed and given to the burning flame. And then came the Son of Man in the clouds of heaven, and there was given him dominion and glory that all men and languages should serve him, and the kingdom and dominion and the greatness of the kingdom under the whole heaven, was delivered to the people of the saints of the Most High.* In the last chapter of this prophecy we have the remarkable declaration that at the time of the end (till which time Daniel represents himself as ordered to seal his words) many should *run to and fro, and knowledge should be increased.*

St. Paul in his second epistle to the Thessalonians assures us that the day of judgment would not come till an apostacy had taken place in the Christian church, and *a man of sin had appeared in it who should exalt himself above all that is called God, and whose coming should be after the working of Satan with signs and lying wonders, but whom the Lord would consume with the breath of his mouth and the brightness of his coming.*

St. John tells us that the *holy city* (by which undoubtedly is meant the Christian church) should be trodden under foot 1260 years, at the end of which term he represents the kingdoms of this world as becoming the kingdoms of the Lord and of his Christ. *The beast and the false prophet*, he says, *will be taken and cast into a lake of fire* (that is, all antichristian corruption and oppression will be abolished), *and Christ shall reign a thousand years, and the saints shall reign with him.* That is, truth and righteousness shall for a long period become prevalent and mankind universally receive and acknowledge Christ as their Head and Lawgiver. I will only add our Lord's prediction in Luke xxi.24. *The Jews shall be led captive to all nations, and Jerusalem shall be trodden down of the Gentiles till the times of the Gentiles are fulfilled.* These words are very striking. They intimate to us a dispersion of the Jews for a certain period, the preservation of them through that period, and some great revolution in the state of the Gentiles at the end of it. It is evident that these predictions in the Old and New Testaments have the same events in view, nor is it possible with any appearance of reason to apply them to any events which have already happened. Certainly, the stone mentioned by Daniel *which was cut out of the mountain without hands* (that is, without the aid of human power) has not yet filled the whole earth. That man of sin who was to usurp the prerogatives of the Deity and to deceive the world with lying miracles, has not yet been destroyed by the brightness of our Lord's second coming. The knowledge of the Lord has not yet covered the earth as the waters fill the channels of the sea. The universal empire of reason and virtue has not yet been established, nor have all the people and nations been yet brought to serve the Son of Man. War has not yet been excluded from the world, nor has liberty taken place of tyranny, knowledge of ignorance, and sanctity of vice and corruption. To such a happy termination of human affairs in this world, next to the happiness of the heavenly state, the Scriptures point our views, and it is an argument in their favour that they do give us an expectation so animating amidst the variety of gloomy prospects with which this world, in its present state, is often presenting us, for it is an expectation no less credible and probable in itself than it is encouraging. This is what I shall now proceed to shew you.

Almost every object in nature grows up gradually from a weak and low to a mature and improved state of being. The condition of mankind, in particular, has been hitherto improving. At first they were rude and ignorant. In time several of the arts were discovered. Civilization and agriculture began and governments were established. By degrees the arts were improved. New ones were discovered and better forms of government were established, and in the present aera of the world it is evident that the life of man appears with greater dignity than ever, and that in consequence of a vast variety of successive improvements and additions produced by them in the sources of human enjoyment, there is the same difference between the state of our species now and its state at first as there is between a youth approaching to manhood and a child just born.

It deserves particular consideration here that it is the nature of improvement to increase itself. Every advance in it lifts mankind higher and makes them more capable of farther advances, nor are there, in this case, any limits beyond which knowledge and improvement cannot be carried. And for this reason discoveries may, for aught we know, be made in future time which, like the discoveries of the mechanical arts and the mathematical sciences in past time, may exalt the powers of men and improve their state to a degree which will make future generations as much superior to the present as the present are to the past. Let us here look back again.

At the first establishment of civil society man was an animal, naked in body and mind, running about in the woods or tending cattle, destitute of arts and laws and ideas. From this low condition he has risen to be the animal we now see him, to command the powers of nature, to fertilize the earth, to traverse the ocean, and to measure the distances and magnitudes of the sun and planets. His progress to this state has been irregular and various. Ages of improvement have been followed by ages of barbarism, and the several climates of the earth have felt the vicissitudes of knowledge and ignorance just as they have of light and darkness. Yet what has been lost in one place, or at one time, has been gained in another, and an age of darkness and barbarism has been succeeded by ages of improvement more rapid than any that preceded them. There was a time when no man was what whole countries are now. And there may come a time when every country will be what many are now, and when some will be advanced to a state much higher.

Nothing can direct us better in judging of the manner in which future improvements are likely to proceed than reflecting on the course of human improvement as it has hitherto taken place. I cannot illustrate what I now mean better than by instancing in natural philosophy.

The highest state of philosophical and astronomical knowledge was, at the beginning of this century, that which it had attained by the discoveries of Sir Isaac Newton. But it had been the work of many ages to prepare mankind for these, and to bring the world to a capacity of understanding and receiving them. To a few wise men above two thousand years ago there appeared some glimmerings of this philosophy, but they were disregarded and soon lost. A barbarous philosophy, called the Peripatetic, prevailed after this for a long period. The inventor of it (like the Pope in the Christian church) was set up as an universal master, and the most wretched jargon was received implicitly for true science. It is scarcely possible to describe the state of darkness with respect to the knowledge of nature in which the world was involved during this whole time. About two centuries ago a glimmering of light again appeared, and a more rational philosophy began to gain ground. The light gradually increased. One great genius rose after another, and one discovery produced further discoveries. A Bacon was followed by a Boyle, and a Boyle by a Newton. Each of these prepared the way for his successor, and the last (the pride and glory of this country, and a name with which no names of kings and princes deserve to be thought of) the last, I say, has struck out a glorious light. He extended on every side the boundaries of science, subjected light itself to dissection, and with a sagacity never before known among mortals unfolded the laws which govern the solar system. Such, however, were the prejudices in favour of former systems of philosophy that even his philosophy, though founded on experiment and demonstration, was not immediately received. For many years it encountered much opposition, but at last it made its way. Foreign nations came over to it, and it is now the philosophy of the world. A state of philosophy so improved could not take place soon among mankind. It was necessarily reserved for an advanced age of the world. What is now known of the relation of this earth to the sun, and of the order of the heavenly bodies, is so contrary to vulgar prejudices and seems to be so contradicted by the testimony of our senses, that had it been proposed, even to the philosophers of Greece and Rome, they would probably have scouted it as much as they did Christianity. False systems of philosophy have occasioned a more thorough examination of philosophical subjects, and their detection has given greater weight and stability to the true philosophy, for truth always shines brighter and stands firmer after growing out of the ruins of error, and an error once prevalent and afterwards detected is never likely to recover itself.

These observations are applicable with strict propriety to the natural course of improvement in religious knowledge, and, particularly, the knowledge of genuine Christianity and its spread among mankind. Till the time of our Saviour the world had been too much in its infancy to be capable of admitting more of the knowledge of Christianity than could be communicated by obscure hints, and a succession of dark preparatory dispensations. And even in the ages immediately following the time of our Saviour, it was by no means ripe for that universal prevalency of Christianity which we expect hereafter. The prejudices of mankind were then of such a nature, and the doctrines of the gospel so much out of the road of their ideas, that had it prevailed every where it must have prevailed in a very imperfect form, and an adulteration of it by the false learning and philosophy of the times was unavoidable. For these reasons it might be necessary that at first there should be only a partial propagation of it, and that its more general establishment should be deferred till the world was more improved and therefore more capable of properly understanding it, till sufficient time had been allowed for a full discussion of its doctrines, till the completion of prophecy became an argument for it so striking as to be irresistible, till the system of nature and the plans of Providence should be laid more open to our views, and there should be a possibility of establishing it among mankind in such purity and with such evidence as should leave no danger of further adulterations of it.

It appears, therefore, that the same preparation of ages which is required to bring about advances in philosophical knowledge is required also in religious knowledge. We are apt to be hasty and impatient. We should learn to wait till seeds have had time to grow and to produce crops. The government of the Deity proceeds gradually and slowly. As He does not bring the individuals of the human race on the stage of mature life before they have been duly prepared for it by passing through the instruction and discipline of infancy and childhood, so neither does he bring the species to that finished state of dignity and happiness for which it is intended without a similar introduction and education.

Religious improvement must be expected to keep pace with other improvements. There is a connexion between all the different branches of knowledge which render this necessary. It would be strange, indeed, if men were not likely to understand religion best when they understood best all other subjects, or if an increase of general knowledge only left us more in the dark in theology. This is what those of our brethren who will admit of no new lights in religion would have us believe. But nothing can be more unreasonable. The age of polite literature in antient Greece and Rome was likewise the age when general knowledge prevailed most, and the period of the revival of letters in these last ages was also the period of the reformation from Popery; and in like manner it must be expected, notwithstanding all the obstacles which the friends of old establishments endeavour to throw in the way, that the present period of more knowledge than ever yet existed in the world will produce a farther reformation.

It is observable that the Scriptures place the downfall of Antichrist before the commencement of the universal kingdom of the Messiah. This must be the order in which these events will happen. It would be absurd to imagine that Christianity, in its corrupt state, will ever become the universal religion. Previously to this it must lose that connection with civil power which has debased it, and which now in almost every Christian country turns it into a scheme of worldly emolument and policy, and supports error and superstition under the name of it. The absurdities fathered upon it must be exploded and it must be displayed to the world in its native and original excellence. Then only will it be fit to triumph over false religions and to reform and bless all nations.

The observations now made may be of use in assisting you to form just ideas of the progressive course of human improvement. Such has it hitherto been, and such the natures of things assure us it must continue to be. Like a river into which, as it flows, new currents are continually discharging themselves, it must increase till it becomes a wide-spreading stream, fertilizing and enriching all countries, and *covering the earth as the waters cover the sea.*

I will here point out to you briefly a few circumstances in the present state of the world which indicates [*sic*] a farther progress and are particularly encouraging.

First, in philosophical knowledge great advances have been lately made. New fields of philosophy have been opened since the time of Sir Isaac Newton. Our ideas of the extent and grandeur of the universe have been carried much farther than he carried them, and facts in the system of nature discovered which could they have been intimated to him would have been pronounced by him impossible. Standing on his shoulders and assisted by his discoveries we see farther than he did. How daring then would be the man who should say that our successors will not see farther than we do?

This increase of natural knowledge must be accompanied with more enlarged views and liberal sentiments in religion, and we find that this has been its effect. There is, indeed, no circumstance in the present state of the world which promises more than the liberality in religion which is now prevailing. God be thanked, the burning times are gone, and a conviction of the reasonableness of universal toleration is spreading fast. Juster notions also of the origin and end of civil government are making way, and an experiment is now making by our brethren on the other side of the Atlantic of the last consequence, and to which every friend of the human race must wish success. There a total separation of religion from civil policy has taken place which will probably read a lesson to the world that will do it infinite service. Alliances between church and state and slavish hierarchies are losing credit, long experience having taught their mischief. The nature of religious liberty is better understood than ever. In the last century those who cried out the loudest for it meant only liberty for themselves because the advocates of truth. But there is now a conviction prevailing that all encroachments on the right of conscience are pernicious and impious, that the proper office of the civil magistrate is to maintain peace, not to support truth. To defend the properties of men, not to take care of their souls. And to protect equally all honest citizens of all persuasions, not to set up one religious sect above another.

Sentiments so reasonable must continue to spread. They promise an open and free stage for discussion and general harmony among the professors of Christianity. O happy time! when bigotry shall no more persecute the sincere enquirer, and every one shall tolerate as he would wish to be himself tolerated. When mankind shall love one another as brethren amidst their religious differences, and human authority in religion be exploded. When civil governors shall know their duty and employ their power for its proper purpose. When the sacred blessing of liberty shall meet with no restraint except when used to injure itself, and all shall be allowed without the fear of losing any rights to profess and practise that mode of faith and worship which they shall think most acceptable to their Maker. Then will come to pass the prophecy of Isaiah, (before recited to you) *The wolf will dwell with the lamb, the leopard lie down with the kid, and the lion eat straw with the ox, the sucking child shall play on the hole of the asp, and they shall not hurt or destroy in all the earth.*

I might now, would the time allow, proceed to recite many other important circumstances in the state of the world which are preparations for that revolution in favour of human happiness which is the object of this discourse. Such as the alleviation of the horrors of war occasioned by the spread of the principles of humanity, and the encouragement arising from hence (and also from the growing conviction of the folly as well as the iniquity of wars) to expect a time when nation shall no more lift up a sword against nation. The softened spirit of Popery, and the visible decline of the papal power. The extinction of the order of Jesuits, and the demolition of convents and monasteries. The shutting of the doors of the infernal inquisition, and the ceasing of acts of faith. The extended intercourse between the different parts of the world and the facility of the diffusion of knowledge created first by the invention of the art of printing, but now carried farther than ever by the increase of commerce and the improvements in the art of navigation. The establishment, at this moment going forward, of an equal representation of the different provinces of France, and the tendencies to it in some of the other countries of Europe. All these circumstances (and many more might be mentioned) render the present state of the world unspeakably different from what it was. They shew us man a milder animal than he was, and the world outgrowing its evils, superstition giving way, antichrist falling, and the Millennium hastening.

Having stated to you the evidence for the doctrine which is the subject of this discourse, I shall now proceed to what I next proposed when I entered upon it. I mean, to take notice of the means by which that happy termination of affairs on this globe which I have been representing is to be brought about. The observations I have made plainly point out to us these means and, therefore, I have, in some measure, anticipated myself on this subject. There are, however, some of these means which I must not omit to recall to your remembrance and to which it is necessary that, on the present occasion, I should more particularly direct your attention.

In general, it is obvious that this end is to be brought about by the operations of Providence concurring with those tendencies to improvement which I have observed to be inseparable from the nature of man. Often Providence works for this end by bringing good out of evil, and making use of human passions to accomplish purposes contrary to those at which they aimed. It would be easy to mention many instances of this. The end of persecutors is to prevent the spread of heterodox opinions, but, instead of answering this end, it generally gives such opinions a wider spread. The progress of Christianity has been assisted in this way, for it is a very just observation that the blood of the martyrs has been the seed of the church. The political views of princes have often, and are now remarkably operating in the same way. The passions of King Henry the 8th, were the means of introducing that period of light and reformation in this country to which we owe our present liberty and happiness. The writings of unbelievers have done service to the Christian religion by causing a stricter enquiry into its evidence and clearing it of the rubbish which has been thrown upon it and the false doctrines which have been mingled with it. And I am greatly mistaken if the obstinacy with which abuses so gross as to be palpable to all the world are retained, in the present age and even in this country, will not in the end prove a great public benefit by causing a more quick and complete overthrow of them and of the establishments that support them, and thus giving a better opportunity for the introduction of establishments favourable to truth and liberty and virtue.

Such are the secret and indirect means by which Providence often carries on its ends. But, in the present case, the most common means which it employs are the investigations and active exertions of enlightened and honest men. These are aimed directly at the melioration of the world and without them it would soon degenerate. It is the blessing of God on the disquisitions of reason and the labours of virtue, united to the invisible directions of his Providence, that must bring on the period I have in view. Inactivity and sleep are fatal to improvement. It is only (as the prophet Daniel speaks) by running to and fro, that is, by diligent enquiry, by free discussion and the collision of different sentiments, that knowledge can be increased, truth struck out, and the dignity of our species promoted. Every one of us ought to co-operate with his neighbours in this great work, and to contribute all he can to instruct and reform his fellow-creatures. His power may be little, but this is no reason against exerting it as far as it will go. The less his power is, the more anxious he should be to employ that little, and not to suffer any part of it to be lost. There are none who have not some degree of power. The rich may help by their fortunes; the great by their influence; the poor by their labour, and the learned by their instruction and counsel. And were all to contribute all they can in these different ways, much would be done and the world would make swift advances to a better state.

The observations I have made shew that our exertions for this purpose ought more especially to be directed to the following points.

First, an improvement in the state of civil government. The dispositions and manners of men depend more than we can well conceive on the nature of the government to which they are subject. There is nothing so debasing as despotic government. They convert the governed into beasts and the men who govern into demons. Free governments, on the contrary, exalt the human character. They give a feeling of dignity and consequence to the governed, and to the governors a feeling of responsibility which has a tendency to keep them within the bounds of their duty, and to teach them that they are more properly the servants of the public than its governors. Much study has been employed, and much pains taken, to find out the best forms of government. Nor is there any subject on which the human understanding can employ itself much more usefully. Many improvements remain to be made and it should be the business of wise and good men to investigate them, and to throw as much light as possible on a subject so interesting to human happiness.[18] I cannot help taking this opportunity to remove a very groundless suspicion with respect to myself by adding that so far am I from preferring a government purely

---

[18] Much assistance in this enquiry may be derived from the *Defence of the American constitutions of government*, lately published by his Excellency Mr. Adams [John Adams, *A Defence of the Constitutions of Government of the United States of America* (Philadelphia, 1787)] where an account is given of most of the governments that have hitherto existed, in order to prove the necessity of providing checks and balances in a constitution of government, by lodging, as is done in our own constitution, the power of legislation in more than one assembly and separating from one another the legislative, executive, and judicial powers.

republican, that I look upon our own constitution of government as better adapted than any other to this country, and in theory excellent.[19] I have said in theory, for, in consequence of the increase of corruption and the miserable inadequateness of our representation, it is chiefly the theory and form of our constitution that we possess, and this I reckon our first and worst and greatest grievance. We have been the most distinguished people under heaven. Lately our glory has been eclipsed. But could we, in this instance, turn the form into the reality (the shadow into the substance) we might recover our former rank, and, with the aid of strong measures for reducing our debts, rise, perhaps, to greater glory than ever.

But, I must hasten to what I meant next to mention as an object necessary to be attended to by the enlightened part of mankind, in order to improve the world. I mean, gaining an open field for discussion, by excluding from it the interposition of civil power, except to keep the peace, by separating religion from civil policy, and emancipating the human mind from the chains of church-authority and church-establishments. Till this can be effected, the worst impediments to improvement will remain. The period to which I have been carrying your views must, as I have before observed to you, be preceded by the downfall of all slavish and antichristian hierarchies. These *let at present, and they will let till they are taken away.* They are, by certain prophecy, destined to destruction. The liberality of the times has already loosened their foundations. The obstinacy of their adherents is increasing their danger, and the wise and virtuous of all descriptions should make themselves willing instruments in the hands of Providence to hasten their removal, not by any methods of violence, but by the diffusion of knowledge and the quiet influence of reason and conviction.

Thirdly, another great object which the friends of reformation ought to attend to is an improvement in the state of education. The importance of education has been so well represented to you by my excellent friend and brother, Dr. Kippis, in the discourse he delivered to you in this place last year, that it is needless for me to dwell much

---

[19] What I here say of myself I believe to be true of the whole body of British subjects among Protestant Dissenters. I know not one individual among them who would not tremble at the thought of changing into a democracy our mixed form of government, or who has any other wish with respect to it than to restore it to purity and vigour by removing the defects in our representation, and establishing that independence of the three states on one another in which its essence consists.

upon it. Nothing, certainly, can be of more importance. Seminaries of learning are the springs of society which, as they flow foul or pure, diffuse through successive generations depravity and misery, or, on the contrary, virtue and happiness. On the bent given to our minds as they open and expand depends their subsequent fate, and on the general management of education depend the honour and dignity of our species. This is a subject with which we are far from being sufficiently acquainted. I often think there may remain a secret in it to be discovered which will contribute more than any thing to the amendment of mankind, and he who should advance one step towards making this discovery would deserve better of the world, than all the learned scholars and professors who have hitherto existed.

The course of improvement, when it has once begun, is (like the motion of a descending body) an accelerated course. One improvement produces other improvements, and these others, and for this reason there may be improvements, apparently little, which may lead to so many more as to be, in their consequences, like the opening of new senses among mankind. There is great encouragement in this consideration. It shews us that the greatest good may arise from the slightest degree of real improvement which we can produce by our exertions, and it should, therefore, quicken our zeal in all such exertions. This observation is, perhaps, more applicable to the subject of education than any other. Improvement, in this case, must be in the highest degree useful. It has a particular tendency to perpetuate itself and may, however inconsiderable at first, increase so far as to bring about an universal reformation. A set of gentlemen, let us suppose, well-informed and of liberal sentiments, see and lament the defects and abuses in the common modes of education. They resolve to try the effect of a new plan. They unite their influence and their contributions for this purpose. They found a college, small perhaps in its origin and narrow in its extent, but wise in its regulations. The care with which it is super-intended and the excellence of its discipline make it an asylum in which young men are saved from the contagion to which they are exposed in other seminaries, and from which they go out, well-instructed and well-principled, to be a comfort to their parents, an honour to their teachers, and blessings to society.

This soon engages general attention and draws to it greater encouragement, in consequence of which it extends its beneficial influence through a wider circle. The example kindles zeal in others and gives rise to institutions formed on plans still more extensive and improved. One generation thus improved communicates improvement to the next, and that to the next, till at last a progress in improvement may take place rapid and irresistible which may issue in the happiest state of things that can exist on this earth. It cannot be amiss for the gentlemen to whom I am addressing myself to fancy themselves in the situation now described. Should it lead them to entertain a delusive expectation, it is a pleasing one, and they will have their reward. The success to which it carries their views is at least the tendency and the possible effect of their exertions. They have, hitherto, been encouraged beyond their expectations, and they have reason to look forward to greater encouragement. Let it appear that they are likely to improve the state of education, and to sow the seeds of catholicism, virtue and rational piety in the kingdom, and there cannot be a doubt but they will receive all the support they can wish for. And who knows what a glorious service they may in the end perform? I feel, indeed, more and more of a hope that they are laying the foundation of an institution which will gather strength for a long period, and cause multitudes in future times to rise up and call them blessed.

One of the best effects which I expect from it is an extension of that catholicism which I have just mentioned, and of a spirit of candour and benevolence. The common effect of education has hitherto been the reverse of this. It has taught a gloomy and sour, instead of a manly and benevolent, religion, a religion consisting in a blind attachment to rites and forms and mysteries, and not in an impartial enquiry after truth, in the love of God and his creatures, and the practice of all that is worthy from a regard to the moral government of the Deity and a future judgment. This has produced some of the worst consequences and, particularly, that *odium theologicum* (that rancour of ecclesiastics) which, because surpassing in virulence all other rancour, has been long proverbial. There is, as I have before observed, less of this than there used to be in the world. But too much of it remains, nor will it be ever totally abolished till a conviction becomes universal of the following truth. 'That nothing is very important except an honest mind, nothing fundamental except righteous practice, and a sincere desire to know and do the will of God.' I wish earnestly I could be, in any degree, the means of propagating this conviction. There is nothing by which any one can better serve the essential interests of society. The institution which occasions the present service will, I hope, do much good in this way. It is intended for the purpose of providing that denomination of Protestant Dissenters to which we belong, with a succession of able and useful ministers. And this is of no less importance than the existence of our dissent from the established church, a dissent which, in my opinion, is derived from the best reasons, from a dislike of the creed[20] as well as the ceremonies of the church – from a regard to Christ as the only lawgiver in his kingdom, and the rejection of all human authority in religion – and, above all, from a conviction that the only proper object of our religious worship is that one undivided and self-existent Being and cause of all causes who sent Christ into the world, and who is his God and Father, no less than he is our God and father. These are reasons which give the cause we wish to support a dignity not to be expressed, and render the preservation of it our duty by all the means that are consistent with the respect we owe to our brethren of different sentiments, and, particularly, by the establishment of an institution, like the present, for educating ministers.

But the education of ministers is far from being the only end of this institution. It is, (as the public has been informed in our printed reports) farther intended for the education of youth in general at that period of approach to mature life when they are most liable to seduction, and most in danger of taking a wrong turn.

In carrying on this undertaking the first aim of its conductors will

[20] It should be attended to that I here speak of the Presbyterian denomination of dissenters only. The whole body of Protestant dissenters consists of a great variety of different sects who have hardly one common principle of dissent. The majority of this very mixed and numerous body are, without doubt, Calvinists and Trinitarians, and therefore cannot dislike the creed of the church, and, at the beginning of this century, the same was true of even the Presbyterian dissenters. A great revolution has taken place in the opinion of this last class of dissenters: but it originated in the church itself with Sir Isaac Newton, Clarke, Hoadley, Whiston, Sykes, etc. and if from these dissenters the faith of the established church is in any danger, it must be more in danger from many of its own members. I will take this opportunity to add that there is a difference of opinion among dissenters on the subject of civil establishments of religion, some approving them in general and only disliking that particular form of religion which happens to be established in this country, while others object to all such establishments and think, as I do, that they encroach on the rights of conscience, obstruct the progress of truth, engender strife and animosity, and turn religion into a trade. The former sort of dissenters must wish to see their own religion substituted for that which is established, but the latter dread such a substitution and can have no other wish than to see all unjust preferences on account of modes of faith and worship abolished, and all honest and peaceable citizens equally protected and encouraged.

be undoubtedly to attach young minds as much as possible to virtue, and at the same time to communicate to them such instruction as shall be best fitted to assist them in judging for themselves, and to engage them to unite liberality and humility, to piety, zeal, and learning.

The best education is that which does this most effectually; which impresses the heart most with the love of virtue and communicates the most expanded and ardent benevolence; which gives the deepest consciousness of the fallibility of the human understanding and preserves from that vile dogmatism so prevalent in the world; which makes men diffident and modest, attentive to evidence, capable of proportioning their assent to the degree of it, quick in discerning it, and determined to follow it; which, in short, instead of producing acute casuists, conceited pedants, or furious polemics, produces fair enquirers endowed with that heavenly wisdom described by St. James, *which is first pure, then peaceable, gentle, easy to be entreated, full of mercy and good fruits, without partiality and without hypocrisy.* An education so conducted is the only means of gaining free scope for the progress of truth, of exterminating the pitiful prejudices we indulge against one another, and of establishing *peace on earth and good will amongst men.*

Think here of the effects of education as commonly managed. Its business is to teach a learning which puffs up and which must be unlearnt before reason can acquire its just influence. Instead of opening it contracts. Instead of enlightening, it darkens, and, by giving a notion of sacredness in disputable doctrines and stuffing the mind with prejudices, incapacitates for the reception of real wisdom and makes men think it their duty to silence, to imprison, and perhaps to kill one another in order to do God service. Such was the effect of education in our Saviour's time among Jews and Pagans. It made self-righteous Pharisees, ostentatious disputants, proud sophists, and cruel persecutors, zealous for the absurdities of superstition and idolatry, and furnished with skill to defend them and to resist conviction. And the consequence was that, not suspecting the necessity of knowing themselves fools before they could be wise, they rejected with disdain the instruction of the Gospel, and that the poorest and plainest men who had never been taught in their schools, or been perverted by the false learning of the times, entered into the kingdom of God before them. It is in this circumstance that our Lord's thanksgiving in Matth. xi. 25. is grounded. *I thank thee, O father, Lord of heaven and earth, because thou hast hid these things from the wise and prudent, and revealed them unto babes.* Let the conductors of this institution take care to avoid this error. Let it be their study to form men who shall, in Christ's sense, be babes rather than wise and prudent, that is, who shall possess the modesty, lowliness, and teachable simplicity of children, rather than the pride and dogmaticalness of men who, having been educated in colleges, think themselves wise and learned, but whose learning produces a worse entanglement of the understanding than common men are subject to, and is nothing but deeper ignorance and more inveterate prejudice. This is the great advantage by which I wish this institution to be distinguished, and it is an advantage which it must possess if your present views are carried into execution. It is to be formed on an open and liberal plan. Our two universities are fortresses created for the security and preservation of the church of England, and defended for that purpose by tests and subscriptions. Most of the seminaries also among ourselves are intended for conveying instruction in the particular systems of the sects that support them, and for making Baptists, Independents, Calvinists, and orthodox believers. The founders of this institution, while they neglect no proper means of making good scholars and enlightened philosophers, will, I doubt not, be anxious above all things about making good men, upright citizens, and honest and candid believers.

This is a design that all must approve who do not think that the truth having been happily found out and established in this kingdom two hundred years ago, nothing remains to be done but to support it and to adopt measures for maintaining the belief of it, and for creating an inviolable attachment to it. Thus did Jews and Pagans think in our Saviour's time, and, therefore, rejected the divine light of Christianity. Thus do Mahometans and Papists now think of their national establishments, and, therefore, continue in darkness and superstition. Is it credible that like consequences should not arise from like sentiments in this country? Is it not as proper in us, as it would be in them, to suspect our public creeds and forms? Can it be imagined that we have reached a degree of perfection which renders farther enquiry needless? I am indeed much mistaken if some very great errors do not still make a part of our national faith. This is at least possible, and this possibility is a sufficient reason for maintaining an openness to conviction with respect to it. Should such errors exist, and the reformed churches themselves want reformation, institutions for liberalizing education must do infinite good by being the means of detecting them. But should they not exist still the best consequences must follow. It will appear that our national code of faith and worship can stand the test of examination. It will gain credit and find a more honourable support than that authority of fallible men and that interference of secular power in religion, which have hitherto, almost everywhere, supported nothing but imposture, superstition and idolatry.

It may be objected that the liberality in education which I have recommended will have a tendency to set men loose from all principles. The observation I have just made proves this to be an unreasonable apprehension. The best way, certainly, of attaching men to true principles is to enable them to examine impartially all principles. Every truth that is necessary to be believed and really sacred, must be attended with the clearest evidence. Free enquiry can be hostile to nothing but absurdity and bigotry. It is only falshood and delusion which fly from discussion and chuse to skulk in the dark.

But I am in danger of wandering beyond the proper purpose of this discourse. Let me now recall briefly to your attention some of the reasons which should quicken your zeal in the great work you have undertaken. I have already taken notice of its great importance. Forming youthful and tender minds to virtue, and pointing their ambition to that moral excellence and resemblance of the Deity which alone constitute true honour and dignity; directing their faculties as they open, and checking in them the risings of criminal passions; assisting them in the acquisition of valuable knowledge, and teaching them habits of patience, modesty, candour, and self-government; guarding them against the influence of the foolish prejudices which blind mankind; and preparing them by judicious discipline and instruction for an easy admission of the light of truth, and thus contributing to the progressive improvement of the world, the enlargement of Christ's kingdom, and the arrival of a period when the will of God will be done on earth, as it is in heaven; – this, brethren, this is a work of the noblest and highest nature. Angels can hardly be more usefully or honourably employed.

But consider next the need there is of your exertions in this instance. It is a narrow and ill-managed education that keeps up discord and malevolence, and that produces most of the evils of life. It is this that is continually sending out into the world coxcombs, pedants, bigots, despots, and libertines to debase the dignity of man, to embroil society, and to perpetuate ignorance, vice and slavery. The smallest degree of success in an attempt to correct these evils by an improvement in the state of education would be an ample reward for the greatest trouble and expence that could attend it. The inattention to this subject which has prevailed is no less astonishing than melancholy. When the resolution was taken to establish this institution, there was but one seminary for education, after passing through the common grammar schools, to which we, as Dissenters of the denomination commonly (though improperly) called Presbyterians, could look, and even this seminary was by the founder of it intended to form Independents and Calvinists. The moderation and wisdom of its trustees and tutors have indeed given it a liberal turn and made it very useful. It is not, however, of sufficient extent to answer all our views. Being situated in the country, it wants many advantages which can be found only near the centre of the kingdom. But I will not enter on a repetition of what you have so well observed on this subject in your reports and circular letters.

Let me, therefore, desire you, in the next place, to consider the obligation under which your constant use of the words of my text lays you, and the encouragement it gives you. To pray for a benefit without using our endeavours to procure it, is a mockery of the Deity and an abuse of prayer. We are commanded to pray for our daily bread, but he that should do this, while he takes no pains to get his daily bread, would be inexcuseable. We are, therefore, bound by our use of that part of the Lord's Prayer which I have taken for my text to employ all the means in our power to cause the kingdom of God to come, and his will to be done on earth as it is done in heaven. And one of the best of all the means we can employ is, I have shewn, the establishment of such a seminary as we have now in view.

Our use of this part of the Lord's Prayer is farther an encouragement to us in employing these means. A command to pray for a blessing, implies that we shall obtain it if we use the means. In the present instance, particularly, it assures us that an extension of Christ's kingdom and an amendment of the state of the world, are blessings which lie in some degree within our reach and that our exertions for this purpose shall be favoured and succeeded.

The encouragement derived from hence is greatly increased by the doctrine on which I have been insisting. A more prosperous state of things is to take place on this earth. The stone which was cut out of the mountain without human force is hereafter to fill the whole earth, and the kingdom of the Messiah to become universal. Reason and Scripture lead to this expectation. Remember then in your endeavours to enlighten and reform mankind that you are co-operating with Providence, that the hand of God has marked out your path, and that his favour will guide and protect you. I have been shewing you how much the state of the world encourages you. A spirit of enquiry is gone forth. A disdain of the restraints imposed by tyrants on human reason prevails. A tide is set in. A favourable gale has sprung up. Let us seize the auspicious moment, obey the call of Providence, and join our helping hands to those of the friends of science and virtue. Think not, however, that you have no difficulties to encounter. It will not be strange if an alarm should be taken about the danger of the church. There is a jealousy natural to church establishments (especially when undermined by time and the spread of knowledge) which may produce such an alarm. In this case it would be a most unreasonable alarm, for if our religious establishment can bear discussion and stands on good ground as its friends must believe, what harm can be done to it by an institution, the design of which is, not to inculcate the peculiarities of any sect, but to communicate such general instruction and to promote such a spirit of enquiry and candour as shall form worthy citizens for the state and useful ministers for the church? This, however, is a consideration that will not prevent opposition. The enemies of reformation may be alarmed. Ignorance and intolerance may clamour. But their opposition cannot be successful. The liberal temper of the times must overpower them. Bigotry and superstition must vanish before increasing light. We see the clouds scattering. We live in happier times than our fore-fathers. The shades of night are departing. The day dawns, and the sun of righteousness will soon rise with healing in his wings. Let us keep our attention fixed on this reviving prospect. Animated by it, let us persevere in our exertions, knowing that, as far as we are on the side of liberty and virtue, we are on that side which must at last prevail.

Let us, however, at the same time take care not to forget a caution which I have before given and cannot too often repeat. While we proceed in our exertions with perseverance and zeal, let them be accompanied with peaceableness and dispositions perfectly charitable. Some of our fellow-Christians are eagerly maintaining a pre-eminence in the Christian church which Christ has prohibited, and struggling to preserve the power they claim as interpreters of Christ's laws and kings in his kingdom.[21] They either do not see the great change that is going forward, or, if they do see it, they have not the wisdom to suit their conduct to it, and to prepare for its effects. Others of our brethren continue to hold as sacred some of the doctrines of the dark ages. The mist, which opening day is dispersing, still lurks round them. Imagining the acceptance of the Deity to be confined within the circle of their own faith, they cannot view mankind with the same satisfaction that we do. They have not yet felt the chearing power of a religion which makes nothing essential but an honest heart, and they look, perhaps, with pain on your attempts to serve the cause of truth and piety. But though, in this respect less happy than ourselves and, as we think, not so well informed, they may be truly worthy and we should learn not to condemn them whatever sentiments with respect to us a mistaken Judgment may lead them to entertain.

My own experience has induced me to speak thus to you. I have been an object of censure for actions which I consider as some of the best in my life. But being conscious that I have meant well, and believing that I have not laboured quite in vain, the censure I have met with has made no impression on me. I look back with complacency and I look forward with joy in hope of a time when those good men who now dislike me on account of the difference of our religious opinions and views will be as ready to embrace me as I am to embrace them.

Excuse this digression. I am growing too tedious, and I have gone

---

[21] Never was a more important service done to the cause of religious liberty, than by the excellent Bishop *Hoadley*, in the controversy occasioned by a sermon in which he confuted these claims. For this sermon, (and also his opposition to a test law which stigmatizes a large body of the king's best subjects, and profanes a Christian ordinance) he was threatened with the vengeance of both houses of Convocation, but the power of government (in this case wisely applied to the restraint of clerical resentment) interposed and saved him. The issue is well known. He was promoted, and the Convocation ruined, for since that time it has never been allowed to sit to exercise its former powers. [On 31 March 1717, Hoadly preached a sermon, 'The Nature of the Kingdom of Christ', in which he argued that the Gospels give no warrant for any visible church authority. On 3 May 1717 the Lower House of Convocation appointed a Committee to examine the sermon, but before it could send its findings to the Upper House, the King prorogued Convocation. Convocation did not meet again, except formally, until 1852.]

beyond my strength. I will, therefore, conclude with directing you to carry your thoughts to another world. The period on which I have been discoursing will pass while we are silent in the grave. But through the grace of God in the great Redeemer we shall be raised up from death and enter on a new world. There a brighter scene than this world can exhibit to us in its best state will open upon us. There a government of consummate order will be established and all the faithful and worthy of all religions will be gathered into it. There peace and love will reign in full perfection, and those who, by such exertions as yours, are the means of enlarging the kingdom of Christ and causing the will of God to be done on earth as it is done in heaven, will be exalted to a happiness greater than can be now conceived, and which will never come to an end. To this happiness, may God of his infinite mercy bring us, through Jesus Christ our Lord and Saviour.

A Discourse on the Love of our Country
(1789)

A Discourse on the Love of our Country,
delivered on Nov. 4, 1789, at the Meeting-House
in the Old Jewry, to the Society for
Commemorating the Revolution in Great Britain.
(1789)

Preface to the Fourth Edition

Since the former editions of the following discourse, many animadversions upon it have been published. Under the abuse with which some of them are accompanied, I have been comforted by finding myself joined to the City of Paris, and the National Assembly of France. I cannot think of employing my time in making any replies. Knowing that it has been the labour of my life to promote those interests of liberty, peace, and virtue, which I reckon the best interests of mankind, and believing that I have not laboured quite in vain, I feel a satisfaction that no opposition can take from me, and shall submit myself in silence to the judgment of the public without taking any other notice of the abuse I have met with than by mentioning the following instance of it.

In p. 195, I have adopted the words of Scripture, *Now lettest thou thy servant depart in peace* and expressed my gratitude to God for having spared my life to see a 'diffusion of knowledge that has undermined superstition and error, a vast kingdom spurning at slavery, and an arbitrary monarch led in triumph and surrendering himself to his subjects'. These words have occasioned a comparison of me (by Mr.

176

Burke in his *Reflections on the Revolution in France*) to Hugh Peters, attended with an intimation that like him, *I may not die in peace*, and he has described me, p. 99, etc. as a barbarian delighted with blood, profaning Scripture, and exulting in the riot and slaughter at Versailles on the 6th of October last year. I hope I shall be credited when, in answer to this horrid misrepresentation and menace, I assure the public that the events to which I referred in these words were not those of the 6th of October, but those only of the 14th of July and the subsequent days, when, after the conquest of the Bastile, the King of France sought the protection of the National Assembly and, by his own desire, was conducted amidst acclamations never before heard in France to Paris, there to shew himself to his people as the restorer of their liberty.

I am indeed surprised that Mr. Burke could want candour so much as to suppose that I have any other events in view. The letters quoted by him in p. 99 and 128 were dated in July 1789, and might have shewn him that he was injuring both me and the writer of those letters. But what candour or what moderation can be expected in a person so frantic with zeal for hereditary claims and aristocratical distinctions as to be capable of decrying popular rights and the aid of philosophy in forming governments, of lamenting that the age of chivalry is gone, and of believing that the insults offered by a mob to the Queen of France have extinguished for ever the glory of Europe?

Psalm cxxii. verses 2 and 4–9

Our feet shall stand within thy gates, O Jerusalem, whither the tribes go up, the tribes of the Lord unto the testimony of Israel. To give thanks to the name of the Lord, for there sit the thrones of judgment, the throne of the House of David. Pray for the peace of Jerusalem. They shall prosper that love thee. Peace be within thy walls, and prosperity within thy palaces. For my brethren and companions sake I will now say peace be within thee. Because of the House of the Lord our God, I will seek thy good.

In these words the Psalmist expresses, in strong and beautiful language, his love of his country and the reasons on which he founded it; and my present design is to take occasion from them to explain the duty we owe to our country, and the nature, foundation, and proper expressions of that love to it which we ought to cultivate. I reckon this a subject particularly suitable to the services of this day, and to the anniversary of our deliverance at the Revolution from the dangers of Popery and arbitrary power, and should I, on such an occasion, be led to touch more on political subjects than would at any other time be proper in the pulpit, you will, I doubt not, excuse me.

The love of our country has in all times been a subject of warm commendations and it is certainly a noble passion, but, like all other passions, it requires regulation and direction. There are mistakes and prejudices by which, in this instance, we are in particular danger of being misled. I will briefly mention some of these to you and observe,

First, that by our country is meant, in this case, not the soil or the spot of earth on which we happen to have been born, not the forests and fields, but that community of which we are members, or that body of companions and friends and kindred who are associated with us under the same constitution of government, protected by the same laws, and bound together by the same civil polity.

Secondly, it is proper to observe that even in this sense of our country, that love of it which is our duty does not imply any conviction of the superior value of it to other countries, or any particular preference of its laws and constitution of government. Were this implied, the love of their country would be the duty of only a very small part of mankind, for there are few countries that enjoy the advantage of laws and governments which deserve to be preferred. To found, therefore, this duty on such a preference would be to found it on error and delusion. It is, however, a common delusion. There is the same partiality in countries to themselves that there is in individuals. All our attachments should be accompanied, as far as possible, with right opinions. We are too apt to confine wisdom and virtue within the circle of our own acquaintance and party. Our friends, our country, and, in short, every thing related to us we are disposed to overvalue. A wise man will guard himself against this delusion. He will study to think of all things as they are, and not suffer any partial affections to blind his understanding. In other families there may be as much worth as in our own. In other circles of friends there may be as much wisdom, and in other countries as much of all that deserves esteem, but, notwithstanding this, our obligation to love our own families, friends, and country, and to seek, in the first place, their good, will remain the same.

Thirdly, it is proper I should desire you particularly to distinguish between the love of our country and that spirit of rivalship and ambition which has been common among nations. What has the love of their country hitherto been among mankind? What has it been but a love of domination, a desire of conquest, and a thirst for grandeur and glory, by extending territory and enslaving surrounding countries? What has it been but a blind and narrow principle, producing in every country a contempt of other countries, and forming men into combinations and factions against their common rights and liberties? This is the principle that has been too often cried up as a virtue of the first rank: a principle of the same kind with that which governs clans of Indians or tribes of Arabs, and leads them to plunder and massacre. As most of the evils which have taken place in private life, and among individuals, have been occasioned by the desire of private interest overcoming the public affections, so most of the evils which have taken place among bodies of men have been occasioned by the desire of their own interest overcoming the principle of universal benevolence and leading them to attack one another's territories, to encroach on one another's rights, and to endeavour to build their own advancement on the degradation of all within the reach of their power. What was the love of their country among the Jews, but a wretched partiality to themselves and a proud contempt of all other nations? What was the love of their country among the old Romans? We have heard much of it, but I cannot hesitate in saying that however great it appeared in some of its exertions, it was in general no better than a principle holding together a band of robbers in their attempts to crush all liberty but their own. What is now the love of his country in a Spaniard, a Turk, or a Russian? Can it be considered as any thing better than a passion for slavery, or a blind attachment to a spot where he enjoys no rights and is disposed of as if he was a beast?

Let us learn by such reflexions to correct and purify this passion, and to make it a just and rational principle of action.

It is very remarkable that the founder of our religion has not once mentioned this duty or given us any recommendation of it, and this has, by unbelievers, been made an objection to Christianity. What I have said will entirely remove this objection. Certain it is, that by inculcating on men an attachment to their country, Christianity would at the time it was propagated have done unspeakably more harm than good. Among the Jews it would have been an excitement to war and insurrections, for they were then in eager expectation of becoming soon (as the favourite people of Heaven) the lords and conquerors of the earth under the triumphant reign of the Messiah. Among the Romans, likewise, this principle had, as I have just observed, exceeded its just bounds and rendered them enemies to the peace and happiness of mankind. By inculcating it, therefore, Christianity would have confirmed both Jews and Gentiles in one of the most pernicious faults. Our Lord and his apostles have done better. They have recommended that Universal Benevolence which is an unspeakably nobler principle than any partial affections. They have laid such stress on loving all men, even our enemies, and made an ardent and extensive charity so essential a part of virtue, that the religion they have preached may, by way of distinction from all other religions, be called the Religion of Benevolence. Nothing can be more friendly to the general rights of mankind, and were it duly regarded and practised, every man would consider every other man as his brother, and all the animosity that now takes place among contending nations would be abolished. If you want any proof of this, think of our Saviour's parable of the good Samaritan. The Jews and Samaritans were two rival nations that entertained a hatred of one another the most inveterate. The design of this parable was to shew a Jew that even a Samaritan and consequently all men of all nations and religions were included in the precept, *Thou shalt love thy neighbour as thyself.*

But I am digressing from what I had chiefly in view, which was, after noticing that love of our country which is false and spurious, to explain the nature and effects of that which is just and reasonable. With this view I must desire you to recollect that we are so constituted that our affections are more drawn to some among mankind than to others, in proportion to their degrees of nearness to us, and our power of being useful to them. It is obvious that this is a circumstance in the constitution of our natures which proves the wisdom and goodness of our Maker, for had our affections been determined alike to all our fellow-creatures human life would have been a scene of embarrassment and distraction. Our regards, according to the order of nature, begin with ourselves, and every man is charged primarily with the care of himself. Next come our families, and benefactors, and friends, and after them our country. We can do little for the interest of mankind at large. To this interest, however, all other interests are subordinate. The noblest principle in our nature is the regard to general justice and that good-will which embraces all the world. I have already observed this, but it cannot be too often repeated. Though our immediate attention must be employed in promoting our own interest and that of our nearest connexions, yet we must remember that a narrower interest ought always to give way to a more extensive interest. In pursuing particularly the interest of our country we ought to carry our views beyond it. We should love it ardently but not exclusively. We ought to seek its good, by all the means that our different circumstances and abilities will allow, but at the same time we ought to consider ourselves as citizens of the world, and take care to maintain a just regard to the rights of other countries.

The enquiry by what means (subject to this limitation) we may best promote the interest of our country is very important, and all that remains of this discourse shall be employed in answering it and in exhorting you to manifest your love to your country by the means I shall mention.

The chief blessings of human nature are the three following: truth, virtue, and liberty. These are, therefore, the blessings in the possession of which the interest of our country lies, and to the attainment of which our love of it ought to direct our endeavours. By the diffusion of knowledge it must be distinguished from a country of barbarians: by the practice of religious virtue, it must be distinguished from a country of gamblers, atheists, and libertines: and by the possession of liberty, it must be distinguished from a country of slaves. I will dwell for a few moments on each of these heads.

Our first concern as lovers of our country must be to enlighten it. Why are the nations of the world so patient under despotism? Why do they crouch to tyrants, or submit to be treated as if they were a herd of cattle? Enlighten them and you will elevate them. Shew them they are *men* and they will act like *men*. Give them just ideas of civil government and let them know that it is an expedient for gaining protection against injury and defending their rights, and it will be impossible for them to submit to governments which, like most of those now in the world, are usurpations on the rights of men and little better than contrivances for enabling the *few* to oppress the *many*. Convince them that the Deity is a righteous and benevolent as well as omnipotent being, who regards with equal eye all his creatures and connects his favour with nothing but an honest desire to know and to do his will, and that zeal for mystical doctrines which has led men to hate and harass one another will be exterminated. Set religion before them as a rational service consisting not in any rites and ceremonies, but in worshipping God with a pure heart and practising righteousness from the fear of his displeasure and the apprehension of a future righteous judgment and that gloomy and cruel superstition will be abolished which has hitherto gone under the name of religion, and to the support of which civil government has been perverted. Ignorance is the parent of bigotry, intolerance, persecution and slavery. Inform and instruct mankind, and these evils will be excluded. Happy is the person who, himself raised above vulgar errors, is conscious of having aimed at giving mankind this instruction. Happy is the scholar or philosopher who at the close of life can reflect that he has made this use of his learning and abilities, but happier far must he be if, at the same time, he has reason to believe he has been successful and actually contributed by his instructions to disseminate among his fellow-creatures just notions of themselves, of their rights, of religion, and the nature and end of civil government. Such were Milton, Locke, Sidney, Hoadly, etc. in this country, such were Montesquieu, Fenelon, Turgot, etc. in France. They sowed a seed which has since taken root and is now growing up to a glorious harvest. To the information they conveyed by their writings we owe those revolutions in which every friend to mankind is now exulting. What an encouragement is this to us all in our endeavours to enlighten the world? Every degree of illumination which we can communicate must do the greatest good. It helps to prepare the minds of men for the recovery of their rights, and hastens the overthrow of priestcraft and tyranny. In short, we may, in this instance, learn our duty from the conduct of the oppressors of the world. They know that light is hostile to them, and therefore they labour to keep men in the dark. With this intention they have appointed licensers of the press, and, in Popish countries, prohibited the reading of the Bible. Remove the darkness in which they envelope the world and their usurpations will be exposed, their power will be subverted, and the world emancipated.

The next great blessing of human nature which I have mentioned is virtue. This ought to follow knowledge and to be directed by it. Virtue without knowledge makes enthusiasts and knowledge without virtue makes devils, but both united elevates to the top of human dignity and perfection. We must, therefore, if we would serve our country, make both these the objects of our zeal. We must discourage vice in all its forms, and our endeavours to enlighten must have ultimately in view a reformation of manners and virtuous practice.

I must add here that in the practice of virtue I include the discharge of the public duties of religion. By neglecting these we may injure our country essentially. But it is melancholy to observe that it is a common neglect among us and in a great measure owing to a cause which is not likely to be soon removed: I mean, the defects (may I not say, the absurdities?) in our established codes of faith and worship. In foreign countries, the higher ranks of men, not distinguishing between the religion they see established and the Christian religion, are generally driven to irreligion and infidelity. The like evil is produced by the like cause in this country, and if no reformation of our established formularies can be brought about, it must be expected that religion will go on to lose its credit, and that little of it will be left except among the lower orders of people, many of whom, while their superiors give up all religion, are sinking into an enthusiasm in religion lately revived, and mistaking, as the world has generally done, the service acceptable to God for a system of faith souring the temper, and a service of forms supplanting morality.

I hope you will not mistake what I am now saying, or consider it as the effect of my prejudices as a Dissenter from the established church. The complaint I am making, is the complaint of many of the wisest and best men in the established church itself, who have long been urging the necessity of a revival of its Liturgy and Articles. These were framed above two centuries ago when Christendom was just emerging from the ignorance and barbarity of the dark ages. They remain now much the same as they were then and, therefore, cannot be properly adapted to the good sense and liberality of the present times. This imperfection, however, in our public forms of worship, affords no excuse to any person for neglecting public worship. All communities will have some religion, and it is of infinite consequence that they should be led to that which, by enforcing the obligations of virtue and putting men upon loving instead of damning one another, is most favourable to the interest of society.

If there is a Governor of the world who directs all events, he ought to be invoked and worshipped, and those who dislike that mode of worship which is prescribed by public authority ought (if they can find no worship out of the church which they approve) to set up a separate worship for themselves, and by doing this and giving an example of a rational and manly worship, men of weight, from their rank or literature, may do the greatest service to society and the world. They may bear a testimony against that application of civil power to the support of particular modes of faith which obstructs human improvement and perpetuates error, and they may hold out an instruction which will discountenance superstition, and at the same time recommend religion by making it appear to be (what it certainly is when rightly understood) the strongest incentive to all that is generous and worthy, and, consequently, the best friend to public order and happiness.

Liberty is the next great blessing which I have mentioned as the object of patriotic zeal. It is inseparable from knowledge and virtue and together with them completes the glory of a community. An enlightened and virtuous country must be a free country. It cannot suffer invasions of its rights, or bend to tyrants. I need not, on this occasion, take any pains to shew you how great a blessing liberty is. The smallest attention to the history of past ages and the present state of mankind, will make you sensible of its importance. Look round the world and you will find almost every country, respectable or contemptible, happy or miserable, a fruitful field or a frightful waste, according as it possesses or wants this blessing. Think of Greece, formerly the seat of arts and science and the most distinguished spot under heaven, but now, having lost liberty, a vile and wretched spot, a region of darkness, poverty, and barbarity. Such reflexions must convince you that if you love your country you cannot be zealous enough in promoting the cause of liberty in it. But it will come in my way to say more to this purpose presently.

The observations I have made include our whole duty to our country, for by endeavouring to liberalize and enlighten it, to discourage vice and to promote virtue in it, and to assert and support its liberties, we shall endeavour to do all that is necessary to make it great and happy. But it is proper that, on this occasion, I should be more explicit and exemplify our duty to our country by observing farther that it requires us to obey its laws and to respect its magistrates.

Civil government (as I have before observed) is an institution of human prudence for guarding our persons, our property, and our good name, against invasion, and for securing to the members of a community that liberty to which all have an equal right, as far as they do not, by any overt act, use it to injure the liberty of others. Civil laws are regulations agreed upon by the community for gaining these ends, and civil magistrates are officers appointed by the community for executing these laws. Obedience, therefore, to the laws and to magistrates is a necessary expression of our regard to the community. Without it a community must fall into a state of anarchy that will destroy those rights and subvert that liberty which it is the end of government to protect.

I wish it was in my power to give you a just account of the importance of this observation. It shews the ground on which the duty of obeying civil governors stands, and that there are two extremes in this case which ought to be avoided. These extremes are adulation and servility on one hand, and a proud and licentious contempt on the other. The former is the extreme to which mankind in general have been most prone, for it has oftener happened that men have been too passive than too unruly, and the rebellion of Kings against their people has been more common and done more mischief than the rebellion of people against their Kings.

Adulation is always odious and when offered to men in power it corrupts them by giving them improper ideas of their situation, and it debases those who offer it by manifesting an abjectness founded on improper ideas of themselves. I have lately observed in this kingdom too near approaches to this abjectness. In our late addresses to the King on his recovery from the severe illness with which God has been pleased to afflict him, we have appeared more like a herd crawling at the feet of a master than like enlightened and manly citizens rejoicing with a beloved sovereign, but at the same time conscious that he derives all his consequence from themselves. But, perhaps, these servilities in the language of our late addresses should be pardoned as only forms of civility and expressions of an overflow of good nature. They have, however, a dangerous tendency. The potentates of this world are sufficiently apt to consider themselves as possessed of an inherent superiority which gives them a right to govern and makes mankind their own; and this infatuation is almost every where fostered in them by the creeping sycophants about them and the language of flattery which they are continually hearing.

Civil governors are properly the servants of the public and a King is no more than the first servant of the public, created by it, maintained by it, and responsible to it; and all the homage paid him is due to him on no other account than his relation to the public. His sacredness is the sacredness of the community. His authority is the authority of the community, and the term *Majesty*, which it is usual to apply to him, is by no means his own majesty, but the majesty of the people. For this reason, whatever he may be in his private capacity and though, in respect of personal qualities, not equal to or even far below many among ourselves – for this reason I say (that is, as representing the community and its first magistrate) he is entitled to our reverence and obedience. The words *Most Excellent Majesty* are rightly applied to him and there is a respect which it would be criminal to withhold from him.

You cannot be too attentive to this observation. The improvement of the world depends on the attention to it: nor will mankind be ever as virtuous and happy as they are capable of being till the attention to it becomes universal and efficacious. If we forget it we shall be in danger of an idolatry as gross and stupid as that of the ancient heathens, who, after fabricating blocks of wood and stone, fell down and worshiped them. The disposition in mankind to this kind of idolatry is indeed a very mortifying subject of reflexion. In Turkey, millions of human beings adore a silly mortal and are ready to throw themselves at his feet and to submit their lives to his discretion. In Russia, the common people are only a stock on the lands of grandees or appendages to their estates, which, like the fixtures in a house, are bought and sold with the estates. In Spain, in Germany, and under most of the governments of the world, mankind are in a similar state of humiliation. Who, that has a just sense of the dignity of his nature, can avoid execrating such a debasement of it?

Had I been to address the King on a late occasion, I should have been inclined to do it in a style very different from that of most of the addressers, and to use some such language as the following:

> I rejoice, Sir, in your recovery. I thank God for his goodness to you. I honour you not only as my King, but as almost the only lawful King in the world, because the only one who owes his crown to the choice of the people. May you enjoy all possible happiness. May God shew you the folly of those effusions of adulation which you are now receiving, and guard you against their effects. May you be led to such a sense of the nature of your situation and endowed with such wisdom as shall render your restoration to the government of these kingdoms a blessing to it, and engage you to consider yourself as more properly the *servant* than the sovereign of your people.

But I must not forget the opposite extreme to that now taken notice of, that is, a disdainful pride derived from a consciousness of equality, or, perhaps, superiority in respect of all that gives true dignity to men in power and producing a contempt of them, and a disposition to treat them with rudeness and insult. It is a trite observation, that extremes generally beget one another. This is particularly true in the present case. Persons justly informed on the subject of government, when they see men dazzled by looking up to high stations and observe loyalty carried to a length that implies ignorance and servility, such persons, in such circumstances, are in danger of spurning at all public authority and throwing off that respectful demeanour to persons invested with it which the order of society requires. There is undoubtedly a particular deference and homage due to civil magistrates on account of their stations and offices; nor can that man be either truly wise or truly virtuous who despises governments and wantonly *speaks evil of his rulers*, or who does not, by all the means in his power, endeavour to strengthen their hands and to give weight to their exertions in the discharge of their duty. *Fear God* says St. Peter, *Love the brotherhood. Honour all men. Honour the King. You must needs*, says St. Paul, *be subject to rulers, not only for wrath* (that is, from the fear of suffering the penalties annexed to the breach of the laws) *but for conscience sake. For rulers are ministers of God, and revengers for executing wrath on all that do evil.*

Another expression of our love to our country is defending it against enemies. These enemies are of two sorts; internal and external, or domestic and foreign. The former are the most dangerous, and they have generally been the most successful. I have just observed that there is a submission due to the executive officers of a government which is our duty, but you must not forget what I have also observed that it must not be a blind and slavish submission. Men in power (unless better disposed than is common) are always endeavouring to extend their power. They hate the doctrine that it is a trust derived from the people and not a right vested in themselves. For this reason the tendency of every government is to despotism, and in this the best constituted governments must end, if the people are not vigilant, ready to take alarms, and determined to resist abuses as soon as they begin. This vigilance, therefore, it is our duty to maintain. Whenever it is withdrawn and a people cease to reason about their rights and to be awake to encroachments, they are in danger of being enslaved and their servants will soon become their masters.

I need not say how much it is our duty to defend our country against foreign enemies. When a country is attacked in any of its rights by another country, or when any attempts are made by ambitious foreign powers to injure it, a war in its defence becomes necessary: and, in such circumstances, to die for our country is meritorious and noble. These defensive wars are, in my opinion, the only just wars. Offensive wars are always unlawful and to seek the aggrandizement of our country by them, that is, by attacking other countries in order to extend dominion, or to gratify avarice, is wicked and detestable. Such, however, have been most of the wars which have taken place in the world, but the time is, I hope, coming when a conviction will prevail of the folly[22] as well as the iniquity of wars, and when the nations of the earth, happy under just governments, and no longer in danger from the passions of kings, will find out better ways of settling their disputes, and beat (as Isaiah prophecies) *their swords into ploughshares and their spears into pruning-hooks.*

Among the particulars included in that duty to our country by discharging which we should shew our love to it, I will only further mention praying for it and offering up thanksgivings to God for every event favourable to it. At the present season we are called upon to express in this way our love to our country. It is the business of this day and of the present service, and, therefore, it is necessary that I should now direct your attention to it particularly.

We are met to thank God for that event in this country to which the name of *The Revolution* has been given, and which, for more than a century, it has been usual for the friends of freedom and more especially Protestant Dissenters to celebrate with expressions of joy and exultation. My highly valued and excellent friend [Andrew Kippis], who addressed you on this occasion last year, has given you an interesting account of the principal circumstances that attended this event,

---

[22] See a striking representation of the folly of wars, in the last sections of Mr. Necker's *Treatise on the Administration of the Finances of France.* There is reason to believe that the sentiments on this subject in that treatise are now the prevailing sentiments in the court and legislature of France, and, consequently, that one of the happy effects of the revolution in that country may be, if not our own fault, such a harmony between the two first kingdoms in the world, strengthened by a common participation in the blessings of liberty as shall not only prevent their engaging in any future wars with one another, but dispose them to unite in preventing wars every where and in making the world free and happy.

and of the reasons we have for rejoicing in it. By a bloodless victory the fetters which despotism had long been preparing for us were broken, the rights of the people were asserted, a tyrant expelled, and a sovereign of our own choice appointed in his room. Security was given to our property, and our consciences were emancipated. The bounds of free enquiry were enlarged, the volume in which are the words of eternal life was laid more open to our examination, and that aera of light and liberty was introduced among us, by which we have been made an example to other kingdoms and become the instructors of the world. Had it not been for this deliverance, the probability is that, instead of being thus distinguished, we should now have been a base people, groaning under the infamy and misery of popery and slavery. Let us, therefore, offer thanksgivings to God, the author of all our blessings. *Had he not been on our side, we should have been swallowed up quick, and the proud waters would have gone over our souls. But our souls are escaped, and the snare has been broken. Blessed then be the name of the Lord, who made heaven and earth.*

It is well known that King James was not far from gaining his purpose, and that probably he would have succeeded had he been less in a hurry. But he wanted courage as well as prudence, and, therefore, fled and left us to settle quietly for ourselves that constitution of government which is now our boast. We have particular reason, as Protestant Dissenters, to rejoice on this occasion. It was at this time we were rescued from persecution, and obtained the liberty of worshipping God in the manner we think most acceptable to him. It was then our meeting-houses were opened, our worship was taken under the protection of the law, and the principles of toleration gained a triumph. We have, therefore, on this occasion, peculiar reasons for thanksgiving. But let us remember that we ought not to satisfy ourselves with thanksgivings. Our gratitude, if genuine, will be accompanied with endeavours to give stability to the deliverance our country has obtained, and to extend and improve the happiness with which the Revolution has blest us. Let us, in particular, take care not to forget the principles of the Revolution. This Society has, very properly, in its reports, held out these principles, as an instruction to the public. I will only take notice of the three following:

First, the right to liberty of conscience in religious matters.

Secondly, the right to resist power when abused. And
Thirdly, the right to chuse our own governors, to cashier them for
misconduct, and to frame a government for ourselves.[23]

On these three principles, and more especially the last, was the
Revolution founded. Were it not true that liberty of conscience is a
sacred right, that power abused justifies resistance, and that civil
authority is a delegation from the people. Were not, I say, all this true,
the Revolution would have been not an assertion, but an invasion of
rights, not a revolution, but a rebellion. Cherish in your breasts this
conviction and act under its influence, detesting the odious doctrines
of passive obedience, non-resistance, and the divine right of kings –
doctrines which, had they been acted upon in this country, would
have left us at this time wretched slaves – doctrines which imply that

---

[23] Mr. Burke in his *Reflections on the Revolution in France* [1790], denies several of the
principles which in these pages are said to be the principles of the Revolution. He asserts
that our Kings do not derive their right to the crown from the choice of their people, and
that they are not responsible to them. And yet, with wonderful inconsistency, he indicates (p. 123) that a wicked king may be punished, provided it is done with dignity and
he is under the necessity of granting that King James was justly deprived of his crown for
misconduct. In p. 19, he mentions the legal conditions of the compact of sovereignty by
which our kings are bound. The succession of the crown he calls a succession by law
(p. 28) and the law, he calls an 'emanation from the common agreement and original
compact of the State', and the constitution also he calls the 'engagement and pact of
society'. In p. 26 he cites, as an authority against the right of the people to chuse their
own governors, the very act for settling the crown on William and Mary which was an
exercise of that right and the words of which are:
'The Lords and Commons do in the name of all the people submit themselves, their
heirs and posterities for ever', etc.
This act having been passed on purpose to establish a change in the succession for
misconduct, it cannot be supposed that it was intended to deprive the nation for ever of
the power of making again any such change, whatever reasons appearing to the nation
sufficient might occur. That is, it cannot be supposed that it was the intention of the act
to subject the nation for ever to any tyrants that might happen to arise in the new line of
succession. And yet this is the sense in which Mr. Burke seems to understand it, and he
grounds upon it his assertion in p. 27, 'that so far was the nation from acquiring by the
Revolution a right to elect our kings, that, if we had possessed it before, the English
nation did then most solemnly renounce and abdicate it for themselves and their
posterity for ever'. Mr. Burke, before he published this assertion, should have attended
to a subsequent act which has been recommended to my notice by the truly patriotic Earl
Stanhope [Charles Stanhope, third Earl Stanhope (1753–1816)]. I mean the act of the
6th of Anne, chap 7th, by which it is enacted that, 'if any person shall by writing or
printing maintain and affirm that the Kings or Queens of this realm, with and by the
authority of Parliament, are not able to make laws and statutes of sufficient validity to
limit the Crown, and the descent, inheritance and government thereof, every such
person shall be guilty of high treason, etc'.

God made mankind to be oppressed and plundered, and which are no less a blasphemy against him, than an insult on common sense.

I would farther direct you to remember that, though the Revolution was a great work, it was by no means a perfect work, and that all was not then gained which was necessary to put the kingdom in the secure and complete possession of the blessings of liberty. In particular, you should recollect that the toleration then obtained was imperfect. It included only those who could declare their faith in the doctrinal articles of the church of England. It has, indeed, been since extended, but not sufficiently, for there still exist penal laws on account of religious opinions which (were they carried into execution) would shut up many of our places of worship, and silence and imprison some of the ablest and best men. The Test Laws are also still in force and deprive of eligibility to civil and military offices all who cannot conform to the established worship. It is with great pleasure I find that the body of Protestant Dissenters, though defeated in their attempts to deliver their country from this disgrace to it, have determined to persevere. Should they at last succeed, they will have the satisfaction, not only of removing from themselves a proscription they do not deserve, but of contributing to lessen the number of our public iniquities. For I cannot call by a gentler name, laws which convert an ordinance appointed by our Saviour to commemorate his death into an instrument of oppressive policy, and a qualification of rakes and atheists for civil posts. I have said *should* they succeed, but perhaps I ought not to suggest a doubt about their success. And, indeed, when I consider that in Scotland the established church is defended by no such test; that in Ireland it has been abolished; that in a great neighbouring country it has been declared to be an indefeasible right of all citizens to be equally eligible to public offices; that in the same kingdom a professed Dissenter from the established church holds the first office in the state; that in the Emperor's dominions Jews have been lately admitted to the enjoyment of equal privileges with other citizens; and that in this very country, a Dissenter, though excluded from the power of executing the laws, yet is allowed to be employed in making them. When, I say, I consider such facts as these I am disposed to think it impossible that the enemies of the repeal of the Test Laws should not soon become ashamed and give up their opposition.

But the most important instance of the imperfect state in which the Revolution left our constitution, is the inequality of our representation. I think, indeed, this defect in our constitution so gross and so palpable, as to make it excellent chiefly in form and theory. You should remember that a representation in the legislature of a kingdom is the basis of constitutional liberty in it, and of all legitimate government, and that without it a government is nothing but an usurpation. When the representation is fair and equal, and at the same time vested with such powers as our House of Commons possesses, a kingdom may be said to govern itself, and consequently to possess true liberty. When the representation is partial, a kingdom possesses liberty only partially, and if extremely partial, it only gives a semblance of liberty; but if not only extremely partial but corruptly chosen, and under corrupt influence after being chosen, it becomes a nuisance and produces the worst of all forms of government: a government by corruption – a government carried on and supported by spreading venality and profligacy through a kingdom. May heaven preserve this kingdom from a calamity so dreadful! It is the point of depravity to which abuses under such a government as ours naturally tend, and the last stage of national unhappiness. We are, at present, I hope, at a great distance from it. But it cannot be pretended that there are no advances towards it or that there is no reason for apprehension and alarm.

The inadequateness of our representation has been long a subject of complaint. This is, in truth, our fundamental grievance, and I do not think that any thing is much more our duty, as men who love their country, and are grateful for the Revolution, than to unite our zeal in endeavouring to get it redressed. At the time of the American war, associations were formed for this purpose in London and other parts of the kingdom, and our present Minister himself has since that war directed to it an effort which made him a favourite with many of us. But all attention to it seems now lost, and the probability is that this inattention will continue and that nothing will be done towards gaining for us this essential blessing till some great calamity again alarms our fears, or till some great abuse of power again provokes our resentment or, perhaps, till the acquisition of a pure and equal representation by other countries (while we are mocked with the shadow) kindles our shame.

Such is the conduct by which we ought to express our gratitude for the Revolution. We should always bear in mind the principles that justify it. We should contribute all we can towards supplying what is left deficient, and shew ourselves anxious about transmitting the blessings obtained by it to our posterity, unimpaired and improved. But, brethren, while we thus shew our patriotic zeal, let us take care not to disgrace the cause of patriotism by any licentiousness or immoral conduct. Oh! how earnestly do I wish that all who profess zeal in this cause were as distinguished by the purity of their morals as some of them are by their abilities,' and that I could make them sensible of the advantages they would derive from a virtuous character, and of the suspicions they incur and the loss of consequence they suffer by wanting it. Oh! that I could see in men who oppose tyranny in the state a disdain of the tyranny of low passions in themselves, or, at least, such a sense of shame and regard to public order and decency as would induce them to hide their irregularities and to avoid insulting the virtuous part of the community by an open exhibition of vice! I cannot reconcile myself to the idea of an immoral patriot, or to that separation of private from public virtue, which some think to be possible. Is it to be expected that – but I must forbear. I am afraid of applications which many are too ready to make and for which I should be sorry to give any just occasion.

I have been explaining to you the nature and expressions of a just regard to our country. Give me leave to exhort you to examine your conduct by what I have been saying. You love your country and desire its happiness, and, without doubt, you have the greatest reason for loving it. It has been long a very distinguished and favoured country. Often has God appeared for it and delivered it. Let us study to shew ourselves worthy of the favour shewn us. Do you practise virtue yourselves, and study to promote it in others? Do you obey the laws of your country, and aim at doing your part towards maintaining and perpetuating its privileges? Do you always give your vote on the side of public liberty and are you ready to pour out your blood in its defence? Do you look up to God for the continuance of his favour to your country and pray for its prosperity, preserving, at the same time, a strict regard to the rights of other countries, and always considering yourselves more as citizens of the world than as members of any

---

' This passage was intended to be and was generally understood as an attack upon Charles James Fox, of whose private and public life Price had long been severely critical. It would appear that what appeared in print was toned down considerably from what was said in the sermon.

particular community? If this is your temper and conduct you are blessings to your country, and were all like you this world would soon be a heaven.

I am addressing myself to Christians. Let me, therefore, mention to you the example of our blessed Saviour. I have observed at the beginning of this discourse that he did not inculcate upon his hearers the love of their country or take any notice of it as a part of their duty. Instead of doing this, I observed that he taught the obligation to love all mankind and recommended universal benevolence as (next to the love of God) our first duty, and, I think, I also proved to you that this, in the circumstances of the world at that time, was an instance of incomparable wisdom and goodness in his instructions. But we must not infer from hence that he did not include the love of our country in the number of our duties. He has shewn the contrary by his example. It appears that he possessed a particular affection for his country, though a very wicked country. We read in Luke [xi]x.42, that when, upon approaching Jerusalem, in one of his last journeys to it, he beheld it, he wept over it and said, *Oh! that thou hadst known (even thou, at least in this thy day) the things that belong to thy peace.* What a tender solicitude about his country does the lamentation over Jerusalem imply, which is recorded in the same gospel, chap. xiii and 34. *Oh! Jerusalem, Jerusalem, thou that killest the prophets, and stonest them who are sent to thee, how often would I have gathered thy children together, as a hen gathereth her brood under her wings, but ye would not.*

It may not be improper farther to mention the love St. Paul expressed for his country when he declared that for the sake of his brethren and kinsmen he could even wish himself *accursed from Christ* (Rom. ix.3.). The original words are an anathema *from Christ*, and his meaning is, that he could have been contented to suffer *himself* the calamities which were coming on the Jewish people, were it possible for him by such a sacrifice of himself to save them.

It is too evident that the state of this country is such as renders it an object of concern and anxiety. It wants (I have shewn you) the grand security of public liberty. Increasing luxury has multiplied abuses in it. A monstrous weight of debt is crippling it. Vice and venality are bringing down upon it God's displeasure. That spirit to which it owes its distinction is declining, and some late events seem to prove that it is becoming every day more reconcileable to encroachments on the securities of its liberties. It wants, therefore, your patriotic services and, for the sake of the distinctions it has so long enjoyed, for the sake of our brethren and companions and all that should be dear to a free people, we ought to do our utmost to save it from the dangers that threaten it, remembering that by acting thus we shall promote, in the best manner, our own private interest as well as the interest of our country, for when the community prospers the individuals that compose it must prosper with it. But, should that not happen, or should we even suffer in our secular interest by our endeavours to promote the interest of our country, we shall feel a satisfaction in our own breasts which is preferable to all this world can give, and we shall enjoy the transporting hope of soon becoming members of a perfect community in the heavens, and *having an entrance ministered to us, abundantly into the everlasting kingdom of our Lord and Saviour Jesus Christ.*

You may reasonably expect that I should now close this address to you. But I cannot yet dismiss you. I must not conclude without recalling particularly to our recollection a consideration to which I have more than once alluded, and which, probably, your thoughts have been all along anticipating: a consideration with which my mind is impressed more than I can express. I mean the consideration of the favourableness of the present times to all exertions in the cause of public liberty.

What an eventful period is this! I am thankful that I have lived to see it, and I could almost say, *Lord, now lettest thou thy servant depart in peace, for mine eyes have seen thy salvation.* I have lived to see a diffusion of knowledge which has undermined superstition and error. I have lived to see the rights of men better understood than ever, and nations panting for liberty, which seemed to have lost the idea of it. I have lived to see thirty millions of people, indignant and resolute, spurning at slavery, and demanding liberty with an irresistible voice, their king led in triumph, and an arbitrary monarch surrendering himself to his subjects. After sharing in the benefits of one Revolution, I have been spared to be a witness to two other Revolutions, both glorious. And now, methinks, I see the ardor for liberty catching and spreading, a general amendment beginning in human affairs, the dominion of kings changed for the dominion of laws, and the dominion of priests giving way to the dominion of reason and conscience.

Be encouraged, all ye friends of freedom and writers in its defence! The times are auspicious. Your labours have not been in vain. Behold kingdoms, admonished by you, starting from sleep, breaking their fetters, and claiming justice from their oppressors! Behold, the light you have struck out, after setting America free, reflected to France and there kindled into a blaze that lays despotism in ashes and warms and illuminates Europe!

Tremble all ye oppressors of the world! Take warning all ye supporters of slavish governments and slavish hierarchies! Call no more (absurdly and wickedly) reformation, innovation. You cannot now hold the world in darkness. Struggle no longer against increasing light and liberality. Restore to mankind their rights and consent to the correction of abuses, before they and you are destroyed together.

FINIS.

Index

Index

Index

CAMBRIDGE TEXTS IN THE
HISTORY OF POLITICAL THOUGHT

Titles published in the series thus far

Aristotle *The Politics* (edited by Stephen Everson)
Bakunin *Statism and Anarchy* (edited by Marshall Shatz)
Bentham *A Fragment on Government* (introduction by Ross Harrison)
Bossuet *Politics Drawn from the Very Words of Holy Scripture* (edited by
Patrick Riley)
Cicero *On Duties* (edited by M. T. Griffin and E. M. Atkins)
Constant *Political Writings* (edited by Biancamaria Fontana)
Filmer *Patriarcha and Other Writings* (edited by Johann P. Sommerville)
Hegel *Elements of the Philosophy of Right* (edited by Allen W. Wood and
H. B. Nisbet)
Hobbes *Leviathan* (edited by Richard Tuck)
Hooker *Of the Laws of Ecclesiastical Polity* (edited by A. S. McGrade)
John of Salisbury *Policraticus* (edited by Cary Nederman)
Kant *Political writings* (edited by H. S. Reiss and H. B. Nisbet)
Leibniz *Political Writings* (edited by Patrick Riley)
Locke *Two Treatises of Government* (edited by Peter Laslett)
Luther and Calvin on Secular Authority (edited by Harro Höpfl)
Machiavelli *The Prince* (edited by Quentin Skinner and Russell Price)
J. S. Mill *On Liberty,* with *The Subjection of Women* and *Chapters on Socialism*
(edited by Stefan Collini)
Milton *Political Writings* (edited by Martin Dzelzainis)
Montesquieu *The Spirit of the Laws* (edited by Anne M. Cohler,
Basia Carolyn Miller and Harold Samuel Stone)
More *Utopia* (edited by George M. Logan and Robert M. Adams)
Nicholas of Cusa *The Catholic Concordance* (edited by Paul E. Sigmund)
Paine *Political Writings* (edited by Bruce Kuklick)
Pufendorf *On the Duty of Man and Citizen according to Natural Law*
(edited by James Tully)
The Radical Reformation (edited by Michael G. Baylor)
Vitoria *Political Writings* (edited by Anthony Pagden)

.

Lightning Source UK Ltd.
Milton Keynes UK
UKHW011958010320
359605UK00001B/12